1001
NASCAR FACTS

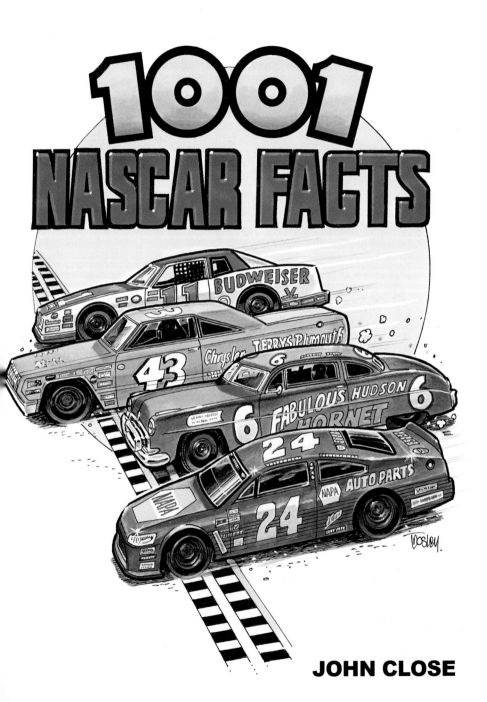

1001 NASCAR FACTS

JOHN CLOSE

CarTech®

CarTech®, Inc.
838 Lake Street South
Forest Lake, MN 55025
Phone: 651-277-1200 or 800-551-4754
Fax: 651-277-1203
www.cartechbooks.com

Edit by Wes Eisenschenk
Layout by Monica Seiberlich

ISBN 978-1-61325-310-6
Item No. CT584

Library of Congress
Cataloging-in-Publication Data
Available at: https://lccn.loc.
gov/2016041641

Written, edited, and designed
in the U.S.A.

Printed in China
10 9 8 7 6 5 4 3 2 1

DISTRIBUTION BY:

Europe
PGUK
63 Hatton Garden
London EC1N 8LE, England
Phone: 020 7061 1980 • Fax: 020 7242 3725
www.pguk.co.uk

Australia
Renniks Publications Ltd.
3/37-39 Green Street
Banksmeadow, NSW 2109, Australia
Phone: 2 9695 7055 • Fax: 2 9695 7355
www.renniks.com

CONTENTS

ABOUT THE AUTHOR

Wisconsin native John Close grew up with racing in the 1950s, cheering on his father's Jalopy stock cars four or five nights a week around the Badger State.

After earning a Journalism/Mass Communications degree from the University of Wisconsin–Oshkosh, Close began covering racing events in the early 1980s. He worked his first NASCAR race as a professional media member in 1986 at Bristol Motor Speedway.

Since then, Close (a former Associated Press newspaper sports editor at the *Daily Jefferson County Union* in Fort Atkinson, Wisconsin) has written countless articles for top racing publications including *Stock Car Racing, Circle Track, NASCAR Illustrated,* and *Speedway Illustrated* magazines. His work has also appeared in *National Speed Sport, Winston Cup Scene, Checkered Flag Racing News,* and *Midwest Racing News* industry trade journals/newspapers.

In 1994, Close became a full-time NASCAR media member and moved to Charlotte, North Carolina, to assume public relations duties for driver Bobby Labonte and the No. 22 Maxwell House Pontiac Winston Cup team. For the next two decades, Close facilitated and managed media and marketing projects for multiple NASCAR Cup, Xfinity,

John Close sits in one of his father's cars in the 1950s.

and Truck Series teams including Richard Petty Motorsports, Hendrick Motorsports, and Ultra Motorsports.

The biggest thrills in Close's racing career came as a spotter in more than 150 NASCAR Cup, Nationwide, and Truck events from 1995 to 2008. His drivers finished in the top-10 in 25 percent of the NASCAR events he spotted; his best effort was a victory with driver Donny Lia in the 2008 NASCAR Camping World Truck Series race at Mansfield, Ohio. Close also called many premiere short-track events around the country during this time including winning efforts in the Snowball Derby at Pensacola, Florida, and the Miller Nationals at Slinger, Wisconsin, with driver Rich Bickle.

Publisher's Note: In reporting history, the images required to tell the tale will vary greatly in quality, especially by modern photographic standards. While some images in this volume are not up to those digital standards, we have included them, as we feel they are an important element in telling the story.

ACKNOWLEDGMENTS

Regardless of what life path you choose, people along the way help guide the direction you go. Here are just a few individuals who shaped my life and career path. In one way or another, each has helped make this book possible.

Lou Close: My dad, and the man who instilled in me the love of fast cars.

Vince Sweeney, Tom Beebe, John Quinn, Phil Hall, Hal Hamrick, Steve Waid, Ben White, Dick Berggren, Chris Economaki, and Glen Grissom: great editors who provided opportunities for me to be a motorsports journalist.

Dick Moore, Wayne Erickson, Terry Tucker, and the Deery family (Jody, Tom, Jack, David, and Chuck): Midwest track promoters who provided racing-related public relations opportunities early in my career.

Dennis Huth: former NASCAR Winston Racing Series and Craftsman Truck Series director who championed my entrance into NASCAR.

Tom Cotter: NASCAR Public Relations firm manager who provided my first NASCAR Winston Cup PR job in 1994.

Benny Parsons, Buddy Baker, and Neil Bonnett: NASCAR legends who befriended and mentored me as a NASCAR "newbie."

Rich Bickle: Wisconsin superstar short-track racer who redirected my life totally when he made me his NASCAR race-day spotter.

Jim Gresham: true gentleman, racer, and friend who provided great opportunities for me in the "twilight" of my professional motorsports career.

Gail and Sam Close: my wife and son, who have provided a life with me I would have never dreamed possible.

INTRODUCTION

The basic definition of a fact is "a piece of information that is known to be true."

The greatest mathematical minds have determined the number of facts to be infinite.

People love facts and support every imaginable topic with countless facts every day.

There are even special ways of stating our facts.

"I know for a fact."

"The fact is . . ."

"It's a well/little known fact."

"Due to the fact that . . ."

"The fact remains."

Okay, you get the picture.

It's always all about the facts, right?

Heck, let's just admit it. We're addicted to facts.

Fortunately, facts aren't much of a health hazard unless you don't have them right. If that's the case, you better be ready to hear, "Get your facts straight." Or "Stick to the facts!"

Always remember to be very careful when you question someone else's facts. If you use the wrong tone to ask someone "Is that a fact?" you'd better be prepared for an argument or worse, a fight over the "facts."

In the end, all this talking about facts and how important they are is a bit silly because, as we all know, "The facts speak for themselves."

As one of America's most popular forms of professional motorsports today, NASCAR can trace its roots back to the late 1800s and the beginning of the motoring age. That history, along with eight decades of organized NASCAR races, milestones, equipment evolution, and personalities has created a list of amazing facts. Breaking them down to just 1,001 was one heck of a challenge.

"That's a fact, Jack."

Enjoy the book.

Chapter 1

BNR: Before NASCAR Ruled

Early cars were hardly anything you'd consider strapping on for some hot laps at Darlington, Bristol, or Talladega. They were little more than motorized horse carriages created by eccentric "tinkerers." By 1900, more than 100 different brands of cars were available and they were offered in all sorts of configurations.

Then, as now, you only needed two cars to race. The earliest races were total "run what ya brung" events contested on primitive roads and later at developed "driving parks." Most early races were time trials, hill climbs, or endurance runs. Eventually, as the automobile became more prevalent at the turn of the century, oval racetracks began to spring up around the country.

During the Roaring Twenties, tracks of all kinds appeared across the nation as a speed-crazy culture contributed to one of America's most explosive decades. Races were held everywhere with most still featuring purpose-built, high-speed racers.

Racing stock cars off the assembly line became more prevalent in the 1930s. For as little as $5, a thrill-seeking daredevil could buy an old roadster, coupe, or sedan at the junkyard, get it running, and take it racing at the local county fairgrounds dirt oval. Regardless of where you lived (New England, California, the Midwest, or the Southern United States) stock car racing was gaining in popularity.

Rajo Jack was also an extremely talented engine builder. Here's a 1930s Champ Car racer proudly announcing he has a Rajo under the hood. (Photo Courtesy Steve Zautke Collection)

By the turn of the 20th Century, half- and one-mile county and state fairgrounds horse racing ovals were among the first tracks to host automobile races. (Photo Courtesy Steve Zautke Collection)

Stock car racing hit the beach at Daytona Beach in 1936 and set the stage for gas station proprietor and racer William Getty France to form a national organization that prompted the founding of NASCAR a decade later.

With that history as a backdrop, these are facts about cars, tracks, people, and events that had an impact on stock car racing in the 50-plus years leading up to the formation of the sport known today as NASCAR.

CARS

1   At the turn of the 20th Century, the total number of automobiles in the United States was estimated at around 10,000, about a quarter of the number of cars in the parking lot at any NASCAR Sprint Cup race today. By 1905, the number of cars in the United States had grown to 25,000; more than 200 companies tooled up to produce the new "horseless carriage." Today, new auto sales in America total nearly 17 million units annually.

Sweepstakes was Henry Ford's first race car. This 2,200-pound, 96-inch-wheelbase racer was built on a steel-reinforced wooden chassis. The 2-cylinder, water-cooled engine featured a massive 7 x 7–inch bore and stroke per cylinder. Mounted horizontally in the chassis, the estimated engine displacement was 538 ci (8.8 liters) topping out at 26 hp at 900 rpm. This is thought to be the first engine to have spark plugs with porcelain insulators. A 2-speed transmission and chain-drive configuration delivered the power payload to the rear axle. The car hit a top speed of 72 mph in testing, which bested the official automobile world speed record of 65.79 mph. Ford drove the car to victory over Alexander Winton in a historic 1901 race at Grosse Pointe, Michigan. He attracted enough financial interest to form the Henry Ford Company and later, the Ford Motor Company. Today, *Sweepstakes* is on display at the Henry Ford museum.

 Steam-powered race cars were common at the dawn of the 20th Century. One of the earliest models to race consistently was the Keene Steammobile Runabout, a formidable car weighing 1,125 pounds. The Steammobile Runabout's water tank capacity was 26 gallons and the chassis wheelbase measured 96 inches. Grounded by 35-inch wheels and 3-inch pneumatic tires, the Steammobile Runabout routinely ran in the 1901 Boston to Keene "endurance races." These 85-mile events were organized and supported by Bay State Automobile Association and the New Hampshire Automobile Club.

 Andrew L. Riker was one of America's first tycoon racers. In 1900, Riker drove the *Riker Torpedo* to an electric-car world speed record of 29 mph over a 5-mile closed course. The record stood for more than 10 years. Riker was later instrumental in designing and producing the 1906 gas-powered, chain-driven Locomobile *Old 16*. With the famed George Robertson behind the wheel, the car went on to win the 1908 Vanderbilt Cup, which was, at the time, America's most prestigious auto race.

 Henry Ford was completely comfortable behind the wheel of *Sweepstakes* while racing Alexander Winton in 1901, but common sense told him he didn't want anything to do with driving the company's next racing creation, the Ford 999. In racing terms, the 999 was a beast. It was named (appropriately) after the famous New York Central Empire Express steam locomotive of the 1800s, which was the first man-made vehicle of any kind to exceed 100 mph. An iron-bar tiller steered 999; it featured a bare bones wood structure frame housing a massive 1,155-ci inline 4-cylinder engine capable of producing an estimated 70 to 80 hp. The car had a giant 230-pound flywheel with no transmission, just a wooden-block clutch and a solid-shaft direct drive to a rear ring and pinion gear. The 109-inch-wheelbase chassis had no rear springs and because the valvetrain and clutch were exposed, the ill-handling beast provided a constant oil bath for its driver. The 999 made its racing debut on October 25, 1902, at the Grosse Pointe track outside Detroit. With newcomer Barney Oldfield behind the wheel, the 999 secured the Manufacturers' Challenge Cup for Ford with a time of 5 minutes 28 seconds, a world record for a 5-mile race on a closed course. Through the next year, Oldfield and the 999 toured the country and set countless speed records.

 The Arrow was a "twin sister" to the Ford 999; both cars were built at the same time in 1902 by Ford engineer Tom Cooper. The Arrow was considered more sophisticated than the 999 because of an enhanced intake manifold that made the Arrow the faster of the two. Unlike the 999 however, the Arrow was star-crossed as it was involved in the first recorded fatality in American motorsports. On September 11, 1903, driver Frank Day was killed at the first automobile race at The Milwaukee Mile in Milwaukee, Wisconsin. Henry Ford brought the Arrow back to Michigan where he repaired it in preparation for a land speed run. Ford, who originally declined to drive either car, wheeled the newly rechristened *Red Devil 999* to a new land speed record of 91.37 mph on Anchor Bay at Lake St. Charles on January 12, 1904. Ford eventually retired both vehicles by the end of 1904.

 Untold thousands of cars have raced at Daytona, both on the beach and at Daytona International Speedway. Only one, however, can claim to be the first at the World Center of Speed. Created by Ransom Olds, the Olds *Pirate* was the first car to make a timed pass at the first

The Olds Pirate *will be forever identified as the first great car to hit the sands and make an official timed speed run at Daytona Beach, Florida. (Photo Courtesy General Motors)*

Daytona Beach Speed Trials in 1902. A bare-bones model of the Olds Curved Dash Runabout, the *Pirate* had no bodywork of any kind. Its most prominent feature was a pair of horizontally mounted torpedo-like gas and oil tanks. Propelled by a 95-ci single-cylinder engine, the *Pirate* and driver Horace T. Thomas cruised to a blazing 54.38 mph in the gasoline-powered 1,000-pound class in the 1902 Daytona trials. Because the event was officially sanctioned and scored by the American Automobile Association, the *Pirate* will forever have the distinction of being the first car to take an official race run at Daytona.

 Built in 1904, the Pope Toledo Racer was a prototype for the company's stock Touring models introduced over the next several years. The car featured a 120-hp 4-cylinder gas internal combustion engine with twin cast heads and integrated copper water jackets. The car also had a gear-driven magneto and multiple-disc clutch. The Pope was one of the first American cars with a 4-speed transmission, as well a fifth "reverse" gear. All were fitted into a frame of chrome-nickel steel construction with a 104-inch wheelbase and 34-inch wheels. The Pope Toledo competed in the first Vanderbilt Cup Race in 1904; it finished third. Over the next several years, Pope continued to race the Torpedo model and use its successes to promote its Touring cars as one of the most advanced, fastest, and reliable cars available. Unfortunately, the strategy didn't work and Albert Pope declared his auto company bankrupt in 1907.

9 Chrysler Corporation took NASCAR by storm in the 1960s when it introduced its 426 Hemi engine. The powerplant, while revolutionary in NASCAR, was not a new concept. The Hemi had made its debut in 1906 in the Pungs-Finch Limited. Built in Detroit, the Pungs-Finch engine was a 600-ci 4-cylinder model featuring hemispherical combustion chambers and angled valves. Thanks to the giant engine, the wooden-frame and -body car had an estimated top speed of 55 mph. Today, only one 1906 Pungs-Finch car remains in existence. The restored classic has won numerous vintage racer awards at both the Pebble Beach and Amelia Island Concours d'Elegance meets. It sold at auction in 2015 for $852,500.

10 Maybe the most important car ever, Henry Ford rolled out his first Model T October 1, 1908. Ford had been actively producing automobiles since 1903 with eight different models (the A, B, C, F, K, N, R, and S cars) before launching the Model T in 1908. The T featured a 4-cylinder 20-hp engine and was available in two models: the Runabout ($825), and the Touring model ($850). It quickly sold 10,000 units in the first year of production which led Ford to drop all other models in order to satisfy the demand for the Model T. With the advent of the automated assembly line in 1913, Ford ramped up Model T production and produced more than 15 million units before ending the car's run in 1927. Due to the massive build numbers, the cost of a new Model T fell to around $300 in the mid-1920s making it the first affordable car for working-class Americans.

11 Few automobile inventions had as big an impact on the automobile as the electric starter. The concept was pioneered and patented in America at Dayton Engineering Laboratories (DELCO) in 1911 by Charles Kettering and Henry Leland. Prior to the electric starter, cars were started by hand cranking, often kicking back and resulting in untold numbers of hand, wrist, and arm injuries. Cadillac was the first major brand to implement the electric starter in 1912; Ford was one of the last to abandon the crank-starting method in 1919. By the 1920s, nearly all of the major U.S. brands featured electric starters, further fueling the automotive craze of the Roaring Twenties.

12 Crafted by the E. R. Thomas Motor Company in 1907, the Thomas Model 35 *Flyer* is arguably the most famous American turn-of-the-century race car. The 5,000-pound car, featuring a 4-cylinder 60-hp engine, won the first, and, to date, only race around the world in 1908. Driver George Schuster took the green flag in Times Square in New York City on February 12, and along with five other teams, headed for Paris, France. However, only three cars finished the 22,000-mile race with the Thomas *Flyer* declared the winner 169 days later on July 30, 1908. The *Flyer*, dubbed *Leslie Special,* was introduced to a new generation of racing fans in the 1965 movie *The Great Race.* Today, the original Thomas *Flyer* is on exhibit at the National Automobile Museum in Reno, Nevada.

13 Organized by General Motors founder William Durant and driver Bob Burman, the Buick Racing Team dominated much of the early racing scene. The team, which was the first factory-backed racing effort, included Burman and the Chevrolet brothers (Louis and Arthur) as drivers. The team won hundreds of events during its run from 1908 to 1911, including a victory by Burman in the first American Automobile Association (AAA) –sanctioned race at the Indianapolis Motor Speedway (the Prest-O-Lite 250) August 19, 1909. With its racing heritage firmly established, Buick became a long-time NASCAR player, capturing two Sprint Cup Manufacturers' Championships (1981 and 1982).

14 Winner of the first Indianapolis 500 in 1911, the Marmon Wasp Model 32 was the only single-seat race car in the field that day. Piloted by the 1910 AAA driving champion Ray Harroun, the first use of a rear-view mirror was employed, allowing Harroun to be the only driver in the field without a riding mechanic. The feat introduced one of countless innovations developed in auto racing that eventually made their way into the production of everyday passenger vehicles.

Ray Harroun's Marmon Wasp, a 6-cylinder car with an engine displacing 477 ci, was based on the 1909 Marmon Model 32 production car. (John Close Photo)

15 While aerodynamic testing is commonplace in today's modern NASCAR, it wasn't a consideration in racing until Frank Lockhart debuted the Stutz Black Hawk Special in 1928. Scale models of the car were constructed and aero-tested in both the Curtiss Aircraft and Army Air Services wind tunnels, one of the first American cars to be tested in such a manner. At 2,800-pounds, the vehicle featured a twin turbocharged Miller U-16 engine. It was also the first land speed record car to use an intercooler for the turbos. After a failed land speed record run at Daytona Beach that ended when Lockhart barrel-rolled the car into the ocean, the Black Hawk was repaired for another run at Daytona Beach on April 25. This time, the right-rear tire blew at more than 220 mph sending the car into a series of prolonged flips. Lockhart (the winner of the 1926 Indianapolis 500) was thrown from the vehicle and killed instantly. The engine was salvaged and later installed in the *Sampson 16 Special* for the 1939 Indianapolis 500, as well as the 1940, 1941, and 1946 Indy 500s. The engine is on display in the Indianapolis Hall of Fame Museum today.

16 Developed in 1929, the Chevrolet inline 6-cylinder engine quickly became a challenger to the Ford Flathead V-8 engine in the early years of stock car racing. The 193.9-ci six-banger produced 50 hp and featured cast-iron pistons and a forged-steel crankshaft. The engine, lighter than the Ford V-8, enabled Chevrolet and other 1930s GM coupes and sedans using the Stovebolt 6 to win countless local stock car, roadster, and Jalopy races against their Blue Oval competitors all the way into the 1960s. The only engine Chevrolet offered from 1929 through 1954 (including a 235-ci model in the new 1953 Chevrolet Corvette) was relegated to a secondary racing option with the 1955 introduction of the Chevy small-block V-8.

17 Although not the first V-8 engine produced, the Ford Flathead V-8 is one of the most important. Introduced in 1932, the engine was the first V-8 offered in an affordable American passenger car. It became a stalwart of the early stock car racing community as 1930s Ford coupes, roadsters, and sedans became the hot iron at local racetracks and stock car events throughout the country. The original engine measured 221 ci and produced about 65 hp. Juiced up with aftermarket items such as multiple carburetors, performance pistons, heads, and crankshaft, the Ford Flathead V-8 could easily be pushed to over 200 hp. The engine made the early stripped-down Fords the cars to beat in the early days of stock car racing and remained a stout competitor into the 1970s.

18 Today's NASCAR Modified division got its start in the 1933 Elgin Road Races. The event was supposed to be for "stock roadster cars" but thanks to Edsel Ford, it turned out to be anything but Ford's car featured a Harry Miller–built Ford 221-ci L-Flathead V-8 with a 3-speed manual transmission and live axle suspension. The 112-inch wheelbase featured transverse leaf springs and four-wheel mechanically actuated drum brakes. Stripped down to its most basic essentials with no fenders, interior, rumble seat, glass, or lighting, it was so fast that Ford immediately ordered Miller to build 10 of them. The day before the Elgin races, driver Fred Frame crashed his car into a grove of trees in Turn 7 and destroyed it. Ford had a back-up car readied and entered it in the race; Frame drove it to

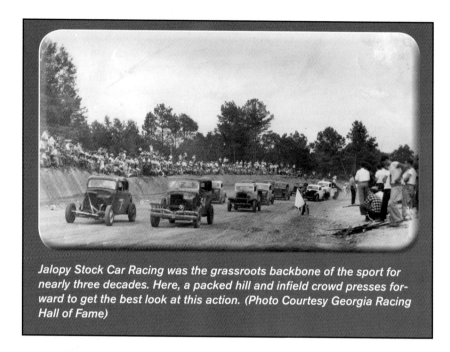

Jalopy Stock Car Racing was the grassroots backbone of the sport for nearly three decades. Here, a packed hill and infield crowd presses forward to get the best look at this action. (Photo Courtesy Georgia Racing Hall of Fame)

what is widely considered one of the greatest early stock car races ever. After a promotional victory tour, the car was stored in a barn for decades before a full restoration in 1988. It remains one of the most important race cars in the history of Ford Motor Company.

19 The engineers who control the building and performance of today's modern NASCAR vehicles have nothing on the men who fashioned Jalopy stock cars from the 1930s through the late 1950s. The lack of money in the 1930s led to the Jalopy movement by using the ever-increasing car parts inventories at local junkyards. Basically stripped of their fenders, running boards, glass, and anything else deemed unnecessary to race, these rudimentary cars featured items such as a belt to strap the doors shut, large stripped bolts as welded braces, and fuel tanks crafted out of wash tubs. As racing became more sophisticated in the 1950s, the Jalopy class began to die out and was eventually replaced by a new brand of purpose-built lightweight modified cars. America's first entry-level stock car racing class, the Jalopies, eventually faded from the racing scene completely by the 1970s.

20 Given that the earliest race cars were production vehicles, getting to and from the racetrack was a simple exercise of driving the car there and back. By the 1920s, Indy and sprint car drivers started using trailers to haul their race cars. Stock car racing, however, didn't adopt this trend until the mid-1950s. Meanwhile, early Jalopy and roadster cars (illegal to drive on the street) were pulled to and from the track by trucks or more powerful production cars using a tow bar.

21 The front fenders of today's NASCAR entries are "stickered up" with the logos of companies offering contingency prize money in addition to the winnings earned in the race. The first time these types of contingency awards were used in American racing was in the 1906 American Grand Prize Race at Savannah, Georgia. There, Continental Tires and Bosch Magneto posted additional contingency money ($4,500 and $1,000, respectively) for the winner while Michelin Tire paid $1,000 to the winner.

22 The 1930s saw car designers literally switch gears. The emphasis from luxury and style to mechanical innovation and reliability. Improvements that became part of NASCAR vehicles in later decades were smooth shifting synchromesh transmissions, hydraulic brakes, power steering, and a sleeker, all-steel aerodynamic body shape. Two other 1930s innovations (a steering column–mounted gearshift and in-dash AM radio) never really caught on with the racing crowd but proved to be popular options with the buying public just the same.

23 Unlike today's modern NASCAR driver who goes into battle with the highest-quality personal safety gear available, early racers wore little to protect themselves from injury. Stock car racing helmets in the 1920s and 1930s were often little more than replicas of leather football helmets or football helmets themselves. Usually a T-shirt, work pants and boots, goggles, and leather driving gloves completed the driver's safety ensemble.

24 Although Goodyear and Firestone churned out racing tires for Indy Cars in the 1920s and 1930s, neither firm made an attempt to create a racing-specific tire for the emerging stock car market. That left the stock car, roadster, and Jalopy racers of the 1920s and 1930s to seek out the best production tires for their racers. These early tires featured an inner tube of compressed air inside a hard rubber outer casing reinforced with layers or plies of fabric cords. Initially made of cotton, the cords were replaced by rayon in the 1930s. The best of these bias-ply tires for racing proved to be harder rubber composition truck tires built to withstand the loads and long distances of commercial vehicles. At a cost of nearly $8 for a set of four, most Depression-era racers didn't have money for new tires, which sent drivers and teams scurrying around the local junkyard for used tires. These racing scuffs usually cost 10 to 25 cents each.

TRACKS

25 There is no record of a NASCAR race ever being held at the Narragansett Trotting Park or Rhode Island State Fairgrounds racetrack, but the sanctioning body owes a tip of the hat to the 1-mile dirt oval just the same. The first automobile oval-track race in America was held at the Narragansett Trotting Park September 7, 1896. With an estimated 60,000 fair-goers on hand to watch the race, seven cars (five internal combustion, one steam, and one electric powered) entered the event. A Riker Motor Company Electric Car won the five-lap race in 15 minutes logging a top speed of 24 mph. Narragansett Trotting Park continued to be the hub for auto racing in the Northeast and hosted numerous events through 1913. The popularity of the races doomed the horse races there. Eventually, the facility was taken over by the state and renamed the Rhode Island State Fairgrounds in 1913. The track was paved and reconfigured with banked turns in 1915. Eddie Rickenbacker, who went on to be America's top flying ace in World War I, won the first race on the new track September 18, 1915. The track continued to host racing events until closing for good after the 1924 racing season.

26 Located in Yonkers, New York, the Empire City Race Track was one of the first facilities in New York State to host auto races. Built

Here is what's left of Frank Day's Ford Arrow after he crashed at Milwaukee Mile's inaugural event in 1903. Day was the first driver to perish in a race. (Photo Courtesy Steve Zautke Collection)

in 1899 as the Empire City Trotting Club at a cost of $780,000, the half-mile dirt oval track featured a 7,500-seat grandstand. Closed for horse racing almost as quickly as it opened, the track began hosting select auto racing–related events including a world record speed run in 1902 by Barney Oldfield and the Ford 999. Oldfield covered the 1.6-kilometer distance in 55.54 seconds. Auto racing continued at Empire City until 1907 when the track was purchased and reopened as a thoroughbred horse racing facility. The last vestiges of Empire City Racetrack came down in 1950 when the track was renamed Yonkers Raceway. In 1972, the Rooney family (owners of the Pittsburgh Steelers) purchased the track. Today, it flourishes as one of the top horse trotting facilities in the United States, hosting nearly 250 events annually.

27 Opened in 1903, The Milwaukee Mile, on the Wisconsin State Fairgrounds in West Allis, today stands as America's longest continuously operating speedway. The Mile first came on the scene as a privately owned, 1-mile horse racing track in 1876. It was then purchased by the Wisconsin State Agricultural Society as part of the property used to create a new, permanent site for the Wisconsin State Fair in 1891. A decade later, interest in staging automobile auto races on the dirt oval sparked the first race. Thousands of spectators flocked to the track on Friday, September 11, to witness the two-day event highlighted by match races between Henry Ford's 999 and Arrow racers. Both cars had mechanical trouble on the first day allowing William Jones of Chicago to wheel a Columbia to victory in the speedway's first auto race. His time of 8 minutes, 21 seconds in the five-lap event was good enough to beat four other competitors including the second-place driver, an unknown African-American racer simply known as Black Jack. Unfortunately, no motorsports events of any kind were scheduled for the Milwaukee Mile in 2017. In all, nearly 40 different NASCAR-sanctioned events were held at the track from 1984 to 2009.

28 It was inevitable that NASCAR would one day race at Indianapolis Motor Speedway beginning with the first Brickyard 400 in 1994. More than 80 years earlier, the track opened on June 9, 1909. Ironically, the first competition at America's motorsports Mecca wasn't a car race but rather a National Hot Air Balloon Championship held on June 5, 1909. Organized by track founder, builder, and president Carl Fischer, the balloon event drew more than 40,000 people providing working capital to complete the unfinished 2.5-mile racetrack. Opened for car racing on August 19, 1909, the track's original crushed stone surface couldn't withstand the pressure of heavy automobiles, so in late 1909, Fischer had the surface repaved with more than 3.2-million bricks held together with grouted cement. After a series of 1910 race festivals featuring as many as 40 events over three days, Indy hosted its first 500-mile race May 30, 1911. A field of 40 cars took a five-wide start in front of an estimated 80,000 fans with Ray Harroun and his Marmon Wasp holding off Ralph Mulford for the victory. The event drew unprecedented exposure for the sport and new fans throughout the country, ultimately setting the stage for decades-long expansion of motorsports in America including the formation of NASCAR.

29 Long before Richmond International Raceway hosted its first NASCAR event, racing was a mainstay at the Virginia State Fairgrounds. In August 1907, the 1-mile dirt oval at the State Fairgrounds hosted the first race in Richmond. The event drew 2,500 fans and set the stage for the Fairgrounds to host countless open-wheel races throughout the next four decades. By 1928, the Richmond Fairgrounds was hosting unmodified stock car races. Jalopy races made their debut at the track in the 1930s and on July 4, 1941, the track held its first sanctioned stock car race. After World War II, racing continued at the Virginia State Fairgrounds at a new site in rural Henrico County, now home to Richmond International Raceway. The track was a mainstay for stock car racing throughout the remainder of the decade and into the early 1950s, joining the NASCAR ranks on April 19, 1953, when Lee Petty won the track's first Grand National event in a Petty Enterprises Dodge. Since then, the facility has hosted more than 200 races in seven different NASCAR divisions.

30 Can you imagine a NASCAR Cup, Xfinity, or Truck Series race being run on a superspeedway made out of wood? Of course not, but that's exactly what made up the racing surface of America's first superspeedways. With both land and wood plentiful and inexpensive, giant wooden racetracks made their first appearance in America in 1910. That's when the first of these Board Tracks (a 1.25-mile oval constructed of 2 x 4–foot wooden planks) was built in Playa del Rey, California. In addition to its unique construction, Playa del Rey also had 20-degree banking in the corners making it the first high-banked speedway in the country. Wooden superspeedway construction surged in 1915 with the addition of a 2-mile banked oval in Chicago, 1-mile banked ovals in Brooklyn, New York, and Des Moines, Iowa, and a 1.25-mile banked oval in Omaha, Nebraska. By far the most unique Board Track constructed in 1915 was a 2-mile Tacoma, Washington, oval banked 18 feet (more than 50 degrees). Eventually, a total of 19 high-banked, 1-mile or longer wooden-surface speedways were built through the late 1920s, most hosting AAA National Championship IndyCar-style races during that period. The Board Track era proved to be short, however, as weather played havoc with the untreated wooden surface. Heat, cold, rain and snow caused warping, cracking, and rotting surface conditions. In the end, most Board Tracks existed two or three years before figuratively rotting into the record books, but they remain a forerunner to Bill France's NASCAR high-banked superspeedway dream that became a reality at Daytona International Speedway in 1959.

31 While Charlotte Speedway on Little Rock Road was the site of the first NASCAR "Strictly Stock" race in 1949, another Charlotte Speedway circa 1924 was the original venue for the Queen City. A crowd estimated at more than 50,000 poured into the 1.25-mile banked oval October 25, 1924, to see an IndyCar-style race featuring top drivers of the day. The 200-lap, 250-mile AAA-sanctioned event featured 12 cars with Tommy Milton taking home the top prize of $10,000. In all, 15 races were held at the track, including 6 in 1926. After just three events in 1927, Charlotte Speedway closed due to the significant cost of maintaining the 2 x 4–inch green pine and cypress board surface that had deteriorated significantly in the hot North Carolina summer conditions.

32 Early auto racing was dangerous and fatalities were then (as they are now) an unwanted outcome. One of the most dangerous and deadly tracks of racing's early years was Ascot Motor Speedway (later Legion Ascot) in California. The 5/8-mile dirt track opened on Thanksgiving Day 1924 and hosted open-wheel and early stock car competitions through 1936. In all, 24 drivers died racing at the killer track with 6 perishing in 1933 alone. The deaths prompted an outcry from local newspapers printing headlines such as "Legalized Murder" and "Is It Worth It?" After driver Al Gordon and his riding mechanic Spider Matlock were killed in a January 26, 1936, crash, Legion Ascot was shut down. A fire four months later destroyed the track's grandstand; the speedway nicknamed "King of the Grim Reapers" was now closed forever.

33 Opened as a 1-mile dirt track October 17, 1931, Oakland Speedway was critical to the growth of auto racing in California. Located in San Leandro, the track was billed as "fastest dirt mile track in the country." A half-mile dirt track was built inside the Oakland oval in 1935 and with it came "low-buck" stock car racing. Oakland stayed active throughout the last half of the 1930s helping to integrate short-track stock car, midget, motorcycle, and roadster races into the California car scene. Oakland Speedway shut down at the outbreak of World War II and the track's grandstand came down in 1942. Never reopened, Oakland Speedway is now the site of the Bayfair Mall.

34 Opened in 1916, Atlanta's Lakewood Speedway (a 1-mile dirt oval with a lake taking up most of the infield) hosted its first stock car race November 11, 1938. Lloyd Seay won the event in a 1934 Ford roadster owned by Raymond Parks, besting a top field of drivers including Roy Hall, Bob Flock, and NASCAR founder Bill France Sr. Shuttered during World War II, Lakewood reopened in September 1945 and stayed busy throughout the rest of the decade and into the 1950s with NSCRA-, AAA-, and, NSCCC-sanctioned events. NASCAR made its first appearance at Lakewood November 11, 1951,

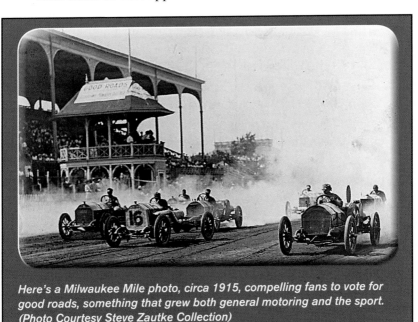

Here's a Milwaukee Mile photo, circa 1915, compelling fans to vote for good roads, something that grew both general motoring and the sport. (Photo Courtesy Steve Zautke Collection)

with Tim Flock besting brother Bob for the victory in the Strictly Stock event. NASCAR records show Lakewood hosted 13 events in the 1950s including a pair of Convertible Division races (1956 and 1958). Lee Petty is shown as the winner of the final NASCAR race at Lakewood in 1959 although his son, Richard Petty was originally declared the winner of the (now) NASCAR Grand National division event. The building of Atlanta Motor Speedway in 1960 marked the end of NASCAR at Lakewood Speedway, which eventually hosted its last auto race on Labor Day in 1979 when Georgia racing legend Buck Simmons took the checkered flag. While just a distant memory now, Lakewood Speedway proved to be one of the most important tracks of NASCAR's early years; its big city Atlanta market and larger-than-most 1-mile length helped further legitimize the sport in the southern United States.

35 With the departure of the land speed record runs to the Salt Flats in Utah, the city of Daytona Beach began looking for ways to continue both the excitement and the financial benefits of hosting auto racing events. In 1936, the city selected Sig Haugdahl to come up with a fresh concept. Haugdahl's response was to create a new event, a race for stock cars on a track that combined both the beach and the paved surface of Florida Highway A1A. Haugdahl, a local racer who set the land speed record of 180 mph in his *Wisconsin Special* on the beach in 1922, designed a track that initially measured 3.2 miles. The oval track used one long paved straight on A1A and another running parallel on the beach connected by a pair of hairpin turns in the sand. Under Haugdahl and later Bill France Sr., the Daytona Beach Course hosted stock car races until closing down for the duration of World War II. After the war, France quickly went back to promoting races on the track, which had expanded to a 4.2-mile distance. That Beach Course has the distinction of staging the first NASCAR-sanctioned race of any kind (a modified event won by Red Byron) in February 1948. The track continued to host NASCAR Modified, Strictly Stock, Convertible, and Grand National races until the opening of Daytona International Speedway in 1959. Paul Goldsmith wheeled a Ray Fox-prepared Pontiac to victory in the last NASCAR race held on the Daytona Beach Course in 1958.

Meanwhile, Banjo Matthews captured a 125-mile NASCAR Sports-man/Modified race. Curtis Turner grabbed top honors in the 160-mile NASCAR Convertible event that same weekend as racing on the beach at Daytona faded into history.

36 Recognized as the first 1-mile dirt speedway in America spe-cifically built for auto racing, Langhorne Speedway opened in 1926. Langhorne was literally a circle with no discernible straight-aways and hosted IndyCar, midget, sprint, and motorcycle racing throughout its early history. In 1940, the suburban Philadelphia track hosted the All American Championships, one of the first big stock car races held on the East Coast. Georgia ace Roy Hall won the 200-mile event with Bill France Sr. coming in second. Eventually, Langhorne showed up on the NASCAR tour as part of the inaugural 1949 NASCAR Strictly Stock season. Curtis Turner won the race, beating 44 other competitors. A total of 19 NASCAR events (includ-ing two Convertible Division races) were held at Langhorne Speed-way through the 1957 season. The track remained open until 1971 when it was demolished for the development of a shopping center.

PIT PASS

37 Born during the middle of the American Civil War, Henry Ford graduated from being an engineering assistant for Thomas Edi-son to one of America's greatest industrialists. His early auto racing efforts not only helped establish the new form of transportation as a viable commodity in American culture and commerce, but they also fueled the sport into the 21st Century through technical innovation and financial support. Ford constructed his first car, the Quadricycle, in 1896. With Edison's encouragement to build a bet-ter model, Ford spent the next 10 years doing that before introduc-ing the Ford Model T, the first affordable car for America's general public. Ford is also credited with implementing the first moving automotive assembly line, dealer franchising, increasing the mini-mum wage, shorter work weeks, and profit sharing for employees. In addition to being one of the wealthiest people in the world, Ford also ran for Senate in 1918 (he lost). He also consulted virtually every American president from the early 1900s through the 1940s. Ford also drew great criticism for his pacifist war, racial profiling, and anti-union activities. Prior to his death in 1947, Ford launched the Ford Foundation, created for the advancement of human welfare. He donated most of his wealth to the foundation, which today is worth an estimated $13 billion dollars.

38 Born in Wauseon, Ohio, in 1878, Barney Oldfield was the first great American race car driver. In 1902, the young bicycle racer agreed to drive Henry Ford's famous 999 race car, a lofty proposition given Oldfield had never driven a car much less raced one. Undaunted, Oldfield and the 999 defeated a host of challengers during the next two years. He was the first driver to average faster than a mile a minute in a race car, turning the trick in 59.6 seconds at Indianapolis in 1903. In 1910, he set the world land speed record by piloting a Blitzen Benz to 131.724 mph on the sands at Daytona Beach. That made Oldfield a star to the American public and led to acting roles and endorsements. Oldfield later became the first to turn a lap at more than 100-mph average at the Indianapolis Motor Speedway in 1916. An advocate for safety, Oldfield was a pioneer in the use of driver safety restraints, roll cage use, and tire development. Oldfield retired in 1918 but stayed connected to motorsports until his death in 1946.

39 The son of a Michigan governor, William Durant wasn't dreaming of an automotive empire when he took over the Buick Car Company in 1904, but that's exactly what happened. He used Buick as the cornerstone to General Motors Holding Company, founded September 16, 1908. By combining Buick, Oldsmobile, and later Cadillac and Oakland (Pontiac), Durant formed the first automotive super-company. A self-made millionaire, Durant believed that avoiding duplication was the automobile's ticket to profitability. It is said that Durant was prepared to spend $8 million to acquire the Ford Motor Company in 1909, but that deal never happened. Later, with finances stretched to the limit, Durant was forced out of General Motors in 1910 only to return to the business a year later after partnering with Louis Chevrolet. By 1914, Durant had bought out Chevrolet and set his sights on taking back General Motors. In

1916, Durant had acquired enough stock to again become president of GM and during the next four years grew the car company to a staggering size. Durant lost control of General Motors again in 1920. His next automotive project, Durant Motors, lasted through the 1920s before falling victim to the Great Depression in 1933. Having lost millions on stock investments when the stock market crashed in 1929, Durant declared bankruptcy in 1935. In the end, the man who created General Motors worked as a bowling alley manager before his death in 1947.

40 Considered the first great American gasoline-powered engine builder, Ransom Olds patented his first gas "hit and miss" engine in 1886 and founded America's first car company, the Olds Motor Vehicle Company, in 1897. Olds was the first to outsource parts and mass-produce cars, specifically the Olds Curved Dash Runabout, producing 425 vehicles in 1901. These vehicles featured transmissions from Horace and John Dodge, engines from Henry Leland (the founder of Cadillac and Lincoln) and bodies from Fred Fisher, who went on to General Motors design fame. In 1902, Olds put his car brand on the auto racing map when he and a stripped down Runabout named *The Pirate* won the first official timed event on the shores of Daytona Beach, Florida. In later years, his Olds Rocket 88 became the engine of choice for modified and late model stock cars as well as in NASCAR; the brand won five of the first eight NASCAR Strictly Stock races during the inaugural 1949 season. The high point for Oldsmobile's racing success came in 1955 when Tim Flock delivered the brand's only NASCAR Manufacturers' Championship. Olds also founded REO Motor Company and the first line of mass-produced trucks in 1908, and later designed and produced the first gas-powered lawnmower in the 1940s. Olds died in 1950 at the age of 86.

41 While most historians remember September 26, 1909, as the start of the International Ladies Garment Workers Union strike in New York City, NASCAR fans celebrate it as the birth of NASCAR founder William Getty France; the son of Irish immigrants Emma Graham and William Henry France. As a teenager, the Washington,

Bill France Sr. grew NASCAR from an idea to one of the most successful professional sports enterprises in America. (Photo Courtesy Ed Samples Jr. Collection)

D.C. native would joyride his father's Model T on a banked board track in Maryland. Later, in the midst of the Great Depression, France moved his family (now consisting of wife Anne and son Bill Jr.) to Daytona Beach, Florida, to escape the brutal winters of the north. There, he became ingrained in the emerging Daytona racing culture and the rest, as they say, is history.

42 One of America's early racing stars, Joe Tracy, rivaled Barney Oldfield as the country's top driver at the turn of the 20th Century. A regular competitor in the early Vanderbilt and Bennett Cup races, he is the only driver to participate in the first five Vanderbilt Cup and Elimination events from 1904 to 1906. Tracy participated in the 1904 Daytona Beach Tournament races and drove a Peerless to a second-place finish in that 5-mile event. He retired after the 1906 season, and was retroactively awarded the 1906 National Driving Championship in 1951.

43 You won't find William Klann's name in any NASCAR record book, but his name will forever be linked to the American automobile just the same. "Pa" Klann, a machinist at Ford, brought the concept of the automated assembly line to Henry Ford. Klann visited the Swift Meat packing slaughterhouse in Chicago where he was impressed with the factory's deconstruction line and the efficiency of one person doing the same job. Klann took the idea to Detroit where he and Peter Martin, head of Ford production at the time, "flipped" the concept, making the first modern moving automobile assembly line. This new system allowed Ford to mass-produce inexpensive cars.

44 Long before lending his name and design instincts to an American car brand, Louis Chevrolet was a top race car driver. Born in France on Christmas Day 1878, Chevrolet first moved to Canada and then to Brooklyn, New York, in 1899. Initially a mechanic, Chevrolet began driving race cars in 1900 and by 1905, was beating Barney Oldfield, Henry Ford, and others in high-profile races. His victories drew the attention of William Durant, president at General Motors, who then hired Chevrolet to drive for his Buick race team. Chevrolet not only delivered on the track, but also in the shop where he designed a car under his own name. The vehicle featured an industry-first 6-cylinder, center-of-floor gearshift, and an emergency brake mounted under the dash. Launched in 1912, the new Chevrolet sold nearly 20,000 cars its first three years.

Chevrolet was unhappy, often clashing with Durant, forcing him to leave the company in 1914. He then founded Frontenac Motor Corporation with his brothers, Gaston and Arthur. Using a Ford Model T as the base chassis, the Chevrolet brothers built three Frontenac race cars, one for each to drive in the 1915 Indianapolis 500. While none of the cars finished, Chevrolet was determined to build a winner, a feat he accomplished when Gaston Chevrolet and Tommy Milton won back-to-back Indy 500s in 1920 and 1921. Meanwhile, Louis competed in the Indy 500 four times, his best finish a seventh-place in 1919. Unfortunately, an economic downturn forced Chevrolet and Frontenac out of business in 1922. Chevrolet continued building cylinder heads for the now "Fronty-Fords" until the Ford Model A all but put him out of business. In the end, Chevrolet never cashed in on the financial success of the brand bearing his name although he returned to the company as a consultant in the 1930s. Chevrolet was forced to retire after suffering a brain hemorrhage in 1938. He lived out his final years in poor health passing away on June 6, 1941. He is buried across the street from the Indianapolis Motor Speedway in Holy Cross Cemetery.

45 The career of Hall of Fame Driver Wendell Scott highlights the history of African-Americans in NASCAR. While Scott is a NASCAR pioneer, others laid the groundwork for his entrance into motorsports. Dewey Gadsen, better known as Rajo Jack, was part of that group. Barred from top competitions in the 1920s and 1930s because of his color, Rajo Jack competed in "outlaw" races on the West Coast. He sometimes claimed to be Native American or a Portuguese driver named Jack DeSoto so he could be allowed to race. Among his biggest wins was the 1936 AAA National Championship 200-mile stock car event at Mines Field in Los Angeles. He also won 300-milers at Oakland and Ascot Speedways in the 1930s and raced into the 1950s before ending his driving career. Gadsen died of a heart attack in 1956 and his death certificate identifies him as Rajo Jack.

46 Frank Lockhart had Daytona International Speedway grandstand named honoring him as one of the great drivers of the 1920s. Born in Ohio, Lockhart mastered the dirt and board tracks of California before moving to IndyCars in 1926; he promptly won the Indy 500, making him the fourth rookie to capture the event. Lockhart won four additional IndyCar events in 1926 and finished second in the AAA National Championship standings. During the off-season, Lockhart, along with John and Zenas Wiesel, designed and produced a manifold to cool the fuel between the carburetor and supercharger. Lockhart secured a patent for the part now commonly called an intercooler. The intercooler provided a significant jump in horsepower and propelled Lockhart to a new world land speed record of 164.02 mph during a pre–Indy 500 test on Muroc Dry Lake in California.

Lockhart and his Perfect Circle Turbocharged racer then won the pole for the 1927 Indy 500 and led the most laps before the car broke a rod late in the race. He won nine Indy Car events in 1927 and again finished second in the AAA National Championship chase.

Buoyed by his land speed record of 1927, Lockhart focused on a new project for 1928: the Stutz Black Hawk land speed racer. The car was plagued by bad luck, crashing on its first outing on the beach at Daytona in February 1928. Two months later, Lockhart and the Black Hawk returned to Daytona for another land speed attempt. This time, Lockhart, at just 25 years old, was killed in the crash, cementing his place as a Daytona and racing legend for all time.

47 While best known as a top official for the Automobile Club of America (AAA) West Coast Region during the 1920s and 1930s, Art Pillsbury made a then-unknown giant contribution to NASCAR and the construction of its banked speedways. Pillsbury was the first to apply the Searle Spiral Easement Curve to racetrack building. The concept was pioneered in the railroad industry; the rails were placed at different heights on a gradual incline in the turns, easing the transition from the flat straights into the banked corners. This allowed for greater overall speed. Pillsbury and speedway construction manager Jack Prince first applied this spiral banking formula when building the 1.25-mile Beverly Hills Speedway in 1919.

At the track's first event in 1920, cars held the track at record race speeds averaging in excess of 100 mph for the entire event, an astonishing mark considering that was faster than the average qualifying speed for the Indianapolis 500 at that time. Thanks to Pillsbury, racing not only got faster, but race car geometry and set up changed forever. Pillsbury went on to build or consult on most major banked superspeedways of the Board Track era. His crowning achievement was a 45-degree banked track at Culver City, California, in 1924. Since then, "Pillsbury's Principles" have been used in the construction of virtually every banked track in America, including those on the current NASCAR tour.

48 Without a doubt, Englishman Sir Malcolm Campbell was the all-time king of the Daytona Beach world land speed record, setting a new record five times from 1928 through 1935. Campbell's *Bluebird* land speed cars were famous worldwide and the 1933 version was the first to break the 250 mph barrier with a 272.465 mph record run. Two years later, Campbell slightly bettered the mark with a

276.710 mph clocking. As Campbell helped put Daytona on the map as the World Center of Speed, he also nearly destroyed that distinction when he moved his land speed record runs to the dry lake beds near Bonneville, Utah. It was there that Campbell realized his dream of becoming the first to break the 300 mph barrier with a 301.129 mph world speed record in September 1935. He promptly retired and never made another land speed record attempt. He passed away from a stroke in 1949.

49 As stock car racing's first great team owner, Raymond Parks' accomplishments are often overlooked. Born in 1914, Parks, the oldest of 16 children, grew up in hardscrabble Georgia. He left home at 15 to work in the illegal moonshine business and began fielding race cars for local Atlanta drivers Roy Hall and Lloyd Seay in 1938. Wrenched by legendary mechanic Red Vogt, Parks' immaculately prepared Fords, with Hall, Seay, and sometimes Bill France Sr. behind the wheel, dominated stock car racing in the south prior to World War II. After the war, Parks returned to racing and his cars won the first two NASCAR championships contested: the modified title with Fonty Flock in 1948 and the first NASCAR Strictly Stock title with driver Red Byron in 1949. Parks, always dressed in a coat, tie, and hat, kept NASCAR alive in its early years, often bankrolling the enterprise for a struggling Bill France. After scoring a fourth-place finish with driver Curtis Turner at Montgomery, Alabama, in 1955, Parks curtailed his support of racing and bowed out as a NASCAR team owner. A member of the International Motorsports and the NASCAR Halls of Fame, Parks passed away in 2010 at the age of 96.

50 Considered by many as the best natural-talent stock car driver of the pre-World War II era, Lloyd Seay's life was cut short in September 1941 when his cousin shot him to death during an argument over an order of sugar for their moonshine business. Before the tragedy, Seay had translated his "whiskey tripper" driving skills to the racetrack, capturing the first race at Lakewood Speedway in 1938. Driving for his cousin Raymond Parks, Seay won multiple events throughout the South in 1939 and 1940 before scoring one of his biggest victories on the beach at Daytona in August 1941.

Two weeks later, Seay again won, this time lapping the field twice in a race at High Point, North Carolina. On Labor Day, September 1, 1941, Seay earned his biggest win to date capturing the 100-mile National Championship Stock Car race at Lakewood. Sadly, the next day, he was shot dead, a premature end to the life of stock car racing's first great driving star.

51 Considered the greatest mechanic of the early stock car era, Louis Jerome "Red" Vogt is also remembered as the man who gave NASCAR its name. Working out of a small garage in Atlanta, Vogt organized and chartered the National Stock Car Racing Association (NSCRA) in 1929, one of Georgia's first racing series. He also built Miller engines for the Indy 500 and one year served as the riding mechanic for Peter DePaolo. In the late 1930s, Vogt's mechanical genius propelled the winning stock car efforts of team owner Raymond Parks and drivers Roy Hall, Lloyd Seay, and Bill France before the formation of NASCAR. Vogt is credited with naming Bill France's new stock car series "NASCAR" at the now famous Streamline Hotel meeting in 1947. Perhaps more important, he is credited with crafting the first set of rules for the sanctioning body.

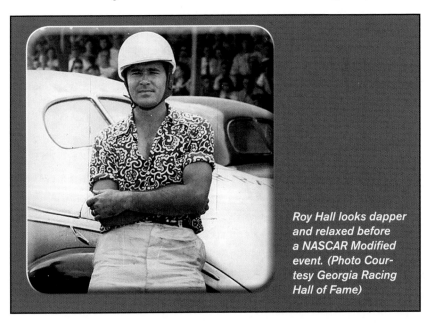

Roy Hall looks dapper and relaxed before a NASCAR Modified event. (Photo Courtesy Georgia Racing Hall of Fame)

Back on track, he created winning Vogt Specials for Bob Flock, Fonty Flock, Red Byron, Curtis Turner, Fireball Roberts, and Jack Smith during the early years of NASCAR. Vogt eventually closed his Atlanta garage, lending his talents to DePaolo's NASCAR factory Ford team, Carl Kiekhaefer's potent Chrysler 300 effort, and the legendary Fish Carburetor Buicks of the 1950s. Vogt eventually moved to Daytona Beach where he opened his own garage. He retired in 1968 and died at the age of 86 in 1991.

52 In 1972, singer Jim Croce released *"Rapid Roy, the Stock Car Boy,"* a song inspired by early stock car racing great Roy Hall. One of the best, and fastest, moonshine runners in Georgia in the late 1930s, Hall made his racing debut at the first Lakewood Speedway race in 1938. Driving for cousin/car owner Raymond Parks, Hall was one of the early kings of the Daytona Beach Road Course, winning there in 1939 and 1940. He was declared stock car racing's "mythical" national champion in 1939 and 1941. Hall, consistently in trouble with the law and often racing under an assumed name to avoid authorities, saw his driving career short-circuited when he was charged and convicted of an Atlanta bank robbery in 1945. He served 3½ years of a six-year prison sentence. Hall returned to racing, wheeling a Parks-owned Oldsmobile to a sixth-place finish in the 1949 NASCAR Strictly Stock race at North Wilkesboro. Two weeks later, Hall was seriously injured in a modified race and never regained his championship racing form. He retired from racing in 1960 and later saw his racing exploits put to song by Croce in 1972. Hall died in 1991 at the age of 71.

MILESTONES

53 While mass production is usually seen as the launching point of American automobile culture, it was the development of several tools during the 19th Century that made construction of early cars a reality. Interchangeable parts on cars and their mass production would have never been possible without the milling machines, lathes, metal planers, and standardized control jigs developed in the late 1800s. All of these tools are still commonly used in the construction of NASCAR purpose-built race cars.

54 NASCAR has had countless epic races, but none of them have ever earned the right to be called the "Race of the Century." That distinction was reserved for the 1895 Chicago to Evanston, and back again, event. Held November 28, 1895, the event is widely considered the first official stock car race held in the United States. The Chicago *Times Herald* newspaper and publisher, Herman H. Kohlsaat, fanned interest for the event. A total of 83 cars entered for the event originally scheduled for November 2, but when only three cars showed up, the race was rescheduled for Thanksgiving Day. On that day, six vehicles attended including one lone American-made gasoline car, the Duryea Motor Wagon. The high, thin-profile wooden-spoke carriage-wheeled car featured a 2-cylinder engine with tiller steering.

Battling near-freezing temperatures and overnight snow making roads nearly impassable, Duryea was the early leader before he hit a rut and broke the steering arm off his car. Undaunted, he found a blacksmith and had a replacement bar formed. Now in second place behind a Benz owned by Macy's Department Store, Duryea regained the lead just before the halfway turnaround in Evanston. On the drive back to Chicago, Duryea's car lost one of two cylinders requiring another near-hour delay for repairs. Despite that, Duryea crossed the finish line at Jackson Park more than an hour ahead of the Macy's Benz, the only other car to finish. Duryea won $2,000 and great celebrity for his win as newspapers across the country hailed his amazing achievement for winning The Race of the Century.

55 The Ford Motor Company has scored more than 700 NASCAR Cup division wins, a foundation of success built when the first victory came in its first race. The October 10, 1901, contest pitted a then-unknown Henry Ford and his *Sweepstakes* car against Alexander Winton, already a major automobile builder. Considered one of the best race drivers of the day, Winton and his *Bullet* race car were clearly the favorite at the Grosse Point, Michigan, horse track located outside of Detroit. Winton quickly pulled away from Ford at the start of the race. Ford, a novice driver at best, eventually steadied his tiller-steered car and began closing the gap on Winton.

When the *Bullet* slowed with mechanical problems in the 8th mile of the 10-mile event, Ford roared by and rolled to an easy win with a time of 13 minutes 23 seconds. The victory attracted investors to Ford's new venture, Ford Motor Company, and signaled the beginning of the brand's long participation in motorsports.

56 Named after Charles Goodyear, an American chemist who developed and patented vulcanized rubber in 1844, the Goodyear Tire and Rubber Company was founded in 1898 by Frank Seiberling. One year later, the Akron, Ohio, company produced its first automobile tire. In 1901, Seiberling provided Henry Ford, what is considered the first racing tires for his *Sweepstakes* car. Goodyear later developed and patented the first tubeless tire in 1903. When Henry Ford introduced his Ford Model T in 1908, it rode on Goodyears. Spurred on by early successes such as providing tires for Barney Oldfield's world speed record run of 131.72 mph in 1910, Goodyear continued developing racing tires and won its first Indianapolis 500 in 1919. After another Indy 500 victory in 1920, Goodyear coined the phrase "Win On Sunday, Sell On Monday" in its advertising. Goodyear eventually came to NASCAR with a series of tire tests for the Convertible Division at Darlington in 1954 and, in 1955, team owner Carl Kiekhaefer used Goodyear "Police Specials" on his potent Chrysler 300 NASCAR champion race cars. In the 1960s, Goodyear survived a tire war with Firestone and fended off Hoosier Tires for NASCAR supremacy in the middle 1990s. Since 1968, every NASCAR Cup, and Grand National champion has raced on Goodyear tires.

57 As it is today, Detroit was a focal point for the American automobile industry and it makes sense for the city to be among the first having organized car races. In one of the first track-rental agreements in motorsports, a local automobile dealer leased Daniel Campo's Grosse Point area track for Detroit's first race. October 10, 1901, was practically a civic holiday as many businesses and even the local courthouse closed for the day. Meanwhile, the event attracted entries from all over the country. The first race was a 1-mile electric car test and was won by a Baker produced in Cleveland, Ohio. The

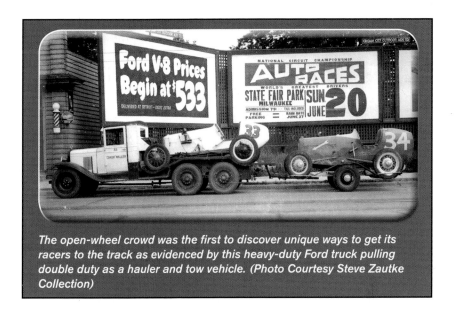

The open-wheel crowd was the first to discover unique ways to get its racers to the track as evidenced by this heavy-duty Ford truck pulling double duty as a hauler and tow vehicle. (Photo Courtesy Steve Zautke Collection)

second 1-mile race was a contest for cars weighing less than 1,500 pounds and was won by a Toledo Steam Car. The third event saw Henry Ford and his *Sweepstakes* racer score a stunning victory over Alexander Winton in a 10-mile clash.

58 Long before NASCAR was established in 1947, the American Automobile Association (AAA) was sanctioning races. Formed in March 1902, the AAA Racing Board sanctioned its first race in 1904, the Vanderbilt Cup. A year later, AAA created the National Motor Car Championship marking the first time in American racing history that a points system was used to decide a national champion. A feud with the Automobile Club of America (ACA) spurred a name change to the AAA Contest Board in 1908 and, with the backing of the Manufacturers Contest Association (MCA), organized a set of rules that outlawed purpose-built European race cars in favor of American "stock configuration" cars. To ensure that stock vehicles were used, the AAA decreed that at least 50 cars had to be produced and sold during a calendar year to be eligible for competition. Many of these AAA types of rules can still be found in the NASCAR rule book. For the next 40-plus years, the AAA Contest Board ruled as America's top motorsports organization sanctioning

everything from the Indianapolis 500 to national sports car, midget, sprint, and stock car events. In 1955, the AAA abruptly ended all racing associations after 83 spectators died and more than 120 more injured when a car launched into the crowd at the 24 Hours of Le Mans event.

59 The 1904 Vanderbilt Cup Race was the first major international automobile race held in America. Organized by William K. Vanderbilt Jr., "Willie K." saw the event as a springboard for American cars to rival their European counterparts. The inaugural race took place on Long Island, New York, October 8, 1904. Seventeen cars from France, Germany, Italy, and the United States took the green flag in two-minute intervals. Disaster struck almost immediately, when George Arents Jr. rolled his Mercedes on the first lap killing his riding-mechanic Carl Mensel. George Heath won the 10-lap race, averaging 52.2 mph in his French Panhard. The Vanderbilt Cup remained one of America's most important races through 1916 before going dark from 1917 until racing resumed in 1936. While several races since have been called the Vanderbilt Cup, none of them have ties to the original concept.

60 Considered the first sanctioning organization for competitive motor racing, the New York-based Automobile Club of America began establishing contest rules in 1904. The club staged the 1908 American Grand Prize race considered to be the first American Gran Prix. Perhaps the club's most important achievement, however, was its tireless lobbying for public motoring safety, laws, and better roads. Its efforts drew the attention of President William Howard Taft, the first President to travel by automobile. Taft helped the group champion automotive expansion in the United States. The ACA continued its public and motorsports efforts until the 1930s when the Great Depression crippled the automotive industry. The organization was disbanded during World War II.

61 The American Grand Prize was the first Gran Prix race held in the United States. The watershed event was held November 26,

1906, in Savannah, Georgia, in front of an estimated crowd of 250,000. Twenty teams took the green flag in the 16-lap, 402-mile race with French Gran Prix driver Louis Wagner wheeling a Fiat to victory. Despite the success, the ACA didn't sanction another American Grand Prize event until 1910 when David Bruce-Brown beat Ralph DePalma for the win. Bruce-Brown won the American Grand Prize race again in 1911 before the event was moved to Milwaukee, Wisconsin, for the 1912 race. Caleb Bragg won the 1912 race on the 7.88-mile course in an event marred by the crash death of Bruce-Brown during practice. No race was held in 1913 and the event moved again, this time to Santa Monica, California. Run on an 8.44-mile course along the Pacific Ocean, Eddie Pullen's Mercer took the top spot in the 1914 race, which, for the first time, featured primarily American drivers and cars due to the outbreak of World War I in Europe. The 1915 American Grand Prize race was run in San Francisco, California, and won by Dario Resta while the 1916 Santa Monica Gran Prix saw Howdy Wilcox and Johnny Aitken co-pilot a Peugeot to victory. The 1916 race, part of the AAA National Championship series, proved to be the last Formula 1 Gran Prix–style race held in the United States until the 1959 United States Grand Prix at Sebring International Raceway December 12, 1959.

62 The preferred distance for many NASCAR races has become 500 miles, but one of the earliest stock production car races in America covered more than twice that distance. Many early races were 24-hour affairs and it was simply a matter of how many miles could be run in that time. On June 22, 1907, nine cars took the green flag on the Michigan State Fairground's 1-mile dirt oval in Detroit. Henry Ford's Model K won the race, covering 1,135 miles. The winning distance was 300 miles more than the previous best in a 24-hour event. Because the rules allowed multiple drivers and cars, drivers Frank Kulick and Bert Lorimer used two different Model Ks to win the event. Herbert Lytle's Pope Toledo finished second with 1,109 miles completed; seven of the nine starters completed the marathon race.

63 From the 1992 through the 1997 Winston Cup seasons, NASCAR Hall of Fame driver Darrell Waltrip sported sponsorship from Western Auto/Parts America. The association represented the peak in motorsports marketing for the company formed by entrepreneur George Pepperdine as Western Auto Supply Company. Pepperdine quickly realized Henry Ford's 1908 Model T was an automotive aftermarket opportunity waiting to happen and formed a mail order business that same year catering mainly to Model T owners. Pepperdine made a fortune selling Model T and other parts and opened Western Auto's first retail store in 1921. Along with other retail giants of the 1920s, including Piggly Wiggly, J. C. Penney, and F. W. Woolworth, Western Auto helped develop today's modern franchise business concepts. Eventually, Western Auto grew to nearly 1,600 outlets providing parts to generations of racers over the next six decades. In 1988, Western Auto was purchased by Sears and rebranded in 1996 as Parts America. Sears sold off its shares of Western Auto/Parts America in 1998 ending its association with Waltrip, but the company has stayed an active NASCAR marketer under its new name, Advance Auto Parts.

64 Each year, NASCAR updates its rulebook with performance and safety initiatives. Prior to the 1914 season, a new rule prohibiting the consumption of alcohol during the Indianapolis 500 was instituted. The edict was deemed necessary after Frenchman Jules Goux reportedly drank up to six one-pint bottles of champagne (one at each pit stop) during the 1913 Indy 500. The bubbly apparently had little effect on Goux; he won the race in a Peugeot. Later, Goux credited the champagne with helping him secure the victory. Race officials didn't quite see it that way and the next year they implemented the first rules against drinking and driving in auto racing.

65 The American Automobile Association and its Contest Board sanctioned one of the first stock car circuits in 1927. Races were held in Atlantic City, New Jersey; Altoona, Pennsylvania; Salem, Indiana; and Charlotte, North Carolina, that year with some events in support of the AAA National Championship Indy Car events. Among the cars that competed were Stutz Bearcat, Auburn, and

Early auto races drew giant crowds, treated to great spectacles on the track and in the air with balloon ascensions and flyovers such as this. (Photo Courtesy Steve Zautke Collection)

Studebaker, all roadster-type stock models with few enhancements. Early top drivers Ralph Hepburn and Frank Lockhart also participated in the races. Unfortunately, few records of the events remain today as the AAA abandoned the series after 1928.

On October 28, 1919, the United States passed the Volstead Act prohibiting the production, storage, transportation, and sale of alcoholic beverages in America. Little did Congress know that the 18th Amendment to the Constitution would be a boon to stock car racing as law-breaking moonshiners and whiskey trippers would become some of NASCAR's earliest driving stars. This was especially true in the Southern United States where Roy Hall, Lloyd Seay, Jimmy Lewallen, Bill Blair, Junior Johnson, and others honed their driving skills running "moon." The act also spurred a technological boom for stock car racing as moonshiners modified their pedestrian-looking cars into lightweight, high-powered vehicles capable of outrunning the fastest police cars of the day. With local and regional bragging rights at stake, the moonshiners headed to local fields, makeshift tracks, and fairground ovals to prove who had the hottest iron in head-to-head competition. These early events drew large crowds of spectators and eventually led to more formalized races in the South during the latter 1930s. The repeal of the Volstead Act on December 5, 1933, did little to slow stock car racing as moonshiners/racers continued to make illegal alcohol, modify their cars, and thrill racing crowds well into the 1960s.

67 Held on August 26, 1933, in conjunction with the Chicago World's Fair, the Elgin Road Races gave stock car racing a giant boost on a grand scale. The Elgin site of many area road races from 1910 to 1920, the 1933 event featured top national driving stars Wilbur Shaw, Mauri Rose, Fred Frame, Ralph DePalma, and Lou Moore. A crowd estimated at 35,000 showed up for two races, the first a 200-mile Indy-car event won by Phil Shafer in a Buick Special over Frame's Miller Duesenberg and Rose's Studebaker-powered Russell 8. The second race was limited to stock roadsters with a maximum engine displacement of 231 ci. The 15-car field included 2 Chevrolets, 1 Plymouth, 1 Dodge, and 11 new 1933 Fords powered by improved Flathead V-8 engines that had been tooled by a new young talent named Harry Miller. The 200-mile stock car event proved to be an all-Ford show as Frame and Jack Petticord's Fords swapped the lead before Frame won in a time of 2 hours 32 minutes 6.1 seconds (80.22 average mph). At one point, Frame's Ford was timed at more than 100 mph on the front stretch as Fords dominated the finish by taking the first seven spots. While Ford and Miller went on to motorsports history, the 8-mile Elgin track was shut down after the race and never opened again.

68 Hailed as a new era for automobile racing by the Los Angeles *Times*, the Gilmore Gold Cup is considered to be one of the very first series for stock cars. Sponsored by Gilmore Oil Company, the four-race series began in 1933 with the Elgin Road Races. The second race of the series was held on February 18, 1934, at Mines Field, a local airport located near what is now Los Angeles International Airport. Sanctioned by the AAA, the race between mostly Ford

Flathead V-8 powered roadsters drew a crowd estimated near 75,000. Each paid $1.50 admission to watch some of the top drivers of the day (Pete DePaolo, Louie Meyer, Rex Mays, and Wilber Shaw) race on a specially created "B-shaped," 2-mile airport oval.

Despite the star power, Hartwell Wilburn "Stubby" Stubblefield drove to the win, but only after a four-day recheck of the scoring to confirm his victory. The Gilmore Gold Cup was completed with two additional 1934 events, one at Ascot Speedway and the other at Oakland Speedway. The Ascot race was run on both the track and roads surrounding the speedway, leading to an epic financial failure because fans could watch the action without buying a ticket. While it was a monetary success, the final event at the 1-mile Oakland dirt oval proved to be the end of the Gilmore Gold Cup as William Pickens (the driving force behind the series) contracted blood poisoning after stepping on a rusty nail at the first Mines Field race and died later in 1934. Despite the demise of the series, the Los Angeles Mines Field event laid the groundwork for municipalities to become involved in stock car racing, a concept that eventually played out on the shores of Daytona Beach two years later.

69 Sponsorship in today's NASCAR is essential to a team's success. The initial marriage of a stock car team and a company sponsorship is believed to have happened at the 1936 inaugural Daytona Beach-Road Course race. Winner Milt Marion's 1936 Ford convertible had sponsorship from Permatex, a northeastern-based sealant company. The idea behind the promotion was to have Marion take a 10,000-mile trip around America to prove the reliability of an engine sealed with Permatex Form A Gasket #2, a shellac-based adhesive designed to repair gasket leaks. For this event, Permatex had Bill France Sr. replace 28 solid gaskets in the car's engine (standard clearances required keeping the cylinder head, fuel pump, and rear end gaskets).

Marion left New York City March 1, 1936, and headed for Daytona where, a week later, he and the "Permatex Form A Gasket Test Car" won. That would be a great ending, but the promotion continued the next day as Marion headed to Texas for the remainder of the trip. Marion made stops in Los Angeles, San Francisco, Denver, and Chicago before the journey ended back in New York City. With the engine still in perfect nick, he drove the car on a daily basis, even racing it throughout the summer of 1936.

In September, when finally disassembled, it had run a full 22,297 miles since being sealed with Permatex Form A Gasket #2. The company used the event to fulfill the sponsorship at the consumer level by featuring it in its advertising, including a 16-page promotional brochure complete with "how-to" shots and a first-person account by Marion. In 1975, the company replicated Marion's drive/promotion with Bobby Allison running a 300-mile test at Talladega Superspeedway. His stock car featured an engine sealed with Permatex products and averaged 157.094 over the 300-mile test with no breakdowns.

70 Despite costing as little as 10 cents, attempts to make money by selling tickets often failed because spectator areas were not clearly defined and were often overrun by non-paying customers. This was certainly true at the first Daytona Beach and Road Course event; the

Race officials line up the competitors prior to the drop of the green flag at the first Daytona Beach Stock Car race March 8, 1936. (Photo Courtesy Ed Samples Jr. Collection)

City of Daytona lost an estimated $22,000 promoting the inaugural beach stock car race. The Daytona Elks Club took over the promotion of the race in 1937 and suffered the same financial fate. For the 1938 race, local gas station owner Bill France Sr. took over the promotion of the Daytona race and charged a modest 50 cents a ticket. In an effort to sell more tickets and run off non-paying onlookers, France posted signs stating "Beware of Alligators" around various parts of the ocean-side Daytona Beach track layout. France sold 5,000 tickets and split the profits with promotional partner and race car owner Charlie Reece. Based on that success, France decided to continue his promotional events and the first thing he did for the 1939 Daytona Beach race was double the price of admission from fifty cents to one dollar.

Chapter 2

The 1940s: Let's Get Organized

The conclusion of World War II flew the green flag on a growth period of never before-seen economic prosperity and individual freedom.

Americans were flush with confidence after winning World War II. Meanwhile, the economy, in the depths of the Great Depression at the onset of the war, was at full steam.

People had money and were ready to spend it. Subsequently, families grew larger with the start of the Baby Boom while another boom in the construction of private homes also began.

Meanwhile, Detroit's Big Three (Ford, Chrysler, and General Motors) didn't disappoint. Dated pre-war designs were ditched for new vehicles featuring updated stylish exteriors and more-powerful V-8 engines. In the four years prior to the end of the decade, these new, sleeker models boasted an array of improvements such as keyed ignition starting, hydraulic disc brakes, turn signals, and torque converter–based automatic transmissions

In addition, new cars were attainable to almost everyone as both GM and Ford pioneered in-house auto financing. Meanwhile, the first driver's

The shoreline of the Atlantic Ocean was flooded with cars prior to the running of a Modified race on the Daytona Beach Road Course. (Photo Courtesy Ed Samples Jr. Collection)

education classes made getting behind the wheel easier and less intimidating than ever.

Throw in a massive government initiative to build roads virtually everywhere in the United States, and the era of the American automobile took off on a journey that continues today.

Of course, all of this was good for stock car racing. During World War II, racing was all but dead, but with new vehicles quickly coming to market, unwanted 1930s and early 1940s cars were available and inexpensive. This fueled a renaissance of the sport across America almost immediately after the final shots of the war.

Meanwhile, forward-thinking impresarios such as Bill France Sr. envisioned organizing the sport on a more professional level and a new form of racing taking stock cars off the showroom floor and racing with little modification. This "Strictly Stock" idea was an immediate hit, but more important, the concept took racing from the track and put it squarely in the driveway of every American home.

To say this convergence of events forever changed stock car racing would be an understatement; the late 1940s made stock car racing, and NASCAR specifically, a part of the American sports landscape.

CARS

71 One of the biggest detriments to launching a Strictly Stock division after World War II was the lack of new cars. Out of production since 1942, auto manufacturers had to retool before they could offer the public more than warmed-over pre-war styles. That put the Strictly Stock racing idea on hold until 1949 leaving the modified division to do most of the racing from 1945 to 1949. These 1937-and-newer coupes and sedans were required to have a stock-appearing look by retaining full fenders and windshields. They were also required to use the original ignition system and gas tank. The engine rules were wide-open as there were no bore and stroke requirements (they could be made as large as the engine could withstand). New and/or multiple carburetors, ground crankshafts and cams, and high-compression heads were also allowed to produce engines that could carry the small, lightweight cars to speeds well over 120 mph.

Red Byron (22) and Swain Prichett (17) battle their way through a pack of cars at the Hall County Fairgrounds in Gainesville, Georgia, on July 4, 1947. (Photo Courtesy Georgia Racing Hall of Fame)

72 While new tubeless and radial tire designs were introduced and manufactured in the 1940s, most racing tires were still bias-ply rayon cord construction. The use of regular passenger car or truck tires got a boost in the late 1940s with the introduction of the 4-ply rayon cord tire. Although the thicker rubber carcass of the tires created more heat at high speeds, the double strength four-plies advanced both safety and speed because they stood up to the rigors of racing better than prior two-ply models.

73 NASCAR legend Ralph Moody's first car (a 1940 Ford Coupe) is typical of the low-buck stock cars that competed throughout the South after the end of the war. Moody's car remained stock to a large degree, with wheelwells enlarged for clearance and the doors welded shut for safety. Both front and rear bumpers were removed and replaced with steel "booger bars." Under the hood, the mostly stock 239-ci Ford Flathead V-8 was bored out to a total displacement of 250 ci. Thanks to performance parts such as an Ed Iskenderian camshaft and a Stromberg 97 carburetor, the engine produced an estimated 100 hp. The power was delivered to the wheels through a stock 3-speed transmission and a Ford 3.78 rear-end gear. As with many stock cars of the day, Moody's car retained its headlights so it could be driven home after the race.

74 Lee Petty was a hardscrabble farmer from Level Cross, North Carolina, when, at the age of 35, he decided to give stock car racing a try in 1948. Petty and his brother Julie built a stock car out of an old 1937 Plymouth coupe and entered it in a race at Danville, Virginia. Amazingly, Petty won and at his next racing event in Roanoke, Virginia, finished second. Buoyed by his success, Petty borrowed a Buick Roadmaster from Gilmer Goode and headed to Charlotte for the first NASCAR Strictly Stock race in 1949. The big car was no match for the hard-cornering racing conditions and Petty wound up barrel-rolling the new vehicle into scrap iron. After the race, Petty swore he'd never race a big, heavy vehicle again and when he returned for the third NASCAR Strictly Stock race at Occoneechee Speedway, it was in a 1949 Plymouth Business Man's two-door coupe. Powered by an inline Plymouth 6-cylinder engine, the lightweight car, producing just 97 hp, proved to be a formidable racer as Petty posted five-straight top-10 finishes, including the brand's first NASCAR win at Heidelberg (Pittsburgh) Speedway October 2, 1949. The $1,500 Heidelberg first prize, and more than $3,300 in season winnings, gave Petty the money and the resolve to continue racing Plymouths to six wins through the 1952 season. Petty switched his efforts to Dodge in 1953 after Chrysler Corporation introduced its new Hemi V-8.

75 The success of NASCAR's new Strictly Stock division in 1949 was based on the premise that each car had to be as close as possible to what an Average Joe could purchase. Meaning, for the first season, 1947–1949 American manufactured cars were eligible to enter. Unlike today's modern rulebook, however, the Strictly Stock had just two rules. The first was that the car must be showroom stock. The second rule allowed for the installation of a steel reinforcing plate on the passenger-side front wheel. This was done in the interest in safety because without the reinforcement, the lug nuts would likely pull through the wheel due to heavy loading in the corners.

76 While duct tape earned the nickname, "200-miles-an-hour tape" in modern NASCAR, the first widely used tape in the sport was masking tape. Drivers spent hours prior to a 1949 NASCAR Strictly Stock race taping off the headlights, signallights, and taillights as well as bright work, including bumpers, grilles, and bodyside and roof moldings. A giant visor made of masking tape was also often placed across the top of windshield. All this was done to protect the car from debris that kicked up off the track or beach at speed during a race. At the conclusion of the event, the "100-mph masking tape" was easily removed, any residue cleaned up with a little body solvent, and the car was ready to drive back home after the race.

77 Initially, the Roadster Division was part of Bill France Sr.'s vision for NASCAR. France knew he couldn't hang his hat on only Modified races, so Roadsters and a Strictly Stock division seemed like complementary add-ons. Besides, Roadsters were already playing to big car counts and crowds, especially across the Northeast and Midwest. As much as he wanted it to succeed, Roadster racing never really caught on with the predominantly Southern fan base. As late as February 1949, France was trying to make the Roadsters part of the mix with the First-Annual National Gran Prix Roadster Classic. The Broward Speedway race attracted the best Roadster drivers of the day including "King of the Roadsters," Dick Frazier, an Indiana driver who won an incredible 21-straight Roadster events in 1948. Bob Flock wound up winning the 100-mile event, but the writing was on the wall for Roadsters in general as NASCAR dropped the Yankee Division in 1950 and the class had all but faded away by the middle of the decade.

78 Chrysler Corporation didn't invent hydraulic brakes, but did introduce the first reliable hydraulic disc brake system as standard equipment in a mass-produced car, the 1949 Chrysler Imperial. The system featured the now-familiar flat pressure plates (or discs) coated with a lining called Cyclebond. Front disc brakes became common in NASCAR for the next two decades. Team owner Roger Penske, driver Mark Donohue, and their AMC Matador became the first to use a four-wheel disc brake configuration on a Winston Cup car at Riverside, California, in 1973.

The Olds nameplate first visited the Strictly Stock and later the Grand National Victory Lane 35 times from 1949 to 1952. Bill Rexford scored one of those wins en route to the 1950 NASCAR Strictly Stock championship. (Photo Courtesy General Motors)

79 New technologies mastered in World War II launched a wave of automobile innovation after the war. One wartime achievement was the development of aviation gasoline formulas that produced higher octane. By mating high-octane gas with higher compression limits, post-war automotive engineers at General Motors created a new overhead valve V-8 and introduced it in select 1949 Oldsmobile and Cadillac models. The 303-ci powerplant featured a shorter, stiffer cast-iron engine block housing, aluminum pistons, and forged steel crankshaft topped with a dual-plane intake manifold and 2-barrel downdraft carburetor. Power was rated at 135 ponies and it could push a 3,580-pound 1949 Olds Club Coupe from 0 to 60 mph in 13 seconds. The new combination (quickly coined The Rocket 88), was the "hot iron" on the block, winning five of eight 1949 NASCAR Strictly Stock events. The ultimate success of the new engine spurred a wave of Big Three V-8 innovations with Chrysler introducing its Hemi V-8 in 1951 and Ford the Y-block in 1954.

80 The first NASCAR Strictly Stock race at Charlotte drew one of the most diverse fields of cars to ever grace a speedway. No less than nine makes were represented with Lincoln, Hudson, Oldsmobile, Buick, Chrysler, Ford, Mercury, and Cadillac in the 33-car field. The last of the original "NASCAR Nine" brands in the inaugural race were a pair of Kaisers, a 1948 driven by Buck Baker and a 1947 wheeled by John Barker. Baker finished 11th in his Penny Mullis Kaiser while Barker hammered his Ralph Chaney–owned Kaiser to a 15th-place finish. Baker drove a second Kaiser owned by Buddy Boehmen to a 23rd-place finish at Daytona in the second race of the 1949 season for his only two career starts in the brand. Chaney, meanwhile, helped keep Kaiser alive into 1951, posting six starts with four different drivers including Barker and Jim Paschal. Internal problems and a partnership breakup at Kaiser-Frazier in 1951 began a rapid decline for the brand, and subsequently its involvement in racing. Production of the Kaiser was discontinued in 1955.

81 On November 25, 1949, Cadillac produced its one-millionth vehicle, quite an accomplishment for the brand launched in 1902. Noted for its strong engines, the 1949 Cadillac shared the same powerful 303-ci platform as the Oldsmobile Rocket 88, making it a prime candidate as a NASCAR Strictly Stock racer that year. Frank Mundy drove the lone Caddy in the inaugural race at Charlotte finishing 30th in the 33-car field. Ethel Flock Mobley wheeled the single Cadillac to an 11th-place finish on the beach at Daytona in the second race of the year while Mundy and Bill Blair gave the brand its best season finish with a 4th and 5th, respectively, at Langhorne. While the 1949 Cadillac failed to win, it earned the consolation distinction of being the first vehicle to win *Motor Trend* magazine's Car of the Year award.

TRACKS

82 After moving his family to Daytona Beach, Florida, Bill France Sr. took the job of operating a gas station at 316 Main Street. The station featured full drive-up service and an open-air service bay. Today, known as Main Street Station, a popular bar and music

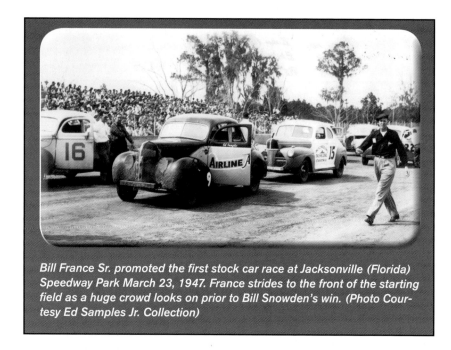

Bill France Sr. promoted the first stock car race at Jacksonville (Florida) Speedway Park March 23, 1947. France strides to the front of the starting field as a huge crowd looks on prior to Bill Snowden's win. (Photo Courtesy Ed Samples Jr. Collection)

venue in Daytona Beach, the site is a popular attraction for NAS-CAR history buffs as well as a place to grab a long, cool one.

83 It's no secret that even today, many Georgia racing fans believe Bill France Sr. "stole" NASCAR and shifted the epicenter of the sport from the Peach State to North Carolina. While there's no real validation of the claim, the fact is that France scheduled 26 of 52 Modified Division races in the inaugural 1948 season in North Carolina. Meanwhile, only 12 races were held in Georgia. France later scheduled the 1949 NASCAR Strictly Stock debut race in Charlotte, the backyard of NSCRA honcho Bruton Smith.

84 Lakewood Speedway was one of the first racetracks to reopen after the conclusion of World War II, hosting its first post-war race on Labor Day, September 3, 1945. The event, featuring a National Hillbilly Jamboree and holiday fireworks show, was met with immediate resistance by the editor of the *Atlanta Journal Constitution*, Ralph McGill. Backed by local Baptist and Methodist religious organizations, McGill campaigned to not allow "unsavory" moonshiners and racketeers to participate in the race, and went so far as enlisting Atlanta mayor William Hartsfield to ban five drivers (Roy Hall, Glen Hall, Bob Flock, Howard Farmer, and Jack Cantrell) from the race at Lakewood, the publicly owned Southern Fairgrounds property.

A giant debate played out in the pages of the *AJC* as fans voiced their displeasure over the fact that their heroes would not be able to race. The chorus got even louder when 30,000 fans showed up on race day as Mayor Hartsfield presented race promoter Mike Benton with a formal city protest. When Benton caved to Hartsfield's pressure, the remaining drivers unanimously voted to not race unless the banned drivers were allowed to compete. The event was delayed for more than an hour and when the crowd grew restless and began chanting "We Want Hall, We Want Hall" Hartsfield and Benton, fearing a riot and backlash at the mayoral election polls the following day, agreed to allow all drivers to complete regardless of their police record. Ironically, Hall won the race. Great public fallout and a crackdown on activities at the Southern Fairgrounds site ultimately kept Lakeland Speedway from hosting another stock car event for more than a year.

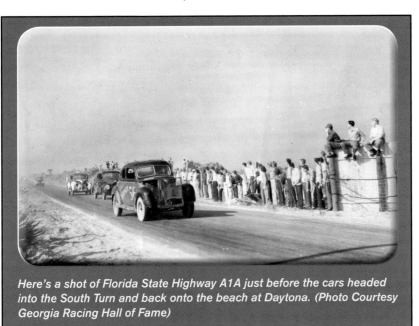

Here's a shot of Florida State Highway A1A just before the cars headed into the South Turn and back onto the beach at Daytona. (Photo Courtesy Georgia Racing Hall of Fame)

85 Seminole Speedway in Casselberry, Florida, hosted some of the first events promoted by Bill France Sr. after World War II. Shortly after the war ended, a group of local investors graded a quarter-mile track on the Orlando track property. With France on board as the promoter, Seminole Speedway held its first race December 2, 1945. France competed in the event and finished second to Atlanta's Roy Hall. The track was quickly converted to a 1-mile dirt oval in January 1946 with its first event, (another Bill France production), taking place in February. War hero Red Byron wheeled a Raymond Parks Ford to a win over a star-studded field featuring Bob and Fonty Flock, Hall, France, and Marion McDonald. Over the next seven years, Seminole Speedway hosted numerous stock car and motorcycle racing events. Although the facility doesn't show up in the record books as ever hosting a NASCAR-sanctioned race, the track (closed in 1954) played an important part in giving NASCAR founder Bill France Sr. the footing needed to launch the organization.

86 The Daytona Beach Road Course (DBRC) was up and running after World War II as Bill France Sr. staged and Roy Hall won a 33-lap, 100-mile stock car race in early 1946. France promoted several races on the same pre-war 3.2-mile DBRC layout before the 1948 season, when the course was changed and moved south to the less populated Ponce Inlet area. The new 2.2- and 4.2-mile tracks used the beach as its front straight and the Florida Highway A1A as the back chute, joined by a pair of treacherous hairpin turns. Initially, cars were to run the shorter track and motorcycles the longer oval, but due to the tendency of the short course to form sand dunes, it was abandoned after just one season. Red Byron won the first NASCAR-sanctioned event (the Rayson Memorial) on the short course on February 15, 1948, while Fonty Flock grabbed a second at the 1948 Buck Mathis Memorial 150 on the 2.2-mile track on August 8. All stock car races held on the Daytona Beach-Road Course from 1949 until it closed after the 1958 season were contested on the 4.2-mile layout.

87 Fans attending early NASCAR races at the Daytona Beach-Road Course knew exactly where to go to see most of the action; the South Turn. Located at the end of the paved Highway A1A back straight, cars at high speed often had trouble negotiating the sandy South Turn hairpin. Despite stripes painted on the highway to give drivers an idea of braking points, car after car overshot the turn and flipped over the sand dune at the top of the corner. As the race wore on and the ruts in the sand grew worse, the South Turn became littered with race cars. The fans watching from this area had to be on their toes and constantly scramble to stay out of the way at NASCAR's first "calamity corner."

88 While the Daytona Beach-Road Course is listed as the first race of the 1948 NASCAR Modified season, Bill France Sr. actually introduced his new organization with a non-points exhibition race at Pompano Beach Speedway in Florida January 4, 1948. Buddy Shuman won the event on the original 1¼-mile dirt Pompano Harness Track, built at a cost of $1.25 million in 1926. According to NASCAR records, Pompano Beach Speedway never hosted an official points-paying race, relegating it to a footnote as the track that hosted the first "unofficial" NASCAR event in 1948.

89 Built by moonshiners Pat and Harvey Charles during the summer of 1948, Charlotte Speedway was the site of the first NASCAR Strictly Stock race on June 19, 1949. The three-quarter-mile dirt track was located just off Little Rock Road on land leased from the C. C. Allison family. The track opened with a NASCAR Modified race on July 11, 1948, with Red Byron wheeling a Raymond Parks–owned Ford to victory. Less than a year later, Bill France Sr. changed the course of stock car racing history with the first NASCAR Strictly Stock race. In an ironic twist of fate, neither Pat nor Harvey Charles attended the inaugural NSS race as both were in prison after a 1949 bootlegging conviction.

90 In an effort to attract as many racers as possible to his first NASCAR Strictly Stock race at Charlotte, Bill France Sr. posted a total purse of $5,000, a giant sum of money in 1949 (approximately $50,000 in today's money). Jim Roper took home the biggest chunk of the kitty earning $2,000 for winning, Fonty Flock got $1,000 for second, and 10th-place finisher Jimmy Thompson got $100. Those

placing 15 through 20 got $25 for their efforts while the remainder
of the field, positions 21 through 33, went home empty-handed.

91 Martinsville Speedway (Virginia) owns the distinction of being
the only track on today's NASCAR tour to have held an event
during the sanctioning body's inaugural 1948 season. One of many
tracks carved out of the rich, red clay of southern Virginia, H. Clay
Earles shaped the small and narrow Martinsville half-mile oval out
of a 30-acre cornfield and opened September 7, 1947. A crowd estimated at 10,000 descended on the 750-seat track to see Red Bryon
wheel a Raymond Parks 1939 Ford to a 200-lap, 100-mile race
win. Less than a year later, Martinsville hosted its first NASCAR-
sanctioned event. The July 4, 1948, holiday race (the 26th event on
the 1948 NASCAR Modified tour) saw Fonty Flock score one of his
division-high 11 wins again driving a Parks Ford to victory.

The success of the 1948 race prompted Bill France Sr. to partner
with Earles and Martinsville to make it one of the original eight
speedways to host a 1949 NASCAR Strictly Stock inaugural season
race. The sixth race on the tour, the September 25 Martinsville SS

*Bill France Sr. works the stopwatch as Red Byron crosses the finish line
during time trials at a 1948 NASCAR Modified race at Greensboro Agricultural Fairgrounds Speedway (North Carolina). (Photo Courtesy Ed
Samples Jr. Collection)*

race drew an estimated 10,000 fans as Red Byron pushed his 1949 Oldsmobile into the lead on the 104th circuit and rolled to a three-lap win over Lee Petty, Ray Erickson, and Clyde Minter. The early success of the two emerging concerns (Martinsville Speedway and NASCAR) along with the personal friendship between France and Earles forged a mutually beneficial partnership that continues today.

92 Pittsburgh Steelers owner Art Rooney lent financial support to build Heidelberg Speedway just southwest of Pittsburgh in 1947. In 1949, Bill France Sr. wanted to bring his Strictly Stock brand to the northeast and Heidelberg's half-mile dirt oval proved to be a willing partner. Lee Petty scored his first NASCAR win in front of a large crowd on October 2, 1949. The 200-lap race took 1:44:25 to complete and Petty averaged 57.458 mph over the 100-mile distance. Dick Linder was second in a Kaiser (ultimately the best finish ever for the brand in NASCAR) with Bill Rexford, Sam Rice, and Sara Christian rounding out the top five.

Heidelberg wasn't part of the 1950 and 1951 Strictly Stock schedules, but returned to the Grand National ranks in 1952 where Herb Thomas scored a dominating win by leading 179 of 200 laps in Hubert Westmoreland's 1951 Oldsmobile. Heidelberg's next NASCAR race wasn't until 1956 when Joe Weatherly topped a 22-car NASCAR Convertible Division field. The track took its last major NASCAR bows with Grand National (now Sprint Cup) races in 1959 (Jim Reed) and 1960 (Lee Petty). NASCAR's final appearance at the now paved track was the Heidelberg-Gulf 100 Grand National East race August 2, 1973. Tommy Collela, the promoter of the track at the time, won the race in his first and only NASCAR career start. Collela closed Heidelberg Speedway after the 1973 season.

93 Fonty Flock must have been happy that Bill France Sr. flew an airplane. While winging his way to a meeting, France flew over an old horse track on a large expanse of land near Hillsboro, North Carolina. France and his investor group built a 1-mile dirt track on the site in 1947 and Occoneechee Speedway hosted its first NASCAR race (a Modified division event) June 7, 1948. Flock won the race and two other Modified events, dominating NASCAR races that season. Flock finished fourth behind his brother Bob in the third race of the 1949 NASCAR Strictly Stock season. The event drew an estimated crowd of 17,500 and cemented a spot on the NASCAR schedule, hosting at least one race each year throughout the 1968 season. On September 15, 1968, a crowd of 6,700 watched Richard Petty take the Hillsboro 150 Grand National race, beating James Hylton by seven laps, at the last NASCAR checkered flag at the now Orange Speedway. France shut the track down after facing opposition from local religious leaders over Sunday events at the track and replaced the 1969 Orange Speedway dates with runs at Talledega, the newest NASCAR track owned by France.

94 Not every early NASCAR race was a classic. The 1948 Modified Series 200-mile race at Langhorne Speedway (Pennsylvania) proved to be a snoozer as Al Keller won by one of stock car racing's all-time largest margins, 18 laps, over runner-up Buck Barr. Keller's Ford led 76 laps of the race covering the distance in a time of 3:17:05. Only 14 of the 48 starting cars finished the event.

Bill France Sr. promoted his first race outside the state of Florida, helping to reopen Greenville-Pickens Speedway July 4, 1946, with a National Championship Stock Car Circuit (NCSCC) event. (Photo Courtesy Gober Sosebee Family)

95 Greenville-Pickens Speedway in Greenville, South Carolina, is a long-time NASCAR track, tracing its roots back to NASCAR Modified Division races in the early 1950s. An early haven for Georgia and South Carolina racers, Greenville-Pickens opened as a half-mile dirt track in 1940 but quickly shut down with the start of World War II. Reconfigured to a quarter-mile, the track reopened July 4, 1946, with a Modified stock car event (the first promoted outside of Florida by Bill France Sr.) and won by Ed Samples of Atlanta. France and NASCAR were shut out of Greenville in the late 1940s and early 1950s when other Modified racing organizations, including the South Carolina Racing Association, were being featured at the track. On October 6, 1955, Tim Flock piloted the famous Carl Kiekhaefer-owned Chrysler No. 300 to a win in G-P's first NASCAR Grand National event. Greenville-Pickens went on to host 28 Grand National races over the next 16 seasons, including the final race June 26, 1971, won by Richard Petty. Over the years, Greenville-Pickens hosted nine different NASCAR division events, the most recent being the NASCAR K&N Pro Series East. The track is also part of the NASCAR Home Tracks program and hosts weekly NASCAR late model stock car races each summer.

96 Enoch Staley was an early convert to Bill France Sr.'s vision of stock car racing, and decided to build North Wilkesboro Speedway in 1946 as long as France organized and promoted his races. With a budget of $1,500, Staley quickly ran out of money leading to the track's odd and now-iconic shape with its downhill front straight and uphill back chute. France staged his first race at North Wilkesboro (a National Championship Stock Car Circuit Modified event) May 18, 1947, with Fonty Flock capturing the win in front of an estimated 10,000 fans. In 1948, North Wilkesboro hosted 6 of the 52 events in NASCAR's inaugural Modified season tour. Curtis Turner was the early master winning 3 of the 6 events with Red Byron earning 2 victories and Marshall Teague winning 1. North Wilkesboro was one of the original eight tracks on the 1949 NASCAR Strictly Stock tour, hosting the final race of the season. The October 16 clash on the then-half-mile dirt oval saw Bill Blair pace the 22-car field for most of the event. Unfortunately, his Cadillac suffered an engine

Weldon Adams (72) rolls his Plymouth stocker onto the track to practice for the 1951 Wilkes County 150 at North Wilkesboro (North Carolina) Speedway. Also identifiable here are the Hudson of Lou Figaro (33) and Ed Massey's Plymouth (4). (Photo Courtesy R. W. Hopkins)

problem allowing Bob Flock's 1949 Oldsmobile to lead the final 20 laps to his first NASCAR Strictly Stock Series victory.

97 The 1946 American Automobile Association "Big Car" season featured events at the top racetracks of the post-war era including Lakewood, Trenton, Winchester, Reading, Langhorne, Williams Grove, Dayton, and Flemington Speedways. Located on the Erie County Fairgrounds site, Hamburg Speedway regularly hosted auto racing before and after the war. The AAA circuit was a regular visitor to Hamburg with four races from 1946 to 1948 before NASCAR came to town in 1949. The September 18 event, the fifth race of the inaugural NASCAR Strictly Stock season, drew a crowd of more than 11,000 fans to the town of just 6,938 residents. Jack White won the race. In the 1950 NASCAR Strictly Stock event, Dick Linder spun and won in front of 8,363 at Hamburg. The 1950 Hamburg race was held the week before the debut of Darlington Raceway and the Southern 500 changed the axis for small tracks such as Hamburg forever. Hamburg was left off the 1951 race schedule and never hosted a major NASCAR event again. The track stayed open for more than 40 years, hosting multiple divisions of car and motorcycle racing highlighted by the DIRTCar Modifieds in the 1980s and the Empire State Sprint cars in the 1990s. Hamburg Speedway closed in September 1997.

98 NASCAR's inaugural 1949 season proved to be a big winner with the ticket-buying public as all eight-races reported attendance of more than 10,000 fans. The hands-down winner of the gate receipt race was the fourth event of the year at which more than 20,000 fans jammed Langhorne Speedway. That race also drew the biggest field of cars with 45 machines taking the green flag.

99 Lakewood Speedway wasn't on the 1949 Strictly Stock schedule, but the track did host a pair of "new car" races that season with great success. Bill France Sr. allowed NASCAR drivers to race in the non-points event at Lakewood held one week after Red Byron won the NASCAR Strictly Stock title. An announced crowd of 33,452 jammed into the Atlanta track and watched Tim Flock steer his Oldsmobile past Curtis Turner with 27 laps remaining and take home $1,650 in first-place prize money. Because of the success of that event, a second race at Lakewood was scheduled for November 13. That day, 22,000 fans showed up only to be disappointed when rain cut the race short after just 39 laps. One week later, when the event was called again after 110 laps because of darkness, June Cleveland was declared the winner; it was Cleveland's first win in any stock car event.

100 Built at a cost of $100,000 as part of a 1937 Great Depression works project, Bowman Gray Stadium in Winston-Salem, North Carolina, originally hosted football games and trotting horse races on the quarter-mile track surrounding the football field. The track was paved for auto racing in 1947 and Bill France Sr. was among the first to take advantage of it, staging a NASCAR Modified race May 18, 1949, won by Fonty Flock. Bowman Gray went on to host 28 NASCAR Grand National Division races from 1958 to 1971. Bob Welborn won the first in a 1957 Chevrolet and Bobby Allison won the last in a 1970 Ford. Meanwhile, BGS also hosted

NASCAR Convertible, Grand National East, Goody's Dash Series, K&N Pro East, and Whelen Southern Modified Tour events over the years. Today, the weekly Saturday night NASCAR Whelan Modified Southern Series races draw massive crowds and are a bucket-list item for fans yet to attend a race there.

PIT PASS

101 Before the formation of NASCAR at the end of 1947, Bill France Sr. promoted races under two different association names. The first was as series director of the National Champion Stock Car Circuit (NCSCC). France even had a slogan for the group, "Where the Fastest That Run, Run the Fastest." France also promoted some events that season under the Stock Car Auto Racing Society. That title didn't last long as a stock car tour named SCARS wasn't exactly the image France wanted to promote.

102 After taking his idea of a national stock car championship to the American Automobile Association in late 1946 only to have the idea turned down, Bill France Sr. launched the National Championship Stock Car Circuit (NCSCC). France and the NCSCC announced a slate of 40 events to begin at Daytona Beach, Florida, in January end in Jacksonville, in December 1947. In between, the NCSCC hit every track it could from Columbus, Georgia, to North Wilkesboro, North Carolina, to Langhorne, Pennsylvania. In the end, Fonty Flock won the 1947 NCSCC championship on the strength of 11 victories in 24 series starts. In keeping with his vision of a structured, professional national series, France awarded Flock a $1,000 championship bonus and a 4-foot trophy. As promised, he also paid $3,000 in point-fund money to other drivers in the series.

Along with establishing the NCSCC's structure as a new stock car racing standard, several 1947 NCSCC races significantly exceeded attendance and profit expectations. In the end, the overall success of the NCSCC proved to France that his ideas about organized stock car racing were on point and gave him the confidence needed to take the next step and schedule a meeting at the Streamline Hotel in December 1947 and begin the formation of NASCAR.

Bill France Sr. (center) and Daytona Beach mayor William Perry (left) present the 1946 National Champion Stock Car Circuit (NCSCC) season championship trophy to Ed Samples. (Photo Courtesy Ed Samples Jr. Collection)

103 With Atlanta's Lakewood Speedway serving as the racing hub of Georgia, dozens of small tracks staged events in front of ever-growing numbers of enthusiastic fans in the 1940s. Unfortunately, not all competitors and fans were welcome at these events and were often denied access. Undaunted, African-American racers from around Georgia formed the Atlanta Stock Car Club (ASCC) shortly after World War II. ASCC races featured Modified Stock Cars (the same late 1930s Ford coupes that dominated southern racing at the time) and flamboyant drivers including Richard "Red" Kines, Arthur "The Decatur Express" Avery, Robert "Juckie" Lewis, and James "Suicide" Lacey. In the early 1950s, ASCC races often drew overflow crowds, many coming on organized bus tours to ensure their safety. Eventually, changing times and legal decisions such as the 1954 U.S. Supreme Court Brown versus Board of Education ruling eliminating "separate but equal" policies in schools played a large part in eliminating the need for groups such as the ASCC, which folded mid-decade.

104 Christened Truman Fontello Flock, "Fonty" delivered moonshine on his bicycle as a teenager in his native Fort Payne,

Alabama. Later, Flock discovered an emerging stock car racing culture while running moonshine to Atlanta and began to compete in events throughout the south in the late 1930s. After his first big win at Lakewood Speedway in 1940, Flock's driving career seemingly ended with a massive wreck on the beach at Daytona in 1941 which left him with head and back injuries as well as a crushed chest and broken pelvis. Flock eventually returned to racing May 5, 1947, sweeping the field by setting fast time, winning his heat, and the 30-lap National Championship Stock Car Circuit (NCSCC) main event in the first race held at North Wilkesboro Speedway. Amazingly, Flock went on to win seven 1947 NCSCC events, beating Ed Samples and Red Byron for the NCSCC season championship.

Flock won a division-high 15 Modified Division races in NASCAR's inaugural 1948 season only to finish second to Byron in the final championship standings. In 1949, Flock won the NASCAR Modified season crown on the strength of 11 wins. That same year, he also participated in six NASCAR Strictly Stock races and finished fifth in the points. Flock's greatest years came in the 1950s by competing in 148 NASCAR Grand National events from 1950 through 1957. His greatest season, 1951, came when he posted eight wins, 22 top-10s, 13 pole positions, and a second-place finish in the championship battle.

After another bad wreck at Daytona in 1957 (a crash that claimed the life of Bobby Myers) Flock retired from racing. He finished his career with 19 Grand National victories and one Convertible Division triumph. Fonty Flock passed away in Atlanta on July 15, 1972.

105 Colorado-born Robert "Red" Byron was one of the most unlikely heroes of post-war stock car racing. After 57 missions as tail-gunner on a B-24 bomber during World War II, Byron's plane was shot down over the Aleutian Islands leaving him with crippling injuries to his left leg. Told he would never walk again, Byron was in military hospitals for more than two years. Byron, who had raced before the war, returned to the sport in 1946 and promptly won his first three races by anchoring his injured leg in a steel stirrup bolted to the clutch pedal. A year later, he finished third in the National Championship Stock Car Circuit championship promoted by Bill

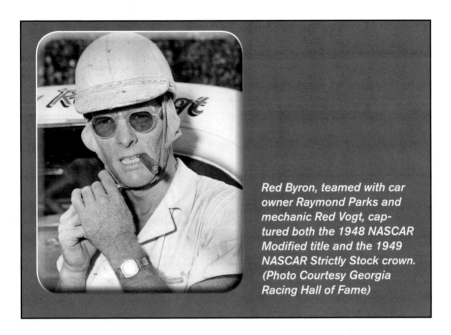

Red Byron, teamed with car owner Raymond Parks and mechanic Red Vogt, captured both the 1948 NASCAR Modified title and the 1949 NASCAR Strictly Stock crown. (Photo Courtesy Georgia Racing Hall of Fame)

France Sr. and winning nine races in the process. Byron was all but unstoppable in 1948, winning the first NASCAR-sanctioned race at Daytona and 10 other events while posting 23 top-3 finishes to earn the inaugural NASCAR Modified championship. He went on to capture two more events and the title in NASCAR's inaugural 1949 Strictly Stock season. Byron ran only nine NASCAR events after the 1949 championship season, retiring due to health issues in 1951. He died in 1960 at the age of 44 and in 1998, was named one of the top 50 drivers in the first 50 years of NASCAR.

106 You won't find Wilton Garrison listed among Big Bill France's inner circle of trusted advisors, but he may have been responsible for rekindling France's interest in creating something more than a regional racing empire. Shortly after auto racing resumed in 1945, France decided to stage a stock car race at Southern States Fairgrounds in Charlotte. France pitched it as a "national championship" race to Garrison, the sports editor of the *Charlotte Observer* at the time. Garrison told France that he didn't believe you could have a national championship based on one event. If France was going to use that kind of promotion, Garrison indicated there had to be a league with a season schedule, point standings, and prize money in order to determine a national champion. Garrison's observations left an impression on France and he incorporated many items into the formation of the NCSCC in 1946 and NASCAR in 1947.

107 Located at 140 South Atlantic Avenue in Daytona Beach, Florida, the Streamline Hotel today stands as the birthplace of NASCAR. The Streamline, named for its rakish art deco lines and interior themes, opened in 1941 as a four-story, 47-room marvel of the times, the first fireproof building in Daytona and the home of the city's first bomb shelter. The lavish hotel was topped by the Ebony Room, a rooftop bar where Bill France Sr. conducted the now-famous December 14, 1947, meeting that led to the formation of NASCAR. Through the years, the Streamline fell into disrepair and disfavor as newer, bigger, and more modern beachfront hotels grabbed customers away from the dated hotel. Since then, the Streamline has served as a youth hostel, a religious retirement home, and an alternative lifestyle bar in an effort to avoid the wrecking ball. In 2014, a development group purchased the Streamline for $950,000 with the intent to restore the hotel (complete with first-floor

Fonty Flock celebrates the 1947 National Championship Stock Car Circuit Modified Division title along with Ed Samples and Bill France Sr. in the rooftop Ebony Room bar at the Streamline Hotel in Daytona Beach, Florida. (Photo Courtesy Ed Samples Jr. Collection)

NASCAR-themed bar) and surrounding property. The renovated hotel and grounds were scheduled to open on April 1, 2017.

108 After the formation of NASCAR in 1947, the company was run from Bill France Sr.'s house at 29 Goodall Avenue in Daytona Beach. Later, the company moved into its first corporate headquarters, an old bank building located at 42 Peninsular Drive in Daytona Beach. The 4,000 square foot building was built in 1920, and cost $40 per month to rent.

109 Sam Nunis traveled the country in the 1920s to learn the business of staging auto races from legendary IndyCar promoter Ralph Hankinson. Like Hankinson, Nunis concentrated on Indy-Car and open-wheel race promotion throughout his career, but he also shared Bill France Sr.'s vision of what stock car racing could be. Like France, Nunis lobbied the American Automobile Association to sanction stock car races in the 1940s. When Nunis got the cold shoulder from the AAA, he helped found the National Stock Car Racing Association (NSCRA) in 1946. Nunis, who conducted most of his business in the front seat of his trademark Lincoln Continental, also controlled the promotional efforts of dozens of racetracks on the East Coast, including Trenton and Lakewood Speedways. He continued to promote Trenton into the 1970s before health concerns forced him to retire in 1973. Nunis succumbed to long-term lung and heart disease in 1980.

110 Early auto racing provided little safety for drivers or fans. That played out tragically on July 25, 1948, when Slick Davis flipped his 1937 Chevrolet several times while racing at Greensboro Speedway (North Carolina) and became the first driver fatally injured in a NASCAR-sanctioned race. Tragedy struck again that same day at another NASCAR-sanctioned event in Columbus, Georgia, when Red Byron's car blew a tire and plowed off the track into the crowd. Seven-year-old Roy Brannon was killed and 16 other people were injured. The twin fatalities had little effect on safety; real reform didn't come until the 1950s.

111 Although NASCAR was formed in 1947 and crowned a Modified champion in 1948, it wasn't the only game in town. The new organization had plenty of rivals in the race for sanctioning supremacy. No less than four major groups, including the American Stock Car Racing Association (ASCRA), National Auto Racing League (NARL), National Stock Car Racing Association (NSCRA), and United Stock Car Racing Association (USCRA), all staged national championship events and tallied points systems in 1948. The glut of racing organizations staging the same basic events was said to have been the spark that ignited Bill France Sr. to try something different in 1949, the NASCAR Strictly Stock division.

112 Bill France Sr. and NASCAR ruled the fledgling sport with an iron fist. France saw the need for rules on the track and rules for behavior away from it. For the inaugural 1949 NASCAR Strictly Stock race at Charlotte, France would not let Marshall Teague, Buddy Shuman, Ed Samples, or Jimmy and Speedy Thompson enter the race. Teague, NASCAR's original treasurer in 1947, had multiple disagreements with France over prize money, campaigning for 40 percent of the gate receipts instead of a flat-dollar-number posted purse. He and Jimmy Thompson had also filed entries for a NASCAR race and then competed in another event that same day. Meanwhile, Shuman, Speedy Thompson, and Samples (all who ran races other than NASCAR-sanctioned events on occasion) all supported Teague's prize money movement and were reportedly suspended because they were nabbed placing thumb tacks on the track prior to a NASCAR Modified race a couple of weeks earlier. In announcing his decision to deny the offenders entry in the Charlotte race, France indicated that the drivers exhibited "conduct detrimental to the best interests of the National Association of Stock Car Racing." It is a phrase that countless drivers who run afoul of NASCAR have heard since then.

113 If you were interested in participating in NASCAR's inaugural 1948 season events, you had to pay for it. For $10, NASCAR provided its members with an identification card, NASCAR membership pin, and newsletter. Also included were a NASCAR car

The first NASCAR Strictly Stock race at Charlotte in 1949 included Sara Christian. Seen here are Christian and her husband/car owner Frank with their NASCAR SS Oldsmobile stocker. (Photo Courtesy Georgia Racing Hall of Fame)

decal and a $10 book of 20 coupons, each worth a 50-cent admission discount at 1948 NASCAR-sanctioned races.

114 Danica Patrick and all of the other female drivers who have graced NASCAR are spiritual descendants of NASCAR's first woman driver, Sara Christian. Christian proved her 14th-place finish in the inaugural 1949 Strictly Stock race was more than a novelty; she notched a 5th-place finish in the sixth 200-mile Strictly Stock event on the ultra-tough Langhorne Speedway oval. The crowd was so awed by Christian's effort that she was escorted to Victory Lane where Curtis Turner graciously stood aside to allow fans to cheer Christian. In her next race one month later, Christian posted an even better effort wheeling her 1949 Ford to a fifth-place finish in a race at Heidelberg Raceway outside of Pittsburgh. Christian finished 14th in the 1949 NASCAR Strictly Stock points championship. Unfortunately, her career as a NASCAR driver was short-lived as she was seriously injured in an NSCRA race at Lakewood Speedway in Atlanta after the conclusion of the 1949 NASCAR season. Christian broke her back in the wreck, barrel-rolling her car seven times. With urging from her family to quit, Christian raced just once more in 1950 running a NASCAR Strictly Stock 100-miler on the half-mile dirt Hamburg Speedway (New York), and finished 14th again, just as in her first race.

115 Sometimes, to beat them, you have to join them. That's what Bill France Sr. decided to do when he allowed NASCAR to co-sanction an event with the National Stock Car Racing Association (NSCRA) in 1949. The "Strictly Stock" concept wasn't exclusive to NASCAR as Lakewood Speedway promoter Sam Nunis and NSCRA announced a 150-mile SS race for October 23. France worked with Nunis to permit a NASCAR co-sanction of the race, allowing top Georgia drivers to compete in the Atlanta race. However, no NAS-CAR championship points were awarded. Georgia's favorite son Tim Flock didn't disappoint the giant Peach State crowd of more than 33,000 fans and wheeled a 1949 Olds to victory.

116 NASCAR's early female drivers got their start in racing thanks to a rival sanctioning organization, the South Carolina Racing Association. The series, founded by former Bill France Sr. supporter Joe Littlejohn, started racing at Greenville-Pickens, Columbia, and Hub City (Spartanburg) in 1949. The schedule of events often featured a 10- or 15-lap "Powder Puff" race for the women prior to the stock car feature event. Sara Christian won several of these early girl-power races, beating out other women racers including Louise Smith, Ruby Flock, and Mildred Williams.

117 Bill France Sr. knew Louis Ossinski played football for Georgia and also coached the nearby Seabreeze High School football team. France also knew Ossinski was a lawyer who just happened to have an office across the street from his filling station. When France needed a lawyer to attend the meeting at the Streamline Hotel and later file the documents to incorporate NASCAR, it was a short walk to find him. Ossinsky proved to be the man for the job and on February 21, 1948, he completed the necessary paperwork making NASCAR a private corporation. For handling the legal part, Ossinsky was given 10 percent of the new company. France owned 50 percent while Bill Tuthill, NASCAR's new secretary, had 40 a percent share in the venture. France later bought out Tuthill and partner Ed Otto. Ossinsky was the last outstanding NASCAR shareholder until his death in 1971 when France bought up the remaining 16.6 percentage owned by Ossinsky's heirs, giving France 100 percent control of NASCAR.

118 Erwin "Cannonball" Baker made a name for himself by making more than 140 cross-country motorcycle and automobile speed runs during the 1920s and 1930s promoting early brands and products. A champion dirt track motorcycle racer from Indiana, Baker also drove in the 1922 Indianapolis 500 and held more than 100 land speed records. Baker had all the criteria Bill France Sr. wanted in a person and was chosen to serve as the first NASCAR "National Honorary Commissioner of Racing" in 1947. Baker served until being replaced by Harley Earl, GM's design wizard and friend of Bill Sr. Baker died of a heart attack in 1960 at the age of 78. The now-famous Cannonball Run transcontinental motor race and Hollywood movie of the same name were attributed to Baker. He is enshrined in the Automotive Hall of Fame, the Motorcycle Hall of Fame, and the Indianapolis Motor Speedway Hall of Fame.

119 At the inaugural 1949 NASCAR Strictly Stock race in Charlotte, the job of "Top Cop" (NASCAR Head Technical Inspector) fell to Al Crisler. A noted and well-respected mechanic and motorcycle racer, Crisler was a Piedmont Airlines captain and lived near the airport and Charlotte Speedway. Crisler had strong character and was often called "Captain" or "Major" by those around him. In the first race at Charlotte, it was Crisler's pre-race job to make sure all the cars were as stock as possible and checking for any slight modifications. His post-race tech was to make sure the stock integrity of the vehicle was still intact. Unfortunately for Glenn Dunaway, who won the race, Crisler found the rear springs on Dunaway's Ford had been altered. Several hours after the event, Crisler disqualified Dunaway. That decision meant that Jim Roper would forever be known as the winner of NASCAR's landmark event.

Hollywood actor and nationally syndicated radio host Edward Everett Horton (right) presents Ed Samples with the 1949 National Stock Car Racing Association (NSCRA) championship trophy. (Photo Courtesy Ed Samples Jr. Collection)

120 One of the top moonshine runners of the day, Georgia's Ed Samples almost didn't have a racing career. Shot three times in 1944 over a moonshine deal gone bad, Samples (who had dabbled in stock car racing prior to World War II) proved to be one the sport's biggest stars after the war. Samples' biggest wins included first race at Greenville-Pickens Speedway on July 4, 1946, and the National Championship Stock Car Circuit (NCSCC) on the Daytona Beach Road Course on June 30 that year. Samples, the 1946 National Champion of Stock Car Racing, finished second in France Sr.'s fledgling modified stock car circuit in 1947.

While Samples attended the famed Streamline Hotel NASCAR organizational meeting in December 1947, he wasn't an early supporter and instead chose to race in the South Carolina Racing Association (SCRA) in 1948, winning the division's championship on the strength of 10-straight victories at one point of the season. A year later, Samples was banned from NASCAR competition and the inaugural Strictly Stock race at Charlotte because he had competed in a National Stock Car Racing Association (NSCRA) race the same weekend as a NASCAR event. Undaunted, he captured the 1949 NSCRA Strictly Stock title and was again leading the NSCRA points when the division shut down midway through the 1951 season.

Over the next three years, Samples concentrated on short-track racing, and won the 1954 and 1955 Birmingham (Alabama) Racing Club championships. Meanwhile, he made 13 NASCAR Grand National starts from 1951 to 1954, his best finish a second at Lakewood in 1952. Samples hung up his helmet in 1956 and lived in the Birmingham area until his death in 1991.

121 Most people know that Glenn Dunaway finished last in the first NASCAR Strictly Stock race, but most don't that he did the same in the second race as well. After winning at Charlotte and then being disqualified in post-race tech, the Gastonia, North Carolina, driver and his Hubert Westmoreland–owned 1947 Ford were credited with last place, 33rd. In the second 1949 Strictly Stock event at the Daytona Beach Road Course on July 10, Dunaway and his 1949 Mercury were the first to fall out, and came in last, 28th, in the final rundown. Dunaway fared better later in the season by picking up three straight top-10 finishes in a 1949 Olds on the way to a ninth-place finish in the final 1949 point standings.

122 Martinsville, Virginia, native Sam Rice has several distinctions in the annals of NASCAR. Rice introduced H. Clay Earles to stock car racing and convinced him to build Martinsville Speedway in 1947. Rice, an original partner in the track, was also an early NASCAR team owner fielding 60 Strictly Stock/Grand National entries from 1949 to 1959. His cars won twice: once in 1950 when Bill Blair wheeled Rice's Mercury to a win at Vernon Speedway and again that year when Fireball Roberts piloted an Oldsmobile to victory at Occoneechee Speedway near Hillsboro, North Carolina. Rice's other connection came as a driver when he competed in the inaugural 1949 NASCAR Strictly Stock race starting 14th and finishing 4th in an Oldsmobile. Later that year, Rice again climbed behind the wheel of one of his cars, a Chevrolet, and finished 4th in the Heidelberg (Pittsburgh) Speedway Strictly Stock race. The two races (twin 4th-place finishes) were the only starts of Rice's NASCAR driving career.

123 Bill France Sr. knew he needed star power if he was going to sell the idea of the first NASCAR race to the ticket-buying public in Charlotte. Never shy to go after the biggest fish in the pond, France enlisted the help of Charlotte radio legend Grady Cole. Cole, a laid-back, down-home Southern type, had dominated the Charlotte airwaves for nearly two decades when France came calling in 1949. Cole's WBT Radio morning show was the most listened-to program in Charlotte at all times of the day. France wanted the audience and enlisted Cole to hype his race by making him a co-owner with Bruce Griffin on the car driven by Fonty Flock. On race day, Cole addressed the crowd he helped create and gave the command to start engines over the public address system. Cole remained a friend to NASCAR for years afterwards. His contributions to establishing NASCAR awareness with the general public, especially those in regard to the first Strictly Stock race, should not be overlooked or underestimated.

124 If Jim Roper didn't read the newspaper every day; he might never have won the first NASCAR Strictly Stock race. Roper found out about the race thanks to a mention of the event in *The Adventures of Smilin' Jack* comic strip. A local roadster champion, Roper decided to enter the race and drove a 1949 Lincoln to Charlotte from Kansas for the June 19, 1949, contest. Roper was declared the winner after Glenn Dunaway was disqualified. Two months later, Roper made his only other career NASCAR start driving the same Millard Clothier–owned Lincoln to a 15th-place finish at Occoneechee Speedway. Roper continued to race until an injury in a sprint car race at Davenport, Iowa, ended his career in 1955. Roper passed away in Newton, Kansas, in 2000.

125 The second-ever NASCAR Strictly Stock race at the Daytona Beach-Road Course on July 10, 1949, holds the distinction of being the only event in NASCAR history featuring four siblings.

On that day, brothers Fonty, Bob, Tim Flock along with sister Ethel Mobley took the green flag with Tim posting the best finish, a 2nd behind winner Red Byron. Meanwhile, Ethel took bragging rights over brothers Fonty and Bob with an 11th-place finish (Fonty was 19th, while Bob came home 22nd). That day remains the only time a brother and sister competed against each other in NASCAR's top division.

126 Jack White made his first and only start of the 1949 NASCAR Strictly Stock season a good one by winning at Hamburg Speedway September 18. The fifth race of eight that year, a 200-lap event, drew just 16 cars. That didn't stop more than 11,000 fans from pouring into the Hamburg half-mile dirt oval to see White take the lead on lap 134 when race-long front-runner Glenn Dunaway lost a wheel. White led the remainder of the race, winning and taking home the $1,500 top prize. White went on to make 11 more NASCAR starts over the next two seasons, but never again realized his winning form, posting just one other top-5 finish. White's final NASCAR race was August 24, 1951, when he came in 41st a Grand National event at Morristown Speedway (New Jersey), earning $10 in prize money for the finish.

127 Ask any NASCAR old-timer who the most naturally gifted driver was and you will most likely receive Curtis Turner as the answer. Turner's first attempt at a racetrack was a 1946 race in Mount Airy, North Carolina. When the race was canceled due to a lack of cars, Turner (a fan at the event) jumped into his 1940 Ford, drove onto the track, and put on a show of impressive power slides and doughnuts. The crowd went crazy and "filled the hat," showering Turner with money afterward. A lumberjack by trade, Turner quickly jumped into racing full throttle and by 1948 was a star in the new NASCAR Modified Division.

128 NASCAR reported that 50 drivers competed in at least one NASCAR Strictly Stock race in 1949. Ken Wagner had the distinction of finishing last in the season championship standings after competing in three 1949 events: Martinsville, Heidelberg, and

North Wilkesboro. The Pennington, New Jersey, driver won the pole for the North Wilkesboro race and his best effort was an 11th-place finish at Martinsville. Wagner's season winnings were $100.

MILESTONES

129 December 14, 1949, will always be remembered in stock car racing history as the demarcation day for NASCAR. Bill France Sr. concluded four days of meetings at the Streamline Hotel in Daytona Beach, Florida, on that date, with the result being the formation of NASCAR. The meetings, attended by 35 promoters and drivers from around the country (labeled "assorted hustlers" by Daytona Beach sportswriter Benny Kahn), laid the groundwork for a unified national stock car racing circuit.

Raymond Parks was a regular in the Ebony Room bar atop the Stream-line Hotel as Bill France Sr. enjoyed using the Daytona Beach, Florida, facility for meetings and awards banquets. (Photo Courtesy Georgia Racing Hall of Fame)

130 On the final day of the 1947 NASCAR organizational meetings, the group took several votes. One named Bill France Sr. as the president of the organization. A second vote was taken to name the new group. Initially, the preferred moniker was the National Stock Car Racing Association (NSCRA), but that was quickly voted down in part to the name being used by another organization in Georgia. The second reason for the dismissal was due to the fact that Georgia NSCRA was becoming an adversary of France's new venture. Atlanta mechanic Red Vogt suggested the group be called the National Association of Stock Car Auto Racing (NASCAR). This time, the vote passed giving the group its new name. Later, "of" was changed to "for."

131 The first officially sanctioned NASCAR race was held at Daytona Beach on February 15, 1948. The event drew a field of 62 cars to the Daytona Beach-Road Course with 50 of them taking the green flag. Named the Rayson Memorial, a 68-lap race on the 2.2-mile beach road course (149.6 miles), was won by Red Byron in a 1939 Ford coupe owned by Raymond Parks. Byron earned $1,000 first-place prize money, while Marshall Teague, the only other car to run all 68 laps, earned $650 for his effort. Only 12 of the 50 starters finished.

132 Easily the strongest challenger to NASCAR in the late 1940s was the National Stock Car Racing Association (NSCRA), an Atlanta-based sanctioning body incorporated March 27, 1947, by Sam Nunis and Weyman Milam. At first, the NSCRA worked in conjunction with other sanctioning groups, but that changed in 1948 when Charlotte businessman O. Bruton Smith took control of the organization. Smith, the promoter of Concord Speedway, immediately butted heads with France, accusing him of scheduling NASCAR races up against his NSCRA events at Concord.

Later in 1948, Smith directly challenged France, announcing that the NSCRA would sanction a Strictly Stock championship in 1949. The move prompted France into launching his own Strictly Stock division and debuted in Charlotte (Smith's hometown) for spite. Meanwhile, the NSCRA conducted its own Strictly Stock season with Ed Samples winning the championship. Buddy Shuman (the 1948 NSCRA Modified champion) captured the 1950 NSCRA Strictly Stock title.

While competition from NASCAR was stiff, it may have been the Korean conflict that spelled the demise of the NSCRA. Smith was drafted into service in 1951 and with him went much of the NSCRA's organization and determination to fight France and NAS-CAR. When NSCRA founder Nunis broke ranks during the summer of 1951 and announced that a NASCAR Grand National race would be held at Atlanta's Lakewood Speedway. The NSCRA was finished. Milam disbanded the organization shortly after Nunis' announcement and the NSCRA could only sit back and watch the group fade into history. A crowd of more than 25,000 cheered Georgia's favorite son, Tim Flock, to victory in the November NASCAR GN event.

133 The 1948 NASCAR Modified championship season featured 52 events from February 15 at Daytona Beach through November 14 in Columbus, Georgia. In a show of dominance, a Ford won each of the 52 races as Red Byron, Fonty Flock, Bob Flock, Skip Hersey, Gober Sosebee, Bill Blair, Johnny Rogers, Marshall Teague, Paul Pappy, Tim Flock, Curtis Turner, Billy Carden, Al Keller, and Buddy Shuman all wheeled a blue oval Flathead V-8 coupe to victory at least once that year. Fonty Flock led with 14 wins while Byron, the division champion, had 11 victories. With Byron and the Flocks driving his Fords, Raymond Parks was NASCAR's first team champion owner.

134 Bill France Sr. and his new organization knew they had something big on their hands when more than 14,000 fans paid $2.50 to witness the first NASCAR-sanctioned race at Daytona Beach on February 15, 1948. The financial and artistic success of that first race at Daytona set the tone for France and NASCAR throughout the 1948 season.

135 Right from the start, Bill France Sr. adopted an aggressive marketing strategy for NASCAR by staging events in more than one location on the same day. In the equivalent of a Sprint Cup event in Atlanta, Richmond, and Pocono, NASCAR also ran events at Macon (Georgia), Danville (Virginia), and Dover (New Jersey), on May 23, 1948. All three races awarded points toward the 1948

NASCAR Modified Championship. Gober Sosebee grabbed the win and points at Macon while Bill Blair rolled to the win at Danville. Johnny Rogers completed the NASCAR tripleheader by coming in first at Dover.

136 In addition to staging events in multiple locations on the same day, NASCAR also featured doubleheaders at some of its 1948 Modified Series events. At the September 5 race at North Wilkesboro Speedway, Curtis Turner won a pair of 30-lap feature events. Driving a Ford for team owner Bob Smith, Curtis captured the pole and beat Jimmy Ingram to win the first 30-lapper. In the second race, Turner started 14th (shotgun on the field after a full-field inversion) and raced through the field to win the second race of the day. This marks the first time in NASCAR history that one driver won two sanctioned races in the same day. Two weeks later, September 19, Fonty Flock repeated the achievement winning both 30-lap NASCAR Modified Series races at Occoneechee Speedway.

137 In 1948, an outbreak of polio gripped the United States. One of the hardest hit areas was North Carolina where more than

Drivers lined up to get their starting positions; official Alvin Hawkins holds a hat while an unidentified person seated in the car draws a number for each competitor. (Photo Courtesy Ed Samples Jr. Collection)

2,500 cases were reported, more than 10 times the number reported the year before. With children most vulnerable to the contagious disease, physicians across North Carolina urged cities to close public playgrounds, recreation centers, and pools while discouraging other public venues such as movie theaters, ballparks, and even churches from opening. In keeping with the times, Bill France Sr. and NASCAR canceled several 1948 events in an effort to help contain the outbreak. It is the only time in NASCAR history that races were canceled due to a public epidemic.

138 NASCAR's first championship battle (the 1948 Modified title) remains one of the most hotly contested in racing history. Red Byron won four races in a row taking an early points lead in April, but Fonty Flock roared back by grabbing 6 of his division-high 15 season victories late in the 1948 campaign. Byron and Flock ended up winning the final eight races of the year between them with Byron taking the lead for good by winning the 49th race in North Wilkesboro. A week later, Byron won at Charlotte with Flock rallying back with a victory at Winston-Salem, North Carolina. Byron wouldn't be denied the championship (and the final race of the season) at Columbus Speedway (Georgia) in mid-November. His championship-winning margin was just 32.75 points. Tim Flock finished third in standings with seven-time winner Curtis Turner fourth and Buddy Shuman, a two-time victor, fifth.

139 Bill France Sr. promised a NASCAR drivers' point fund and delivered at the end of the 1948 season. In all, France paid the top-20 drivers a total of $5,000 out of the $64,000 collected in ticket sales. Champion Red Byron got the lion's share of the kitty taking home a $1,250 check signed by NASCAR treasurer Bill Tuthill. Byron gave $834 of the winnings to the car owner, Raymond Parks.

140 The idea of racing showroom stock cars was good, if it worked. The only way to find out was to hold an experimental race. The first one (a 10-mile Novice race for Strictly Stock late-model cars) was held January 23, 1949 as part of a NASCAR tripleheader at

Broward Speedway in Florida. The 2-mile speedway used taxiways at the Ft. Lauderdale-Davie Airport. Lloyd Christopher won the event with little fanfare. France then staged a second experimental 10-mile Strictly Stock race February 27, 1949, pairing it with a 100-mile National Gran Prix Roadster event and a 25-mile Sports Car clash. After Bob Flock won the Roadster race and Tom DeMetry the Sports Car event, local driver Benny Georgeson of Fort Lauderdale, Florida, wheeled his Buick to the win. Eddie Mitchell, a Mercury driver from Defiance, Ohio, was second.

141 While Bruton Smith and NSCRA were battling Bill France Sr. and NASCAR to grab control of Strictly Stock racing in the southeast, a group in Kansas may have beat them to the punch in staging the first race. The International Motor Contest Association (IMCA) claims to have run races for "New Model Strictly Stock Cars" as early as 1947 and one reportedly at the Hutchinson, Kansas, State Fairgrounds, just three weeks before NASCAR's June 1949 debut. While records are sketchy, due in part to a 1950 fire at IMCA headquarters, remaining records show Jim Roper, winner of NASCAR's first Strictly Stock race at Charlotte, finished third in an IMCA 100-mile Strictly Stock event at the Kansas State Fairgrounds just weeks later on July 4. Meanwhile, IMCA is said to have crowned Eddie Anderson as its 1949 Strictly Stock champion. Regardless of who was first, NASCAR eventually gained control of the Strictly Stock division and later the full-bodied stock car world against a host of challengers. Meanwhile, IMCA (originally founded in 1915) is the oldest race sanctioning organization in America, running hundreds of short-track sprint, modified, late model, and hobby stock car events annually.

142 When Glenn Dunnaway's winning 1947 Ford was disqualified after the 1949 NASCAR Strictly Stock race in Charlotte, the car's owner, Hubert Westmoreland, lawyered up. Westmoreland immediately filed a lawsuit against NASCAR asking for damages of $10,000. Greensboro, North Carolina, court judge, John J. Hayes threw the case out on December 16, 1949, ruling that NASCAR had the right to disqualify any car not meeting technical specifications.

143 Bob Flock wheeled his 1946 Davis Brothers' Hudson to the pole in the first Strictly Stock race with a speed of 67.958 mph on Charlotte's dirt oval. Flock led the first five laps before an engine failure on Lap 38 made him the first driver out. Flock avoided the "first to worst" distinction when apparent winner Glenn Dunnaway was disqualified in post-race tech, putting Flock 32nd in the final 33-car rundown.

144 Bill France Sr. knew one of the biggest pieces in creating a national series was putting together a points system. Without points (or a way to quantify results), no champion could be legitimately determined. The points system NASCAR used for the 1948–1951 seasons was based on prize money paid. For instance, if an event had a total purse of $1,000, the winner received 50 points while second got 45, third place 40, fourth place 35, and fifth 30 points. Meanwhile, bigger purses carried more weight and awarded more points, so a race paying $3,500 total purse earned the winner 175 points while second garnered 157.5. Third, fourth, and fifth place earned 140, 122.5, and 105 points, respectively. This system was dropped prior to the 1952 season when the minimum NASCAR Grand National race purse was raised to $4,000 and points were boosted to 200.

145 One success of the first NASCAR Strictly Stock race at Charlotte noticed by Bill France Sr. was the popular driver Sarah Christian. France wasted little time appealing to the female audience by convincing Christian, Louise Smith, and Ethel Flock Mobley to enter the second 1949 Strictly Stock race at Daytona. To promote their appearance, France had new NASCAR publicist Houston Lawling put out a press release proclaiming, "The woman racer is here to stay, like the atom bomb, rum, and home hair waves." The press release went on to say "Women have come a long way since suffrage," and "Anybody who has ever tried to pass a woman driver with one hand clutching her cigarette and the other the wheel knows with a futile and near-fatal effort this can be."

146 The final 1949 NASCAR Strictly Stock national championship standings showed not a single driver competed in all eight races. In fact, only eight drivers competed in six races: Red Byron, Lee Petty, Bob Flock, Bill Blair, Fonty Flock, and Curtis Turner. All finished in the top-6 in points. Frank Mundy (10th) and Sara Christian (13th) rounded out those competing in six events in 1949.

Chapter 3

The 1950s: Sandbanks to Highbanks

The 1950s proved to be one of the most dynamic decades in American history as the United States fueled the newest global economic trend: consumerism.

After years of personal sacrifices inflicted by the Great Depression and World War II, Americans went on a buying spree. New cars were gobbled at a record pace evidenced by the leap from approximately 25 million vehicles on the road in 1950 to nearly 70 million cars and trucks by the end of the decade.

This growth curve changed the country and by 1960 one in six Americans was directly employed by the United States automobile industry or by firms supplying the world's largest industrial complex.

Detroit's Big Three embraced that freedom, producing cars unlike any others ever created. Influenced by the new "jet age," body styles became lower, longer, wider, sleeker, and more angular than their predecessors as hardtop and giant finned cars rolled out of the design studios.

While new, over-the-top body styles may have defined the automotive industry during the decade, technological breakthroughs such as development of more powerful overhead valve V-8 engines, independent front suspension, power steering, and automatic transmissions as standard equipment, made cars more reliable and easier to drive than ever before.

The grandstand is packed to the horizon as the fastest American production cars prepare to do battle at Langhorne (Pennsylvania) Speedway in 1950. (Photo Courtesy Georgia Racing Hall of Fame)

The government aided the automobile industry's growth by passing the Federal Aid Highway Act of 1956, which built the Interstate Highway System. Americans now could now drive (and more important, live) practically anywhere; it gave them more personal freedom than ever before.

Unfortunately, not everyone could keep up; Ford, Chrysler and General Motors took over the market, garnering 70 percent of new car sales by the end of the 1950s. Their success forced several smaller automobile manufacturers including Kaiser, Frazier, Hudson, Henry J, and Packard to close their doors for good.

Despite the loss of nameplates to fuel his Strictly Stock concept, Bill France Sr. had to be giddy with the meteoric growth of the new car industry in the early 1950s. Attendance at NASCAR events jumped dramatically as new Ford, GM, and Chrysler product owners started taking their family cars to the racetrack to cheer on their favorite driver. Now, battle lines were being drawn on both the tracks and in the neighborhood driveways. NASCAR was picking up steam, and fast.

In the end, the birth of the modern American automobile-centric "car culture" helped propel NASCAR from a little known entity racing at small, regional dustbowls to a recognizable national sport showcasing the best cars in the world on a new and modern stage, the giant 2.5-mile Daytona International Speedway.

CARS

147 One of the bonuses of NASCAR's new Strictly Stock division was that it was open to any American production car. That made for an interesting brand mix that included Studebakers, the first independent U.S. automaker to produce an overhead valve V-8 engine. Driver Ralph Zrimsek introduced the brand to NASCAR at Heidelberg (Pittsburgh) Speedway in 1949 with little fanfare. Studebaker had its biggest success in NASCAR in 1951 when Georgia's Frank "Rebel" Mundy wheeled a Perry Smith–owned bullet-nosed Studebaker Commander to wins at both Columbia Speedway (South Carolina) and Mobile Speedway (Alabama). Studebaker continued to perform in various divisions into the 1960s despite an ill-fated merger with Packard in 1954. The company ceased automobile production in 1966.

148 One of the most radical early 1950s cars was the Nash Ambassador. Introduced in 1949 as part of Nash's Airflyte line, the 112-inch-wheelbase vehicle was one of the first production vehicles to be wind tunnel-designed with a lower drag coefficient in mind. The result was a smooth, rounded shape featuring a one-piece safety glass windshield and enclosed fenders. A 234-ci overhead valve inline 6-cylinder engine producing 115 hp propelled the car. After modest success in 1950, Nash hired Curtis Turner and Johnny Mantz to drive a pair of factory-sponsored Ambassadors on the 1951 NASCAR Grand National tour. The move paid off as Turner gave the company its first and only NASCAR Grand National premier series win on April 1 at Charlotte Speedway.

149 Early "rollover bars" were nothing like the bars welded into the chassis of a modern NASCAR stock car. Many of these early devices were made of wood and few organizations required their use. That changed in 1952 when Bernard "Pancho" Alvarez wildly

What's left of a NASCAR Modified (check out the decal on the hood) after what was surely a harrowing ride for the driver. (Photo Courtesy Georgia Racing Hall of Fame)

flipped his No. 94 Oldsmobile on lap 112 of the 200-circuit season-opening event at Palm Beach Speedway (Florida). The force of the accident crushed the roof of the vehicle, briefly trapping Alvarez in the car. Escaping injury, Alvarez never made another NASCAR start. Meanwhile, NASCAR immediately amended its rules, henceforth requiring steel roll bars on all cars.

150 One of the most unlikely cars to become a NASCAR legend, the Hudson Hornet dominated the ranks in the early 1950s. Thanks to its step-down design (with the floor pan located below the frame), the Hornet had a lower center of gravity than many other cars. Combined with a potent 262-ci inline 6-cylinder engine, the Hornet's superior handling allowed it to dominate its V-8-powered competition, winning 12 of 41 races on the 1951 Grand National tour. A year later, Hudson added "Twin H Power" dual carburetors and an "L-Head" to the mix allowing the Hornet to pretty much shut out the competition by capturing 27 of the 34 GN events. The now "Fabulous Hudson Hornet" followed its 1952 success with 22 victories out of 37 Grand National events in 1953. The 1954 season was the last great year for the "racing bathtub," winning 17 out of 37 NASCAR Grand National races. Unfortunately, the company's showroom success was no match for powerful Chevy and Ford competitors, forcing the brand to merge with Nash-Kelvinator in 1954. Beginning in 1955, the Hudson Hornet, now manufactured on Nash-based chassis as part of the new American Motors Corporation in Kenosha, Wisconsin, bore little resemblance to the car that crushed the competition in NASCAR's early years. The last Hudson Hornet rolled off the production line in 1957.

151 Despite rainy conditions that red-flagged the 1952 Southern 500 at Darlington Raceway (South Carolina), driver Fonty Flock made it a sunny day by wearing a short-sleeved shirt, Bermuda shorts and a pair of argyle socks while competing in the event. Flock, starting from the pole, led 341 of the 400 laps to win the race. Flock unveiled his unique fashion statement to the delight of a Labor Day crowd of more than 32,000, when he pulled his 1952 Air Lift Special Oldsmobile into Victory Lane.

Fonty Flock, wearing his special driver's suit, celebrates with the crowd in Victory Lane after winning the Southern 500 at Darlington (South Carolina) Raceway. (Photo Courtesy Georgia Racing Hall of Fame)

152 Introduced in 1954, the Ford/Lincoln Y-Block engine was a replacement for its legendary Flathead V-8. The engine got its name thanks to deep cylinder block skirting that made it look like the letter "Y." The new engine initially proved to be no match for the hot iron and was shut out of the Grand National win column in 1954 and most of 1955. In the second-to-last race of the 1955 season, Buck Baker finally gave the engine its first NASCAR victory at North Wilkesboro. Over the next two seasons, a new and improved Y-block–based "Thunderbird Special V-8" propelled Ford drivers to 45 victories and both 1956 and 1957 NASCAR Manufacturers' Championships. Ford produced the Y-block for American cars and trucks through 1964, but the engine's NASCAR Grand National run all but ended with the introduction of the FE big-block in 1958 and the Windsor small-block in 1962.

153 General Motors was the last of the "Big Three" to introduce an overhead valve V-8 engine, but when it did, it was a doozy. Launched in 1955, the 265-ci Chevy Turbo Fire with the 4-barrel carburetor Corvette option produced 195 hp. In 1957, the engine was beefed up to 283 ci and, when outfitted with twin 4-barrel carburetors, kicked out a hefty 270 hp. Mated with a lightweight 1957 Chevy 150 body and "Black Widow" race-ready option package, the combination was an instant hit with the NASCAR crowd. It cruised to 21 NASCAR Grand National victories in 53 races in 1957 compared to just three the previous season. Despite the success, Ford still won the NASCAR Manufacturers' Championship in 1957, but it was a short-lived success as the new Chevy small-block V-8 powered the brand to the next four NASCAR Manufacturers' titles.

154 An interesting development in the 1950s was the Fish Carburetor, designed by John Robert Fish. Unlike conventional carburetors, the Fish used pressure differential (not air speed) making it instantly self-adjusting regardless of weather or altitude. This eliminated the need for a Venturi as well as both the main and corrector carburetor jets. The Fish Carburetor replaced conventional 4-barrel carburetors in both the NASCAR Modified and Grand National ranks in the mid-1950s. Led by legendary mechanics/engine builders Raymond Fox Sr. and Red Vogt, the team fielded as many as five cars in a race at one time including Fireball Roberts, Cotton Owens, Joe Weatherly, Speedy Thompson, Ralph Moody, LeeRoy Yarbrough, and Milt Hartlauf among the many stars of the era to wheel the famed "M" designated cars.

155 Tim Flock wheeled one of Carl Kiekhaefer's potent Chrysler 300s to 18 victories and captured the 1955 NASCAR Grand National title by a staggering 1,508 points over Buck Baker. Flock also won 18 poles and led every lap in 11 of his victories. These accomplishments are even more impressive when you consider that Flock, who quit NASCAR in 1954 after his winning run at Daytona was disallowed, was out of racing and didn't even have a ride at the start of the 1955 campaign.

156 NASCAR allowed few modifications in the early years of the Strictly Stock/Grand National division. Hudson was the first to test these rules by making "Severe Usage" parts an option on its Hornet Club Coupe model, the same car used in NASCAR. Included in the offerings were the Twin H-Power dual carburetor engine with dual exhaust manifolds and multiple camshaft options. Hudson offered several heavy-duty suspension upgrades as well. Hudson produced more than 9,200 Hornet Club Coupe models from 1951 to 1954, making the car and the parts options eligible for NASCAR competition. Coincidentally, Hudson won 66 of 108 NASCAR Grand National events during that period. That success led to other manufacturers, notably Oldsmobile and Lincoln, to introduce parts branded as Heavy-Duty and Police Car Parts on passenger cars. Ultimately, the parts (and the need for increased safety as speeds climbed) led to the demise of the Strictly Stock concept and summoned the birth of the purpose-built NASCAR race car.

157 In 1995, the NASCAR Craftsman Truck Series was presented at Phoenix International Raceway (Arizona) with Mike Skinner taking the victory. Meanwhile, the first win by a truck at a NASCAR event came on June 11, 1950, when Gwyn Staley captured the Wilkes County Championship Fan's Car Race. The event, although not an official NASCAR race, was held in conjunction with the NASCAR Modified race that day at North Wilkesboro Speedway. It was a 10-lap affair and open to non-race vehicles driven to the track by fans. Staley, the brother of North Wilkesboro Speedway promoter Enoch Staley, started third and drove his Ford pickup to victory.

158 Always looking for a way to compete against the American Automobile Association, Bill France Sr. launched a new Speedway Division for the 1952 season. The series featured open-wheel Indianapolis-style cars with stock passenger car engines. The first official race was held at Darlington Raceway May 10 with Buck Baker driving a Cadillac-powered entry to victory in the 200-mile event. Six additional Speedway Division races were contested at various tracks in 1952 including Martinsville, Lakewood, and Charlotte. A lack of entries and a nationwide steel strike brought the series to a halt after Tom Cherry's wins at Langhorne Speedway June 29. The series returned briefly in 1953, running three events as part of NASCAR's Sportsman Division before fading into the history books forever.

159 Buck Baker not only won the first NASCAR Speedway Division race at Darlington and the division's inaugural championship in 1952, but he also posted a trio of speed records in his Cadillac-powered open-wheel car at the Daytona Beach flying mile. The division made its first appearance February 4, 1952, on the beach with Baker roaring to speeds of 132.940, 142.290, and 140.410 mph during the three-day Speedweeks test. Seven cars took part in the final day's event with Fireball Roberts driving a Ford-powered car to second with a speed of 131.580 mph.

160 While it is a bit sketchy regarding the first to use two-way radio communication in NASCAR, there's no debate about who gave the practice of "spotting" its name. That honor goes to Al Stevens. He used World War II surplus radio/telephone equipment to communicate to his pits and corner crewmembers during the February 9, 1952, Modified and Sportsman race at the Daytona Beach-Road Course. Stevens' first used the equipment in World War II when he served as an Army field artillery spotter.

161 Early attempts at car and crew chief communications were serious, but laughable at times. In the 1952 NASCAR Speedway Division race at Darlington Raceway, driver Tony Bonadies wore an old-style Cromwell helmet with an Army-style walkie-talkie strapped to it. Bonadies wore the oversized, heavy contraption throughout the race until falling out just past the halfway point of the race. In a strange twist of fate, his Chrysler-powered Kurtis-Kraft racer was declared out of the race due to a blown head gasket.

162 Most NASCAR fans aware of the success of the Chrysler 426 Hemi engine in the 1960s, but the famed Mopar powerplant was introduced in 1951. The Firepower V-8 featured domed (or hemispherical) pistons and combustion chamber cylinder heads along with larger cross-flow intake and exhaust valves. While the design was heavier than most engines of the day, the 1951 Hemi measured a stout 331.1 ci and produced an impressive 180 hp. The newly-coined "Hemi" received immediate acclaim, powering a Chrysler Saratoga to third place in the grueling 1951 Carrera

Panamericana Mexican Road Race behind a pair of Ferraris. Lee Petty was the first in NASCAR to benefit from bolting the engine into a Dodge Diplomat for the 1953 season, winning five races and finishing second in championship standings. Petty's hemi-powered Chrysler Windsor Club Coupe then captured seven wins, including Daytona, en route to the 1954 Grand National title and earning the original engine its place in NASCAR history.

163 Both the Hudson and Nash brands had significant success in the early years of NASCAR. Each brand saw its fortunes wane mid-decade after Hudson merged with Nash-Kelvinator Corporation. The 1954 merger was estimated at $200 million and, at that time, considered the largest financial deal between two companies in American history. AMC later made a comeback in 1973 as Mark Donohue drove Roger Penske's AMC Matador to victory in the first race of the season at Riverside Raceway (California). Bobby Allison also took a Penske Matador to Victory Lane at Riverside in the final NASCAR race of 1974 and the first race of 1975.

Tiny Lund in a T-shirt, light pants, and regular shoes, standard attire for the time, scurries away from his burning racer during a 1950s event at Lakewood Speedway in Atlanta, Georgia. (Photo Courtesy Georgia Racing Hall of Fame)

164 As safety concerns grew in the 1950s, companies such as Treesdale Laboratories offered items to protect drivers, making safety options more available and commonplace. Included were the Treesdale Permaproof Fyre Safe Fisher Fabric coveralls. Halfway through the 1954 season, the Pittsburgh, Pennsylvania, company started selling NASCAR drivers its baggy, flame-retardant coveralls for $9.25. By the end of the season, all but a few NASCAR regulars were wearing the sanctioning group's first fire suits.

165 Throughout the 1930s and 1940s, the Cromwell helmet was the standard for both the motorcycle and auto racing industry. The round, hard-shell helmet with leather straps was introduced as a military item in 1924 and adapted to a motorcycle safety helmet in 1926. The "brain bucket" was eventually replaced by General Textile Mills GenTex 70. Developed for the Navy as a fighter pilot helmet after World War II, the GenTex 70 was a significant upgrade in safety gear. It featured a form-fitting padded head sling designed to lessen shock and prevent concussions upon hard impact. The GenTex 70 was made available to NASCAR drivers in the 1954 season for $35.

166 By the 1952 season, more companies were finding creative ways to become contingency sponsors of NASCAR. One such sponsor, Pure Oil Company, not only added cash to the purse during Speedweeks at the Daytona Beach-Road Course, but also pumped 7,856 gallons of free gas into the competitors' tanks.

167 Prior to the 1952 season, all Grand National cars raced on regular passenger (or truck) tires. In addition to its free gas arrangement, Pure Oil Company became the first to offer an all-nylon cord tire specifically designed for racing. Unlike the gas, the company charged NASCAR competitors $37.90 for each tire.

168 To date, Chevrolet has scored more NASCAR top division wins than any other manufacturer. Chevrolet's first victory came on March 26, 1955, when Fonty Flock piloted a Chevy Bel Air with an all new 265-ci overhead valve V-8 engine to the win in a 100-mile Grand National event at Columbia Speedway (South Carolina).

169 While most cars were driven to, raced at, and wheeled home from the racetrack in the 1950s, many competitors started using a tow bar to pull their NASCAR Grand National racers. In 1955, Carl Kiekhaefer forever changed the way cars traveled to the track after introducing a fleet of box trucks to transport his Chrysler 300s to and from the track. The leviathan Mopars were so long, they hung off the end of the box. The trucks are considered to be the introduction of the modern race hauler.

170 NASCAR, and all forms of auto racing in the United States, took a blow June 6, 1957, when the directors of the Automobile Manufacturing Association voted unanimously to recommend that car manufacturers divorce themselves from all events emphasizing speed and horsepower. Given that the AMA board was made up of American car executives, the "gentlemen's agreement" virtually ended factory assistance in NASCAR. By 1962, automakers had had enough of the ban and Ford petitioned the AMA to rescind it. Chrysler, meanwhile, openly defied the ban while General Motors, with 53 percent controlling interest of the market at the time, continued to honor the agreement through the 1970 season.

171 On the surface, Chevrolet appeared to be the biggest supporter of the Manufacturers' Ban. In reality, it worked the hardest to get around the ban. During the 1957 season, Chevrolet commissioned former Hudson engineer Vince Piggins to form the Southern Engineering and Development Company (SEDCO). Based in Atlanta, SEDCO built six *Black Widow* stock cars, one of which Buck Baker drove to the 1957 NASCAR Grand National Championship. The company also issued a *1957 Chevrolet Stock Car Competition Guide* detailing how to convert a Chevy 150 into a NASCAR Grand National vehicle using GM parts. The guide was distributed to more than 400 Chevrolet dealers nationwide giving Chevy "faux" factory support during the ban.

172 When the American Manufacturing Association nixed car company support of auto racing due to concerns over rising traffic fatalities involving high-performance cars, Bill France Sr. banned the use of Chevrolet's new fuel injection system on small-block V-8 engines and turbochargers on Ford's V-8 offerings. Buck Baker won the 1957 NASCAR Grand National title running a Chevy V-8 outfitted with conventional dual 4-barrel carburetors. Much to the dismay of France, Baker proudly displayed the words "Fuel Injected" on the front fenders of his No. 87 black and white *Black Widow* Chevy 150 throughout the 1957 season.

173 With the 1957 Manufacturing Association digging into the NASCAR teams' pockets, Bill France Sr. help bridge the financial gap by encouraging race promoters to increase their event purses. France also reached into NASCAR's wallet, guaranteeing racers at least $300 for every Grand National race attended. That marks the first time that NASCAR offered what is now known as "travel" or "tow" money to racers and teams.

174 In 1956, 23 of the 56 events on the NASCAR Grand National tour paid less than $1,000 to win. On the low side, several races paid $650 to win while the biggest winner's share came at Darlington where Curtis Turner banked $11,750 for his Southern 500 triumph. After the 1957 Manufacturing Ban, all GN events paid at least $1,000 to win.

TRACKS

175 Located on more than 100 acres at the corner of Sugar Creek Road and North Tryon Street in Charlotte, Southern States Fairgrounds Speedway played host to 17 NASCAR Grand National events from 1954 to 1961. Lee Petty captured the most checkered flags (three) at the half-mile dirt oval including one in the first NASCAR event held there August 13, 1954. Petty also scored a win in one of five NASCAR Convertible Division races at the Charlotte oval. The opening of Charlotte Motor Speedway in 1960 spelled the demise of NASCAR events at the track and the final Grand National race (won by Joe Weatherly) was held November 6, 1960.

Darlington (South Carolina) Raceway hardly ever had an empty seat as evidenced by this packed grandstand at the 1955 Southern 500. (Photo Courtesy Ed Samples Jr. Collection)

176 Built by Harold Brasington on a farm owned by Sherman Ramsey, the 1.25-mile ultra-wide Darlington Raceway opened in 1950 featuring multiple racing grooves and a pedestrian walkover bridge on the backstretch. The track's egg-shaped layout was a matter of necessity; it was constructed so it wouldn't disturb Ramsey's minnow pond outside Turn 2 (now Turn 4). Dubbed "The Lady in Black" by sportswriter Benny Phillips, the track opened September 4, 1950, with a NASCAR Grand National race. The first Southern 500 was co-sanctioned by the Central States Racing Association. A field of 75 cars (25 rows three-abreast) took the green flag in front of 25,000 fans with Johnny Mantz the victor. Later that year, Darlington also hosted an AAA/USAC IndyCar race at which Johnny Parsons took the win. Since then, Darlington Raceway has become NASCAR's most storied superspeedway, hosting more than 180 Cup, Convertible, Xfinity, Truck, and K&N Series events.

177 When the Central States Racing Association announced that it would sanction the first 500-mile stock car race at the new Darlington Raceway on Labor Day weekend 1950, Bill France Sr. didn't think it would work. France doubted the ability of Strictly Stock vehicles to complete the 500-mile test and felt that a rash of mechanical failures would not only doom the race, but also slow the growth of the sport with the ticket-buying public. When the CSRA indicated that it was having trouble filling the field with entries and NASCAR rival Sam Nunis announced he was also staging a 500-mile race Labor Day weekend, France partnered with CSRA to co-sanction Darlington. The rest is history as Lakewood dropped the plans for its event and NASCAR roared into the era of 500-mile stock car races unopposed.

178 After years of racing on dusty dirt bullrings across the country, Darlington Raceway was the first paved track to host a NAS-CAR Grand National race: the 1950 Southern 500. Johnny Mantz won, in large part, by being one of a few drivers to have raced on an asphalt surface.

Check out the makeshift mud screen on Marshall Teague's 1951 Hudson Hornet. It was an effort to keep dirt and debris from clogging or puncturing the radiator. (Photo Courtesy Russ Lake)

179 NASCAR made its first West Coast appearance April 8, 1951, at Carell Speedway in Gardenia, California. Marshall Teague drove his Hudson Hornet to a Grand National victory beating Johnny Mantz to the finish in the 200-lap event. Lou Figaro and Bill Norton also won Grand National events at Carell in 1951. The half-mile dirt oval hosted one other GN clash, a May 30, 1954, event won by John Soares in a Dodge.

180 On August 15, 1952, the Monroe County Fairgrounds in Rochester, New York, was the site of one of the most unusual scoring decisions in NASCAR history. After a review of the race scoring showed that Neil Cole was inadvertently left out of the top-10, both he and George Gallup were awarded eighth place. Officials determined that the pair tied for the position by completing 170 laps each in the 176-circuit contest.

181 Southland Speedway in Raleigh, North Carolina, a 1-mile, paperclip-shaped dirt oval featuring 1,850-foot flat straights and 16-degree banking in the turns, opened in 1952 with a AAA

Bill France Sr. (in Hawaiian shirt and Pure Oil hat) and a host of Pure Oil representatives tip a cold drink at Raleigh (North Carolina) Speedway in the early 1950s. (Photo Courtesy Ed Samples Jr. Collection)

IndyCar race won by Troy Ruttman. The track, which had been heavily opposed by local and state legislators, immediately filed bankruptcy after the event. Enter Bill France Sr., who, with partner Jim Chestnutt, formed J&W Corporation and purchased the speedway. On May 30, 1953, the newly named Raleigh Speedway opened, hosting a 300-mile NASCAR Grand National event won by Fonty Flock. Later that year, France made Raleigh the first superspeedway with lights and held events on Saturday to skirt a local Sunday racing ban. In all, Raleigh Speedway hosted seven NASCAR Grand National and three Convertible Division events from 1953 to 1958. Fireball Roberts won the final NASCAR GN held at Raleigh in 1958. France moved the track's Independence Day weekend event to the new Daytona International Speedway in 1959. The track closed shortly after and was torn down in 1967.

182 By 1951, Detroit, Michigan, was the epicenter of the American automobile industry. As NASCAR was gaining credibility with both the public and the manufacturers, it came as no surprise when Bill France Sr. partnered with the Detroit Junior Chamber of Commerce to stage an event celebrating the 250th anniversary of the city. This partnership resulted in a 250-mile Grand National race on the 1-mile dirt oval on the Michigan State Fairgrounds. The August 12 event attracted a crowd of more than 16,000 and was won by Tommy Thompson driving a Chrysler. In all, 16 different makes comprised the 59-car starting grid. A year later, Tim Flock won the second (and last) Motor City 250. Although the track hosted just two NASCAR events, its importance can't be understated as it showcased NASCAR to the movers and shakers of the auto industry, further establishing the division as one of the leading stock car organizations in the country.

183 One of the earliest speedways, dating back to 1900, Trenton Speedway, on the New Jersey State Fairgrounds, gave NASCAR huge exposure on the Eastern Seaboard. Fireball Roberts won the first Grand National race (the 500-lap Northern 500) held on its 1-mile kidney bean–shaped dirt surface May 30, 1958. Tom Pistone won NASCAR's second event at the track, a 150-miler (a year later before NASCAR packed up only to return in 1967 for the Northern 300 won by Richard Petty). Petty won two more times in the next five years before NASCAR's Modern Era spelled the end of racing on dirt tracks.

184 A half-mile dirt horse-racing oval, Stamford Park in Niagara Falls, Ontario, Canada, has the distinction of being the site of the first NASCAR race held outside the United States. The July 1, 1952, event drew a field of just 17 cars. Herb Thomas took the pole and Buddy Shuman grabbed his first NASCAR Grand National win driving a 1952 Hudson owned by B. L Pless. Shuman won by two laps over Thomas as only six cars finished the race on the tight, rough track. It was the only NASCAR race ever held at Stamford, which closed to auto racing in 1954.

185 Located in West Palm Beach, Florida, the half-mile dirt oval at Palm Beach Speedway has the distinction of hosting the first and last race in the 1952 NASCAR Grand National tour. Tim Flock piloted Ted Chester's 1951 Hudson Hornet to a victory in the season opener at January 20 while Herb Thomas garnered the win in the final race of the season in a 100-miler November 30. The track hosted five more NASCAR Grand National events throughout the 1956 season; Thomas dominated with three more victories. Billy Myers drove a 1956 Bill Stroppe Mercury to his first career Grand National victory on Sunday, March 4, 1956, the final top-division NASCAR event at the track.

186 NASCAR's Grand National Series contested 381 events from its inception as the Strictly Stock division in 1949 through the final race of the 1959 GN campaign on October 25 at New Concord Speedway (North Carolina). A whopping 293 of those 381 races were contested on dirt oval tracks, 1 mile or less in length as NASCAR spent the 1950s barnstorming its way across America, one track at a time.

187 One of America's oldest speedways, opening in 1914, Winchester Speedway (Indiana) hosted its first and only NASCAR

Atlanta (Georgia) Speedway hosted weekly Jalopy and Modified Stock Car events such as this one in 1952, before a packed house on a perfect summer afternoon. (Photo Courtesy Georgia Racing Hall of Fame)

Grand National event on October 15, 1950. The second-to-last race of the GN season marked the farthest west a NASCAR race had been held to date and was won by Lloyd Moore in a 1950 Mercury. It was the only victory of Moore's 49-race Grand National career.

188 Nearly 40 years before the Winston Cup Series debut at Phoenix International Raceway, NASCAR held events at the 1-mile dirt oval at the Arizona State Fairgrounds. The April 22, 1951, Grand National event was part of NASCAR's western expansion that included events at Carrell Speedway (Gardena, California) and Oakland Stadium (California). Marshall Teague won it in a Hudson Hornet. NASCAR staged three additional events at the fairgrounds track with Tim Flock (1955), Buck Baker (1956), and John Rostek (1960) all taking home the winner's trophy. Despite its short inclusion on the NASCAR tour, the facility was instrumental in turning the brand into a series with national importance in the 1950s.

189 NASCAR made the first of three appearances at the famed Oakland Stadium in the early 1950s. The track, built in 1931, saw several reconfigurations, one greeting NASCAR Grand

National drivers at an October 14, 1951, event. At that time, the .625-mile oval featured 45-degree banking in the first and second turns while the third and fourth turns were banked at a death-defying 60 degrees, the highest banking for any track hosting a NASCAR Grand National event.

190 Built on a former 320-acre rice plantation and billed the largest stock car racing facility in the country, Memphis-Arkansas Speedway in Lehi, Arkansas, opened with the Grand National Mid-South 250 October 10, 1954. Buck Baker wheeled his 1954 Oldsmobile to victory on the massive 1.5-mile wooden-guardrail oval. Fonty Flock, Speedy Thompson, Ralph Moody, and Marvin Panch also captured Grand National wins there and Curtis Turner won a Convertible Division battle before financial problems forced the track to close in 1957.

191 At the start of the 1953 season, NASCAR informed drivers not submitting pre-event entry forms that they would not receive championship points if they showed up and competed on race day. Among those penalized for the paperwork infraction that season were Bill Blair, Harold Nash, Coleman Lawrence, and Fred Dove. This move helped promoters advertise, in advance, the drivers who would be competing.

192 More than a decade before the Chicago Bears called Soldier Field home, NASCAR strutted its stuff at the sports stadium. A long-time home for Midwestern Midget and Stock Car races; Soldier Field's half-mile paved oval was the site of the 33rd race of the 1956 NASCAR Grand National tour. Fireball Roberts led a FoMoCo sweep of the first three places, beating Jim Paschal and Ralph Moody to the finish. The event proved to be the only NASCAR GN race ever held at the track, which also hosted three NASCAR Convertible Division events won by Tom Pistone, Curtis Turner, and Glen Wood.

193 NASCAR made its first appearance in Wisconsin when it staged a Grand National Series road race at Road America on August 12, 1956. Much of the 283.3-mile event on the twisting 4.1-mile

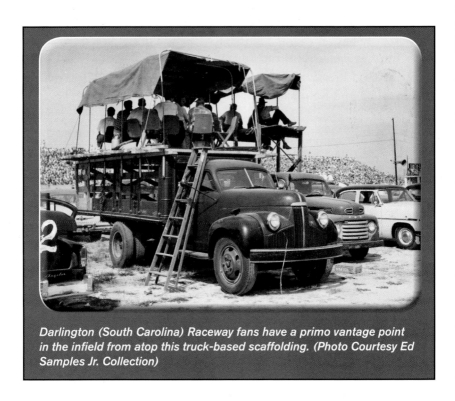

Darlington (South Carolina) Raceway fans have a primo vantage point in the infield from atop this truck-based scaffolding. (Photo Courtesy Ed Samples Jr. Collection)

Elkhart Lake layout was run in the rain. Tim Flock proved to be the best in the wet as he wheeled a Bill Stroppe Mercury to a 17-second win over Billy Myers in a second Stroppe Merc. The event remains the only time NASCAR's top division raced at the iconic track.

194 Depending where the race was and where you were sitting, the cost of a general admission ticket to a NASCAR Grand National race in the mid 1950s was $2.50 for a Saturday Night Special and $10 for a prime seat at Darlington for the Southern 500. While that sounds inexpensive, if you adjust for inflation, that's around $22.50 and $85 in today's money.

195 Built in 1924 as a 5/8-mile dirt track and paved as a half-mile in 1946, Portland Speedway (Oregon) has long played a critical part in the growth of NASCAR in the Northwest United States. Portland hosted seven NASCAR Grand National races in just over

14 months during the 1956–1957 seasons. The track also played a big part in the history of the NASCAR Grand National West/Winston West Series, hosting 36 division events from 1971 to 2000. The track helped launch the NASCAR Craftsman Truck Series with an event in each of the division's four seasons from 1995 to 1998.

196 On July 19, 1958, Buffalo Civic Speedway (New York) hosted its one and only NASCAR Grand National event. Jim Reed won the 100-lap race in front of a crowd of 7,700. The race on the quarter-mile track, later named War Memorial Stadium (the early home of the Buffalo Bills), is the shortest race in NASCAR top-tier division racing at just 25 miles.

197 Beginning in 1903 at nearby Ormond Beach, the Daytona Beach area was king of speed trials as all manners of prototype and production cars tried to prove their mettle in standing and flying-mile test runs. Speed trials continued even after the opening of Daytona International Speedway and in 1960, Greg Ziegler powered a Chrysler 300 F Special to a top speed of 144.927 mph, a mark that still stands as the fastest recorded speed for a stock car on the beach. The annual speed trials ended in 1961 as development along the beach and racing at the new 2.5-mile track took center stage.

A 1957 Chevy takes the green flag for its Measured Mile run. (Photo Courtesy Georgia Racing Hall of Fame)

198 With multiple road courses ranging from 2.5 to 3.25 miles in length, Riverside International Raceway (California) hosted its first NASCAR Grand National event June 1, 1958. Gardena, California, driver Eddie Gray drove a 1957 Ford owned by Vel Miletch to victory in the Crown America 500 beating 45 other competitors. The 90-lap, 500-mile event took more than 6 hours. For the next 30 years, Riverside was the West Coast home for NASCAR delivering the critical Los Angeles media market. In all, NASCAR's Grand National/Cup divisions competed at Riverside 47 times and its West series raced there 41 times. The track closed in 1989.

199 NASCAR made its New York City debut August 2, 1958, at Bridgehampton Raceway, a 2.85-mile road course. Jack Smith won the 35-lap, 99.8-mile Grand National event in a 1957 Chevrolet. The Long Island track eventually hosted three more NASCAR GN events with Richard Petty (1963), Billy Wade (1964), and David Pearson (1966) visiting Victory Lane.

200 The .9-mile Kitsap County Airport paved road course outside Bremerton, Washington, hosted its only NASCAR Grand National event August 4, 1958. Up-and-coming Torrance, California, driver Rufus "Parnelli" Jones won his first NASCAR GN event in a 1957 Ford.

201 The opening of Daytona International Speedway in 1959 turned a dream into a reality. Built on 447 acres, the 2.5-mile paved track features massive 31-degree banking in the turns. Meanwhile, the straight in the "tri-oval" area is banked 18 degrees, much higher than at many other tracks of that time. The final cost of building DIS is estimated as high as $3 million, (more than $24 million today). Bill France Sr. took a second mortgage on his home to help finance to project. France's vision was rewarded and the facility was an immediate hit when 42,000 turned out for the inaugural Daytona 500 February 22, 1959. Since then, Daytona has hosted numerous sports car and motorcycle events as well as more than 270 NASCAR races drawing millions of fans to what is called the World Center of Speed.

Bill France Sr. calling the action over the Greensboro Agricultural Fair-grounds Speedway public address system. (Photo Courtesy Ed Samples Jr. Collection)

202 Have you ever showed up at a NASCAR race and been unable to find your seat? If so, you can only imagine rolling into Wilson Speedway (North Carolina), March 29, 1959, to find the grandstand on fire. Despite the structure burning, the Grand National event was run with 8,000 fans watching from the other side of the retaining fence. Junior Johnson won the 200-lap race without incident.

PIT PASS

203 Lee Petty scored 2,399 points during the 1950 NASCAR Grand National season, 440 more than Bill Rexford. Unfortunately for Petty, NASCAR docked him 809 points for competing in non-sanctioned events during a three-week period when NASCAR had no races scheduled. Petty had more top-5 and top-10 finishes than both Rexford and Fireball Roberts, but was relegated to third in the final standings due to his participation in outlaw events.

204 Lee Petty wasn't the only driver to feel the heavy hand of NAS-CAR during the 1950 season. Red Byron was docked championship points not once, but twice. Byron had all his points stripped early in the year after finishing second at Daytona and fourth at Charlotte for competing in non-sanctioned races. Byron returned to finish third in the inaugural Southern 500 at Darlington and later competed in the Grand National race at North Wilkesboro. After the event, Byron was stripped of all his points a second time for the same infraction. Byron's total of 1,630 points in the four events would have placed him fourth in the final standings. Instead, Byron was credited with zero points for the season and not listed in the championship rundown.

205 A dirt-track racer in his early years, Harold Brasington became a trailblazer when he built NASCAR's first paved superspeedway: Darlington Raceway. Using land provided by farmer Sherman Ramsey, Brasington carved out a 1.25-mile egg-shaped oval and opened on September 4, 1950, with the first Southern 500. Brasington sold his interests in Darlington in 1954 and in the late 1950s partnered with Curtis Turner to build the proposed Charlotte Motor Speedway. Brasington later sold his interests to Bruton Smith, and partnered with Bill Land to create North Carolina Speedway (Rockingham) in 1965. Brasington is credited with building both Darlington and Rockingham Dragway along with multiple short tracks throughout the South. Brasington passed away February 4, 1996, in Florence, South Carolina, at the age of 86.

206 When 1949 Indianapolis 500 champion Bill Holland was suspended by the American Automobile Association Contest Board for participating in a charity race in 1951, Bill France Sr. immediately invited him to try his hand at NASCAR. Holland never quite got a handle on stock car racing, scoring just one top-5 finish (a fourth at North Wilkesboro) in seven 1951 events. Holland returned to the IndyCar ranks in 1954, ultimately ending his career with 21 victories. Despite his lackluster results, Holland's participation in NASCAR during the 1951 season drew significant media and fan attention, helping legitimize the sanctioning body in its early years.

Jocko Flocko on the hood of his 1953 Hudson Hornet with drivers (from left) Tim Flock, Herb Thomas, and Fonty Flock. (Photo Courtesy Brandon Reed Collection)

207 The youngest of the racing Flock brothers, Julius Timothy "Tim" Flock, proved to be the greatest driver in the family, winning 39 NASCAR Grand National races and two division championships (1952 and 1955). Flock ran afoul of Bill France Sr. more than most drivers, the final time earning him a lifetime suspension in 1961 when he took part in a movement to unionize the drivers. He was reinstated in 1966, after his driving career ended. Named one of NASCAR's 50 greatest drivers in 1998, Flock was inducted into the NASCAR Hall of Fame in 2014. Flock died March 21, 1998, at the age of 73.

208 Atlanta's Ted Chester was one of NASCAR's greatest team owners, his cars wining 20 Grand National events from 1950 through 1957. More important, Chester gave NASCAR Jocko Flocko. Chester purchased "Jocko," a Rhesus monkey to partner with driver, Tim Flock. The pair hatched a plan to have "Jocko Flocko" ride with Flock in a race. They got Jocko a helmet, made him a driver's suit and added a secure racing seat complete with safety harness to the passenger's side, all mounted high enough so Jocko could see out. Jocko made his NASCAR debut April 5, 1953, when the team secretly strapped him in for a Grand National event at Charlotte.

"The Flocks" led seven times for 87 laps before fading in the final laps and finishing fourth. After the race, Flock took Jocko into the crowd where he was an instant hit. When the pair finished sixth in the Grand National race at Macon Speedway (Georgia) two weeks later, word quickly spread that Flock had a monkey riding with him fueling a surge in ticket sales for upcoming events. Meanwhile, NASCAR was happy to accept the publicity and revenue even if people were coming to see a monkey. Jocko rode shotgun in eight 1953 Grand National events, the highpoint being a win on May 16 in a 200-lap event at Hickory Motor Speedway.

Unfortunately, Jocko's ride to fame came to an end two weeks later at Raleigh Speedway after he escaped his harness and began leaping around inside Flock's speeding Hudson Hornet. Leading at the time, Flock had to make a pit stop to get Jocko out of the car. The resulting third-place finish got Jocko fired as co-driver, ending his run as the only co-driver in the NASCAR history.

209 NASCAR added another division to the mix in 1951: the Short-Track Division. In all, 11 races were contested on tracks of a half-mile or less. Roscoe "Pappy" Hough won the division title the first year, while Jim Reed, a Peekskill, New York, driver and part-time GN competitor from 1951 to 1962, earned five-straight NASCAR Short-Track Division titles from 1953 to 1957. Lee Petty captured the 1958 title with West Coast driver Parnelli Jones winning the most division races at five. Marvin Porter garnered the final NASCAR Short-Track title before the division was discontinued at the conclusion of the 28-race 1959 season.

210 One of the all-time legends of the Modified ranks, Frankie Schneider won the 1952 NASCAR Modified Division championship. He started 27 Grand National and nine Convertible Series events in his career, winning once at a 150-lap GN race April 28,

1958, at Old Dominion Speedway in Manassas, Virginia. Later that year, Schneider got into an appearance money flap with NASCAR, loaded up his car, and never raced in Grand National again. He returned to his Modified roots, winning hundreds of races over the next two decades. He was victorious in his last race, a Modified event at Nazareth Speedway (Pennsylvania) July 31, 1977.

211 The NASCAR Strictly Stock Series was more a concept than a name, so when the schedule for the 1950 season was announced, it had a new title: NASCAR Grand National Series. The new moniker was selected to mirror the success of the English Grand National steeplechase, the world standard of horse racing since its inception in 1839.

212 Anticipation was high as NASCAR moved the 1950 season-opening Speed Weeks to February. The two-day event featured a 100-mile Modified race on the Daytona Beach-Road Course February 4, won by Gober Sosebee. The Sunday Grand National opener on the beach was caution-free and produced a surprise winner as East Point, Georgia, driver Harold Kite, in his first appearance at a NASCAR Grand National event, wheeled a 1949 Lincoln to victory, earning $1,500 for the win.

213 Known as The King of the Beach, Daytona native Marshall Teague played multiple parts in the early years of NASCAR. Teague was elected treasurer at the initial 1947 meeting and later became NASCAR's first back-to-back Grand National division winner at the Daytona Beach-Road Course in 1950 and 1951. Teague took a trip to Detroit prior to the 1951 season and convinced the Hudson Motor Car Company to back his efforts, effectively creating the first driver/team/manufacturer agreement in NASCAR. Teague scored all seven Grand National career wins in his "Fabulous Hudson Hornet" from 1951 to 1952 before quitting in 1952 after a dispute with Bill France Sr. over money. Undaunted, Teague and his Hudson won the 1952 AAA championship and another AAA title in 1954. He also competed in the Indianapolis 500 three times from 1954 to 1957 with his best finish (seventh) in the 1957 classic.

Eventually, Teague and France settled their differences and Teague was chosen to do tire testing prior to the opening of Daytona International Speedway in 1959. Unfortunately, Teague became the first driver to die at the new speedway when he crashed the *Sumar Special* experimental IndyCar during an attempt to set a closed course speed record. He died instantly, thrown from the car February 11, 1959, 11 days before the first running of the Daytona 500.

214 These days, the Darlington Raceway Southern 500 winner takes home more than $300,000 for capturing NASCAR's oldest superspeedway event. That's considerably more than the $10,510 Johnny Mantz banked for winning the first Southern 500 in 1950, although, at the time, the prize was the largest winner's share in racing history.

215 Tony Bonadies, a Bronx, New York, driver, scored his only NASCAR victory July 14, 1951, when he and his Nash Rambler captured a 400-lap NASCAR Short-Track Grand National race at Lanham (Maryland) Speedway. Bonadies bested Ronnie Kohler and Fonty Flock in large part due to being the only competitor in the event who never made a pit stop.

216 Buckshot Morris was a top mechanic in NASCAR's early days. In 1951, Morris turned all the wrenches for team owners Ted Chester and Frank Christian and their drivers, Tim, Bob, and Fonty Flock. Between them, the Flock brothers won 16 NASCAR Grand National races that season.

217 Racing on the beach at Daytona posed challenges such as completing the race before the Atlantic Ocean's tide rolled in. On February 10, 1952, NASCAR officials had to call the event two circuits short of the 39-lap distance. Marshall Teague, who had more than a minute lead and had paced since the second lap, was declared the winner over runner-up Herb Thomas. Pat Kirkwood was third, the only other car on the lead lap when the waves came crashing in.

218 Despite huge success, early efforts to gain mainstream publicity for NASCAR were difficult at best as the sport was viewed

as a regional phenomenon. A measure of success and public awareness came December 8, 1952, when *Time* magazine featured a story
about Grand National champion Tim Flock. It was the first time a
national, non-traditional sports or automotive magazine featured
the emerging form of motorsports.

219 The first superspeedway night race was held September 19,
1952, at the 1-mile Raleigh Speedway. The 60-car Modified
Sportsman starting field roared off only to come to an abrupt
halt when it plowed into Bill Blevins' car, which had stalled on the
back straight during the final pace lap. 15 cars were destroyed and
Blevins and Jesse Midkiff are killed in the incident. After more than
an hour delay to clear the wreckage, the race was restarted and won
by Buddy Shuman. The next day, newspapers labeled the event
Black Saturday.

220 Tim Flock suffered serious injuries July 4, 1953, while sleep-
ing in the infield before a NASCAR event at Piedmont

Tim Flock was the center of attention, receiving a kiss from his wife,
Frances, and his brother, Fonty, after winning the 1952 Motor City 250 at
the Michigan State Fairgrounds outside Detroit. (Photo Courtesy Georgia
Racing Hall of Fame)

Interstate Speedway in Spartanburg, South Carolina. A representative from Champion Spark Plug backed his car over Flock and a crewman with the vehicle coming to rest on Flock's head. Flock's injuries keep him out of competition for nearly two months before he hit the track at Hickory Speedway for a Grand National event August 29.

221 Few drivers posted the kind of year that Lee Petty turned in during the 1954 NASCAR season. Petty won the 1954 GN championship thanks to 32 top-10 finishes in 34 starts, posting a 5.6 average finish for the season. Just two DNFs marked his record: a 38th-place in the Southern 500 at Darlington from a burnt coil and a last-place finish (32nd) in the final race of the season at North Wilkesboro after a broken hub just 12 laps into the race.

222 Harrisburg, Pennsylvania, driver Dick Kaufman was the first to perish in a NASCAR race on the Daytona Beach-Road Course when he flipped his 1949 Oldsmobile on the second lap of the February 20, 1954 event. Kaufman, a Korean War veteran, had been discharged from the Army two weeks earlier. He was 23.

223 Like his father, Bill France Jr. did everything from selling programs to driving a track grader. At age 21, "Little Bill" took a shot at driving and competed in a pair of 1954 NASCAR Short-Track Division events. In his second career start on July 24, France Jr. and his Nash crashed hard in a race at Bowman Gray Stadium in Winston-Salem, North Carolina. The incident ended his driving career as it was determined he would be safer working in other areas of the family business.

224 NASCAR post-race tech has always been tough as evidenced by the disqualification of Fireball Roberts' winning run at the Daytona Beach-Road Course February 27, 1955. Roberts powered his 1955 Buick to the lead on the first lap and paced all 39 circuits seemingly giving car owner Bob Fish and his famed Fish Carburetor team their first NASCAR Grand National victory. Roberts was disqualified 24 hours later after tech officials determined the push-

Some of the greatest early stars of NASCAR are in this 1950s pre-race shot. Included are (front row, left to right), Ralph Ligouri and Donald Thomas. The back row, left to right: Speedy Thompson, Herb Thomas, Bill Welborn, Buck Baker, Hershel McGriff, and Slick Smith. (Photo Courtesy Ed Samples Jr. Collection)

rods in his Buick's engine were .41 millimeters (.016 inch) too long. Ironically, Tim Flock, disqualified after winning a year earlier at Daytona, was declared the victor.

225 Dale Earnhardt's daddy and Dale Jr's. granddaddy made his NASCAR Grand National debut November 11, 1956, at Hickory Motor Speedway (North Carolina). A local fan favorite, Earnhardt wheeled a Pete DePaolo Ford to a second-place finish just behind Tommy Thompson. After the race, Thompson is booed so loudly by the crowd of 3,500 that NASCAR rechecks the scoring. Later, over the track's PA system, Earnhardt quells the unruly throng and assures the fans that the results are correct.

226 In 1947, Jackie Robinson was the first African-American to break the color barrier in Major League Baseball. On February

26, 1956, Charlie Scott did the same in NASCAR when he became the first African-American to compete in a Grand National race on the Daytona Beach-Road Course, navigating a Carl Kiekhaefer-owned Chrysler 300 to a 19th-place finish. It was the only NASCAR start for Scott, a Forest Park, Georgia, native who died with little fanfare in 1984.

227 In the six seasons from 1951 through 1956, Herb Thomas was the most dominating stock car driver in America, winning two NASCAR Grand National championships and finishing second in the GN points standings three times. His one off-year came in 1955 when he finished fifth in the final standings. Although the first of his 48 career GN wins came in a Plymouth at Martinsville Speedway in 1950, Thomas is synonymous with the Fabulous Hudson Hornets that he drove to 36 GN victories. Late in the 1956 season, a multiple-car accident at the Cleveland County Fairgrounds in Shelby, North Carolina, left Thomas in a coma with head and internal injuries. Thomas competed in just three races after recovering. The Olivia, North Carolina, native was named one of NASCAR's top-50 drivers in 1998 and elected to the NASCAR Hall of Fame in 2013.

228 After seeing Fireball Roberts score a rare 1956 victory over his potent Chrysler 300 cars, team owner Carl Kiekhaefer protested Roberts' car by claiming that the flywheel was overweight. With no scales available in the pit area at Raleigh Speedway, NASCAR took the part to a local fish market where it was determined to be the proper weight, allowing Roberts to keep his Independence Day triumph.

229 Oklahoma was the epicenter of the Dust Bowl era in the 1930s. On August 4, 1956, Lee Petty must have felt like times hadn't changed as he and 12 other competitors took the green flag in front of 6,200 fans for a Grand National race at Tulsa Fairgrounds (Oklahoma). The dust on the half-mile dirt oval was so bad that Petty parked his car after 32 of the 200 laps. He immediately headed to the flag stand, grabbed the red flag and waved it to end the race.

NASCAR declared the event over and no prize money or points were awarded. The event was never rescheduled and remains the last time a NASCAR race was held at the track.

230 Today, NASCAR races draw a multitude of fans to its events, but it wasn't always that way, A meager 900 racing faithful showed up for the NASCAR Grand National race at Newbery Speedway (South Carolina) on October 12, 1957. Fireball Roberts started 10th in the 23-car field and led 181 of the 200 laps, putting his Ford in Victory Lane. This sparse crowd remains the smallest ever to witness a NASCAR top division event.

231 The team of John Holman and Ralph Moody took over the management of Ford Racing from Peter DePaolo prior to the 1958 season. The pair (who revolutionized the sport in the early 1960s with their "Competition Proven" Fords) got their first NASCAR Grand National win March 15, 1958, as Curtis Turner rolled to victory in a 150-lap event on the .333-mile Champion Speedway in Fayetteville, North Carolina.

232 After finishing second to Curtis Turner in a NASCAR Convertible race at Charlotte August 25, 1956, driver Gwyn Staley and team owner Julian Petty installed a snap-on roof to his 1957 Chevrolet and drove it to victory the following Saturday afternoon in a Grand National event at Costal Speedway near Myrtle Beach, South Carolina.

233 Buck Baker became the first driver to win consecutive NASCAR Grand National championships, earning both 1956 and 1957 titles. Baker won 24 times and posted 61 top-5 finishes in 88 events over two seasons. At one point during his hot streak, the former Charlotte bus driver scored 35-consecutive top-10 finishes.

234 High Point, North Carolina, driver Ken Rush scored six top-10 finishes in 16 Grand National starts as well as 11 top-10 efforts in 21 Convertible division starts en route to his 1957 NASCAR Rookie of the Year Award. Sponsored by Purolator Products, the award marks the first-time NASCAR officially recognized the accomplishments of a rookie driver.

235 Known as one of America's top wildcat natural gas and oil speculators, Clinton "Clint" Murchison also proved to be one of the biggest benefactors to NASCAR's early success. Murchison and his Texas-based Southern Union Oil Company provided Bill France Sr. the initial $600,000 of the $3 million it took to construct Daytona International Speedway. Murchison, who also provided all the heavy machinery for the project, passed away in 1969.

236 Anyone who ever raced at Daytona, Talladega, or Michigan Speedway owes Charles Moneypenny a tip of the hat. Moneypenny, a Daytona Beach resident, was the chief designer and lead engineer for the building of all three tracks. In 1957, Moneypenny began turning Bill France Sr.'s dream of a 2.5-mile Daytona International Speedway into reality by creating innovative solutions to complex construction problems. These solutions included anchoring paving equipment to bulldozers at the top of Daytona's high banks so they wouldn't slide down the incline. Moneypenny later patented the technique and used it in the construction of Talladega and Michigan.

237 Like most drivers, Ned Jarrett has a soft spot for his first NASCAR Grand National victory. "Gentleman" Ned's first career triumph came in a 100-mile race at Rambi Speedway outside of Myrtle Beach, South Carolina, on August 1, 1959. Strapped for cash, Jarrett bought his winning 1957 Ford just a few days before the event, paying the car dealer with a post-dated check scheduled to clear the bank on August 3. Jarrett took home $800 for the victory and made good on his promise to pay by covering the check.

238 As the sole supplier of racing tires to the NASCAR Cup Series, the Goodyear Tire and Rubber Company visits Victory Lane at every race these days. The first major superspeedway win for the Akron, Ohio, based company came September 7, 1959, when Jim Reed piloted a Goodyear-shod Chevy to victory in the Southern 500 at Darlington Raceway.

239 The record shows Jack Smith won nearly $150,000 in his 15-year NASCAR career. On October 25, 1959, Smith drove his Chevy to a win in the final race of the Grand National season, the Lee Kirby 300 at Concord Speedway (North Carolina). Instead of banking the top prize of $1,500, the Sandy Springs, Georgia, driver opted to receive a new 1960 Ford courtesy of race promoter O. Bruton Smith.

MILESTONES

240 Vehicle styling in the 1950s was cool to be sure, but the decade also saw several passenger car performance and comfort breakthroughs as well. Included in the advancements were overhead valve V-8 engines from all Big Three carmakers by 1955. Meanwhile, drivers could use all that power thanks to better handling cars from independent front suspension. By the end of the decade, nearly 80 percent of cars sold featured an automatic transmission. On the comfort side, power windows, power seats, air conditioning, and in-dash transistorized radios became available on all cars by 1960.

241 If you had to guess what car company was the first to become a benefactor of NASCAR, you probably wouldn't choose the Nash Motor Company. In 1950, the Kenosha, Wisconsin, automaker offered cash contingency prizes in select races. Meanwhile, Bill France Sr. personally drove a 1951 Nash Ambassador, the official pace car at the Motor City 250. Tim Flock won the race at the Michigan State Fairgrounds (outside Detroit) in a Hudson. In addition to his $7,001 first-place prize money, Flock also won a new Nash Ambassador as part of the company's promotional program.

242 Conowango Valley, New York, driver Bill Rexford drove three makes of cars en route to his 1950 Grand National championship. Rexford piloted an Oldsmobile in 15 races and a Mercury and Ford in one each scoring 1,959 points (110.5 more than Fireball Roberts) and winning the title. In all, seven drivers led the title chase to the crown with Rexford coming out on top due to a stellar 10.9 average finish in 17 events. His one win of the season was on

Memorial Day weekend at Canfield Speedway (Ohio) leading 80 of the 200 laps. Lee Petty finished third in standings followed by Lloyd Moore. Curtis Turner, the top winner in the series that year with four victories, finished fifth in the final standings.

243 Bill France Sr. and Curtis Turner had their share of disagreements over the years, but put their differences aside to co-drive a Nash Ambassador in the inaugural 1950 Carrera Panamericana road race. The 2,172-mile endurance test-race across Mexico proved an adventure as France wrecked the car in the early stages of the race. Prior to the final leg of the race, they bought Roy Pat Connor's Nash and ultimately finished sixth in the final running order with Turner behind the wheel and France riding shotgun. Later, they were disqualified because crewmembers (France) were not allowed to ride along in the car.

244 On July 18, 1950, officials at the newly constructed Darlington Raceway announced that the first Labor Day Grand National event would be titled the Southern 500. Johnny Mantz won the inaugural event by a whopping nine laps over runner-up

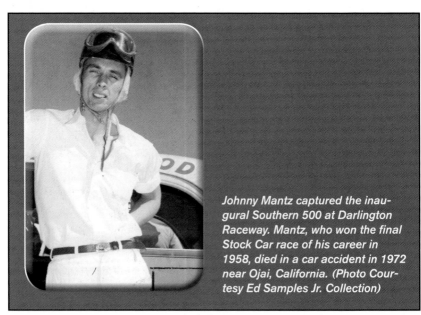

Johnny Mantz captured the inaugural Southern 500 at Darlington Raceway. Mantz, who won the final Stock Car race of his career in 1958, died in a car accident in 1972 near Ojai, California. (Photo Courtesy Ed Samples Jr. Collection)

Fireball Roberts. After that, the Southern 500 earned a top-tier spot in NASCAR lore as the event continued through 2003 before being moved to November as part of NASCAR's first Chase to the Championship series. In 2005, the event was held in May and stayed there until being shifted to April in 2014. It returned to the traditional Labor Day weekend slot in 2015. Jeff Gordon is the all-time leading winner of the Southern 500 capturing the checkered flag six times: 1995, 1996, 1997, 1998, 2002, and 2007.

245 After back-to-back wins at Charlotte and Langhorne earlier in the 1950 season, Curtis Turner outdoes himself by wheeling his Eanes Motor Company Oldsmobile to wins at Rochester Speedway (New York) and again at Charlotte Speedway. Turner's second double-down marks the only time in NASCAR history that a driver captured the pole and led every lap, winning two-consecutive Grand National events.

246 The first NASCAR Grand National night race was held on June 16, 1951, at the half-mile dirt Columbia Speedway (South Carolina). Frank "Rebel" Mundy roared to a one-lap margin of victory over Bill Blair to notch the first of his career NASCAR Grand National wins. Mundy made it a NASCAR-first trifecta by driving a Studebaker to its first series victory.

247 Many early NASCAR events were more survival tests than speed fests. On July 8, 1951, the rough 1-mile Bainbridge Fairgrounds Speedway (Ohio) dirt oval took its toll on a 34-car starting field leaving only 5 cars running at the finish. Fonty Flock started his 1950 *Red Devil* Oldsmobile on the pole and ran to an easy victory in the 100-mile event.

248 Tim Flock's career was littered with instances of running afoul of NASCAR's rule-makers. One of his more bizarre infractions was a disqualification after winning the 1952 NASCAR Modified Sportsman race at the Daytona Beach-Road Course. The reason? The roll bar in his 1939 Ford was made out of wood.

249 Ted Chamberlain pulled off the 1952 season's most unusual driving feat by completing 120 laps of a race at Dayton Speedway (Ohio) with no steering wheel. Chamberlain managed to keep his 1950 Plymouth in the race on the half-mile oval by gripping the steering hub after the wheel portion broke off around Lap 40. Chamberlain, running at the finish, was credited with 13th in the final rundown.

250 After winning pole position in the 1953 Daytona Beach-Road Course event, Bob Pronger bet time trial runner-up Fonty Flock that he would lead the first lap. Pronger's attempt to collect came to a halt when he overdrove the first turn and flipped his Olds 88 through the wooden guardrail, rolled down a sand dune coming to rest on its wheels. Incredibly, Pronger immediately rejoined the race and scored 16th out of 57 starters at the end of the first circuit. Pronger retired his wounded racer on Lap 5 and was credited with 51st place. Meanwhile, Flock won the bet by leading the first 38 laps, but ran out of fuel on the last circuit, finishing 2nd to Bill Blair.

251 Cleveland, Ohio, driver Jimmy Florian competed in 26 Grand National events from 1950 to 1954. On June 25, 1950, Florian scored his first and only victory on a scorching hot day at Dayton Speedway. Florian beat the heat and 24 other competitors by driving the 200-lap race without a shirt on.

252 Jimmy Florian's victory at Dayton is often more remembered for his shirtless antics than for another significant milestone set that same day. Florian's win in a 1950 Ford sponsored by the Euclid Motor Company in Cleveland was the first victory for the Blue Oval manufacturer in NASCAR Grand National competition.

253 The second running of the Southern 500 saw 16 makes of American-made passenger cars start the race on the then-1.25-mile Darlington oval. Frank Mundy won pole position only to finish last when his Studebaker lost oil pressure on Lap 12. Mundy officially scored 82nd in the largest field ever to start a NASCAR Grand National stock car race.

254 Tim Flock took the Grand National championship points lead into the final race of the 1952 season at Palm Beach Speedway (Florida). On lap 164 of 200, Flock retired from the race after flipping his No. 91 Hudson. Thanks to heavy attrition, only eight cars finished the race and Flock was credited with 12th in the final rundown. This allowed Flock to beat out Palm Beach winner Herb Thomas by a narrow 106 points for the 1952 NASCAR Grand National title.

255 After seeing the success of NASCAR's first paved superspeedway, Darlington International Raceway, Bill France Sr. dreams of building his own giant paved track. France takes the first step toward his vision April 4, 1953, announcing his plan to replace the Daytona Beach-Road Course with a new speedway. France has a plan to be ready and open in time for the 1955 season at a yet-to-be determined location.

256 NASCAR notched another first by allowing both domestic and foreign cars to enter the June 21, 1953, International 200 at Langhorne Speedway (Pennsylvania). Six Jaguars, two Porsches, an Aston Martin, and a Volkswagen are in the 38-car starting field led to the green flag by pole sitter Lloyd Shaw in a Jaguar. Outside front row starter Dick Rathmann hammers his 1953 Hudson into the lead on the first lap and paces all 200 circuits to the win. Dick Allwine is the top foreign car finisher coming home sixth in a Jaguar, while Nick Fornoro and Billy Oswald, in Porsches, notch top-10 efforts finishing eighth and ninth, respectively.

257 Prior to the 1954 season, only drivers are awarded points money. During the off-season, NASCAR announces that it will now award equal shares of cash to both drivers and team owners. This came after team owners complained of certain drivers not sharing the year-end financial prizes.

258 By 1954, NASCAR had expanded its slate of races on the Daytona Beach-Road Course to include Grand National, Sportsman, and Modified events. Lee Petty rolled to a second-place finish

Bob Flock (14) speeds away from eventual winner Gober Sosebee (50) and Fireball Roberts (11) at the start of a 1950 Modified Race at the Daytona Beach Road Course. (Photo Courtesy Gober Sosebee Family)

in the Grand National event, and later nabs his first and only victory on the Daytona Beach-Road Course after apparent winner Tim Flock is disqualified. Meanwhile, Orlando, Florida, driver Dick Joslin and his 1939 Ford took home the trophy for winning Friday's 100-mile Sportsman event while Cotton Owens and his 1938 Plymouth grabbed Saturday's 125-mile Modified event. The Daytona Week of Speed slate is completed with time-trials open to all brands of cars (foreign and domestic) on a 5-mile strip along the Atlantic Ocean.

259 Heading into the 1954 season, every Grand National event had been run on an oval track. That all changed June 13, 1954, when Al Keller drove Paul Whiteman's Jaguar XK-120 to a win in NASCAR's first road course race, the International 100, held on a twisting makeshift 2-mile track layout at the Linden Airport (New Jersey). Keller's victory is a first for foreign cars in NASCAR competition as 21 of 43 starters are non-American vehicles.

260 Moments after winning the road race at Linden, Al Keller took a hard left and informed everyone in Victory Lane that he was quitting NASCAR to join the AAA Championship Series. On the 1955 Indianapolis 500, he qualifies 22nd in the 33-car field. In Lap 57, Keller is involved in a back-straight wreck with Rodger Ward and Johnny Boyd. Leader Bill Vukovich Sr. plows into the stalled trio and launches outside the speedway, flipping his car several times, eventually landing upside down and on fire. Vukovich is killed in the wreck. Keller continues to race the Champ Car circuit until he is killed in a wreck at the Arizona State Fairgrounds November 19, 1961.

261 NASCAR Hall of Fame driver Robert Glenn "Junior" Johnson scored 50 victories during his 14-year Grand National career. His first win came in his 16th career start by capturing a 200-lap affair at Hickory Motor Speedway May 7, 1955. Johnson and his 1955 Oldsmobile lead 123 circuits to win over Tim Flock in a Carl Kiekhaefer-owned Chrysler 300.

262 Thanks to Chevrolet, NASCAR got a giant marketing boost when the automaker backed its new 1955 NASCAR factory team support program in a massive national advertising campaign. An estimated 16,000 billboards nationwide featured Chevy's improved V-8 performance and NASCAR branding while print ads in thousands of newspapers and magazines also had NASCAR mentions. Chevrolet television commercials cited NASCAR successes, especially after Herb Thomas drove one to a win in the Southern 500. Chevy later took Thomas' winning car on a public-display Fair Tour around the country making it NASCAR's first show car.

263 Bill France Sr. took a run at the American Automobile Association with the formation of the NASCAR Auto Association in 1954. France touted the fee-based organization as offering the highest standards and finest accommodations not only to NASCAR's then-11,000 members, but also to the motoring public. As it turned out, the idea was a hard sell (even to NASCAR members) and the NASCAR Auto Association quietly faded into history in 1957.

264 Early NASCAR history is littered with scoring controversies that often led to disputed finishes, boycotting of events, or quitting altogether. Scoring, done by hand, was often a nightmare, evidenced by the 136-car starting grid for the February 20, 1954, Modified Sportsman race at the Daytona Beach-Road Course. Cotton Owens bested the field, the largest in NASCAR history, to take the green flag in a race that reported no scoring issues at the finish.

265 While today's teams have their share of success, few dominated like Carl Kiekhaefer's Mercury Outboard-sponsored Chrysler 300s and Dodge Coronets. In a record that is unlikely to be broken, Kiekhaefer's cars scored 16-straight Grand National wins in 1956. The streak started March 25 when Buck Baker drove a Kiekhaefer Chrysler to a 100-mile win at Lakewood Speedway in Atlanta and ended with Herb Thomas and his 300 dominating a 200-lap clash on the half-mile dirt oval at the Merced Fairgrounds (California) June 3.

266 Curtis Turner has the distinction of being the only NASCAR driver to win due to being the only driver left in the race. Turner scored the unusual victory September 30, 1956, when a giant 14-car wreck occurred on Lap 181 of a Convertible race at Asheville-Weaverville Speedway. Because Turner was the only one left in the race, NASCAR red-flagged the race and awarded Turner the win.

267 The modern NASCAR era requires teams to have fleets of cars to complete the season. In 1956, Curtis Turner used the same car (a 1956 Ford Fairlane prepared by Peter DePaolo) to win 22 of 42 NASCAR Convertible Series races entered.

268 Cotton Owens set what became an all-time record when he breezed to a win in the February 17, 1957, event on the Daytona Beach-Road Course. Owens' average speed of 101.541 mph in his Ray Nichels-owned stocker is the fastest ever posted on the 4.1-mile course. This victory was the first of his NASCAR Grand National career.

269 Cotton Owens' win in the fourth race of the 1957 season at Daytona Beach-Road Course also gave Pontiac its first NAS-CAR victory. The brand goes on to capture 154 Grand National wins with the high point in 1961 and 1962 when *The Chief* captured 30 and 22 victories, respectively.

270 It seems fitting that a guy named Speedy was the first driver to average over 100 mph while winning a Grand National race at Darlington Raceway. Alfred Bruce "Speedy" Thompson captured the 1957 Southern 500 with a speed of 100.094 mph, nearly 25 mph faster than the 75.25 mph average winning speed set by Johnny Mantz in the inaugural Southern 500 just seven years earlier.

271 NASCAR has many historic dates and November 27, 1957, is certainly one of them. On this date, Bill France and local dignitaries broke ground on what became Daytona International Speedway. France leased the 447-acre site near Daytona International Airport (mostly marsh and swampland), from the city for $10,000 a year over a 50-year period.

272 After 22 seasons of racing the sand and surf, stock cars made their final appearance on the Daytona Beach-Road Course February 23, 1958. Paul Goldsmith drove a 1958 Pontiac to victory after capturing the pole and leading all 39 laps, besting Curtis Turner, Jack Smith, Joe Weatherly, and Lee Petty before an estimated 35,000 fans. Goldsmith earned $14,065 and averaged 101.113 mph in the landmark victory. The final Speedweeks on the beach also included a win by Banjo Matthews in the 125-mile Sportsman/Modified race. Turner capped a solid weekend with a victory in the 160-mile Convertible event.

273 Richard Petty took his first steps toward becoming NASCAR royalty when he made his first Grand National start July 18, 1958. "The King" started 7th in a 19-car field at Toronto's Canadian National Exposition Speedway, eventually finishing 17th after plowing the Petty Enterprises Oldsmobile into the fence on the 55th circuit of the 100-lap event.

274 Today, fines for activity outside the written rules, or the spirit of NASCAR, can run into six figures. Tommy Thompson and Curtis Turner used their cars to engage in several instances of questionable and intentional bad behavior. For example, after slamming on the brakes, each while in front of the other in a July 1957 race at Hickory Speedway, Bill France Sr. came down on them with a stiff $50 fine each and a stern lecture about sportsmanship.

275 In 1955, every one of the 50,000 printed tickets for the Southern 500 at Darlington Raceway was sold in advance, which made it the first sell-out in the five-year history of the event. An even more amazing crowd estimated at 70,000 witnessed Curtis Turner win the Labor Day Southern 500 classic a year later on September 3, 1956.

276 There was a lot of trepidation when drivers got their first look at Daytona International Speedway in 1959. The new 2.5-mile oval would surely produce disaster. Some even predicted that the cars would not stay up on the steep banking. Their fears were unfounded, however, as the inaugural Daytona 500 was run without a single caution flag. Today, it remains the only Daytona 500 to be run caution-free.

277 Due to all 200 laps being run under green-flag conditions, the inaugural Daytona 500 produced the fastest average winning speed to date in a Grand National race as winner Lee Petty averaged 135.521 mph, 33 mph faster than any previous NASCAR average race-winning speed.

278 Johnny Beauchamp was all smiles in Victory Lane after capturing the 1959 Daytona 500 at the all-new speedway. Days later, Bill France Sr. awards the victory to Lee Petty after photos, (specifically, one by T. Taylor Warren), indicate Petty's Oldsmobile nosed out Beauchamp's Ford for the win. It is the first time in NASCAR history that a race is determined by a photo finish.

279 Richard Petty would have scored 201 career wins if not for his father, Lee. The younger Petty appeared to have scored his first NASCAR Grand National victory at Atlanta's Lakewood Speedway June 14, 1959, with his father in the runner-up spot. Lee Petty protests the win and a review of the scorecards indicates the elder Petty did win the race, bumping his son to second place.

Chapter 4

The 1960s: Growing The Brand

The 1960s proved to be one of the most turbulent decades in American history as the county worked, and sometimes fought its way through a myriad of social and political issues at home and abroad.

And, for the first time, nearly everyone in America got a close-up look at what was happening in the world as 9 out of 10 homes now had a television set. The power of the tube was never more apparent than when nearly the entire world stopped to witness a man's first steps on the moon in July 1969.

While Americans were glued to an estimated 52 million television sets in the early 1960s, with nearly 62 million passenger vehicles on the road at the start of the decade, they were more dedicated to owning a car. Continuing the epic growth of the 1950s, that number grew to nearly 89 million when the calendar turned over to 1970.

Where we lived, where shopped, how we vacationed, who we were, all factored into how the automobile impacted life.

Wherever Americans were going, they wanted to get there faster, ushering in the performance or muscle car era. It was akin to the American automobile industry being on steroids as engines grew bigger and cars

Rex White had his biggest NASCAR Grand National season in 1960, winning six times on the road to his only GN title. (Photo Courtesy Georgia Racing Hall of Fame)

became much faster, and nothing could be better for the Detroit kings of high-speed passenger cars than NASCAR.

More than 10 years earlier, racing American-made stock passenger cars was a novel idea. The insight to race them proved to be more astute than anyone could have predicted as NASCAR spent the 1960s investing in new and bigger tracks to accommodate faster cars. Meanwhile, NASCAR fans chose sides as Chevy, Ford, Pontiac, Plymouth, Dodge, and Mercury all took turns as the hot iron in Victory Lane and driveways across America throughout the decade.

In the end, NASCAR grew by leaps and bounds (more in step with the Detroit auto manufacturers than ever) profiting on and off the track as the automobile became more central to American life and culture.

CARS

280 While 1950s cars capitalized on flamboyant Jet Age styling, Detroit's offerings in the 1960s were more about performance. The change in philosophy came at the perfect time as

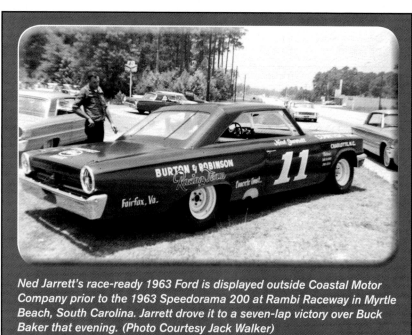

Ned Jarrett's race-ready 1963 Ford is displayed outside Coastal Motor Company prior to the 1963 Speedorama 200 at Rambi Raceway in Myrtle Beach, South Carolina. Jarrett drove it to a seven-lap victory over Buck Baker that evening. (Photo Courtesy Jack Walker)

NASCAR was transitiovning into its superspeedway age of new, bigger tracks including Daytona, Atlanta, and Charlotte. Companies such as Ford, Chevrolet, and, Chrysler could use these venues to showcase their giant cubic-inch/horsepower engines in front of a speed-hungry buying public.

281 Oil was plentiful and gas was cheap in the 1960s. Most filling stations offered full service and gas priced around 25 cents per gallon. The deal was even better for NASCAR competitors when the Pure Oil Company began providing free gas to drivers who qualified for Grand National races in 1960.

282 NASCAR drivers used primitive restraints, such as seat belts, which arrived in the passenger cars of the 1950s. By the 1960s, teams abandoned the standard issue belts and began using three-inch wide racing-specific belts developed for the sports car ranks. The belts featured large hook and eyelet metal buckles covered by a leather flap on each end of the thick, woven belt for comfort. The new belts, with the addition of shoulder straps later on, significantly improved driver safety.

283 Driver and passenger safety became more of a priority in the 1960s with the United States government setting the trend for American carmakers. In 1966, President Lyndon Johnson signed the National Traffic and Motor Vehicle Safety Act. The edict required all new cars manufactured in America in 1968 to include front seat shoulder belts as standard equipment. In part, NASCAR's (and racing in general) experimentation and implementation of shoulder safety harnesses influenced the law.

284 At the start of the 1960s, most Grand National stock cars didn't have door bars much less roll cages. Because most cars were built from new production automobiles, many GN stockers retained interior appointments such as seats and door padding. Also, because NASCAR didn't mandate the removal of side glass until 1970, many 1960s race cars didn't have door bars because their installation prevented the windows from rolling down.

Other than a highly modified stock bucket seat, the production car look of the interior of Richard Petty's 1967 Plymouth was all but gone by the mid-1960s. (John Close Photo)

285 The fact that smaller cars became more popular in the 1960s was nothing new to Detroit. The Nash Rambler, America's first compact car, pushed Nash to third on the sales charts in 1958 behind Chevrolet and Ford. That success, as well as the success of imports, had American manufacturers producing smaller, more fuel-efficient and ultimately, less expensive cars in 1960, including the Ford Falcon, Mercury Comet, Chevy Corvair, and Plymouth Valiant. NASCAR, always eager to jump onto a new automotive trend, quickly embraced the new Detroit offerings and featured them in a pair of races during 1960 Daytona Speedweeks.

286 Detroit's new compact cars took to the Daytona International Speedway January 31, 1960. The first event was 38.1-mile race on the DIS 3.81-mile road course. The race featured 27 cars and was won by Marvin Panch in a Plymouth Valiant. In fact, it was an all-Valiant show as the new Mopar model swept the first seven positions in a field featuring three Ford Falcons, five Chevy Corvairs, eight Volvos, and one each of Rambler, Simca, Morris, and Studebaker Lark. Later that day, Panch won a second race for the division, this one a 20-lap, 50-mile test on the Daytona 2.5-mile high-banked oval. Panch's winning mount was powered by Chrysler's 170-ci slant-6 engine featuring a dealer-optioned Hyper Pack aluminum intake manifold and Carter AFB 4-barrel carburetor, The car was equipped with heavy-duty brakes, shocks, front torsion bars, rear springs, and clutch, as well as a hand-fabricated stainless steel tube exhaust system making it considerably different than a production model.

287 Based on the success of the 1960 Compact Car races at Daytona and Detroit's 1961 introduction of Buick Special, Pontiac Tempest, Oldsmobile F-85, and Dodge Lancer, Bill France Sr. announced that NASCAR would sanction a small-car division. The 1961 Cannonball Compact Division featured three tiers: a Compact Class with engines up to 150 ci, a Standard Compact class with engines ranging from 151 to 200 ci, and a Super Compact Class for cars with engines measuring 201 ci and above. The new division debuted at Daytona on February 19, 1961, with top drivers Lee Petty, Fireball Roberts, Curtis Turner, Ned Jarrett, Tim Flock, Ralph Moody, Joe Weatherly, Cotton Owens, Marvin Panch, and Ralph Earnhardt in the field. Unfortunately, many of the cars in the 49-lap contest were hardly race vehicles, rather, they were more like glorified street cars. A Corvair and a Tempest still had radios and defroster-heater units on board, along with a Volvo reportedly purchased at a used car dealer just hours before the event. Petty won what turned out to be a lackluster race, and that, along with the number and quality of cars entered, caused NASCAR to quietly kill the division.

288 Because of NASCAR master mechanic Red Vogt, Marvin Panch nearly missed turning the double in the 1960 compact races at Daytona. After winning the road course event, Vogt decided to change the rear-end gear of Panch's Valiant. Unfortunately, Vogt was still making the changes when the second race took the green flag for the 50-mile oval-track event. Panch joined the race one-lap down with little chance of winning until the top four cars, including Petty's

For the 1960 season, the power for Jack Smith's Pontiac Catalina Grand National stocker came from a 389-ci engine producing approximately 333 hp. (Photo Courtesy Brandon Reed)

Valiant, crashed on Lap 2 bringing the caution flag out. Panch caught up and quickly dispatched of the rest of the 25-car field to win the race and sweep both ends of NASCAR's first compact car event.

289 Detroit automakers went "big" in the early 1960s fueling the horsepower race with a wide array of powerful V-8 engines. Chevrolet's 409-ci engine, Pontiac's 421, and Chrysler's 413 powerplants set the stage for NASCAR's horsepower race against the Mopar 426 Hemi, the 427 Chevy, and the Ford Boss 429.

290 While the 1964 Ford Mustang is widely acknowledged as the first "pony car," the era actually debuted two weeks earlier with the introduction of Plymouth's Barracuda. The design, featuring low compact body lines with long hoods, small rear seats, sloping back glass, and short trunks, quickly caught on with Detroit carmakers. While the smaller, shorter-wheelbase cars were not eligible for Grand National competition, the Mustang, Camaro, Firebird, Challenger, 'Cuda, Cougar, and AMC's Javelin and AMX all earned a place in NASCAR history as part of the Grand Touring Series.

291 In 1968, NASCAR introduced the Grand Touring Series. The division featured pony cars (Camaros, Firebirds, Javelins, Mustangs, Cougars, Barracudas, and Challengers) outfitted with 305-ci max displacement engines and twin 4-barrel carburetors. The rules so closely resembled those of NASCAR's Grand National division that the new division quickly became known as the "Baby Grands." They raced as part of Grand National events on many occasions, most notably at Talladega in 1969 as a result of the Professional Driver's Association strike. The division was renamed the Grand American Series in 1970, calling it quits after just four 1972 events, with a total of 109 division races from 1968 to 1972.

292 Initially, pony cars were not considered muscle cars. While both were introduced in 1964, the muscle car designation was reserved for the larger, intermediate-sized cars powered by a high-output V-8 engine. The 1964 Pontiac GTO is considered the first of these cars followed by Chevrolet Chevelle SS, Dodge Coronet and Charger R/Ts, Plymouth Road Runner and GTX, Ford Torino, and the SC/Rambler from AMC. Most were quickly retooled into Grand National race cars while the pony cars and their smaller engines were relegated to the Grand Touring division. Pony cars were eventually accepted into the muscle car club after featuring larger, higher horsepower engines in 1968. Despite the change, the shorter-wheelbase pony cars were never full-time participants in GN competition racing; only a handful of events were run into the early 1970s.

293 Goodyear, battling for race tire supremacy against Firestone, reportedly spent $60 million running tire tests in 1966. The result was the Lifeguard Inner Liner Safety Spare. The "tire within a tire" concept allowed the driver to maintain control of the vehicle if the outer tire was compromised. The technology proved a giant safety breakthrough and today, all NASCAR divisions require every tire used on a track of 1 mile or more to have an inner liner.

294 Fonty Flock was considered colorful for wearing Bermuda shorts on his way to a win in the 1952 Southern 500. How-

In the 1960s, headlights and turn signals were no longer taped but replaced by lightweight aluminum cutouts while stock latches gave way to hood pins. (Photo Courtesy Brandon Reed)

ever, in the 1960s, there was a keener eye cast on protective driver wear. Nomex, a fire-retardant material developed by the DuPont Corporation for the U.S. Navy, began use in racing by mid-decade, providing a new level of safety for drivers. Other driver wear usage includes gloves, hoods, underwear, and socks. Nomex continues as a staple material used in firefighting, military, and outer space applications for which protection from extreme heat or cold is necessary.

295 Sam McQuagg scored his first and only Grand National victory July 4, 1966, at the Firecracker 400 at Daytona International Speedway. While testing for the race, McQuagg's fastback Dodge Charger exhibited a tendency toward rear lift at speeds in excess of 180 mph. To correct this, engineers installed an inch and a half aluminum spoiler across the rear deck. This immediately stabilized the vehicle, giving it more down force and grip. McQuagg wheeled Ray Nichel's Dodge to a win, making it the first spoiler-equipped car to win a NASCAR race.

296 NASCAR continued its Strictly Stock mantra in the 1960s by policing carmaker vehicle and parts production runs. For example, in 1963, the rulebook mandated that any Grand National vehicle presented for racing must have a production schedule of at least 1,500 units with at least 100 units on dealer lots to be eligible for competition.

297 With improved block casting, forged and counterweighted crankshaft, forged pistons and connecting rods, cross-bolted mains, and a deep oil sump, the second-generation race-only Hemi engine made its debut in 1964. Topping out at 426 ci while boasting an estimated 780 hp, Chrysler's "elephant" engine was the most powerful to hit NASCAR. Dodge and Plymouth drivers were told not to show off the new engine in practice before the 1964 Daytona 500. However, qualifying tipped their hand as 426 Hemi-powered Mopars swept the first seven spots. Paul Goldsmith's pole run of 174.910 mph was a full 23 mph faster than the 151.566 mph pole run by Fireball Roberts just a year earlier. The 500 proved to be an all-Hemi show with Richard Petty leading a 1-2-3 sweep. In all, the 426 Hemi won 26 of the 62 Grand National events in 1964 and countless others throughout 1971, when the Chrysler Corporation discontinued engine production.

298 Prior to 1965, NASCAR mandated the number of cars produced and delivered to dealers to make them NASCAR eligible. However, the rule wasn't extended to engines, which were still being built as "racing only" parts. When NASCAR got wind of Ford's plans to build a 427-ci single overhead cam engine to combat the 426 Hemi, it established a 500 engine minimum production rule to slow the horsepower race. This meant that at least 500 of the high-performance powerplants needed to be on dealer lots and available to the public before the engine could be used in NASCAR. The 500 rule applied to all brands, including Mopar. Chrysler, campaigning the engine without restriction in 1964, promptly pulled its team factory support and boycotted the 1965 season. Ford withdrew the engine from 1965 NASCAR competition and used it in drag racing. Even without the big engine, Ford still took 48 of 55 Grand National events in 1965 while Chrysler and GM sat out the season.

299 Chrysler Corporation execs were considering moving their 1964 turbine engine concept car into production for the 1966 model year. A new, angular body with a giant sloping rear window was created by Elwood Engel and his Chrysler design support team and a 500-unit production run was ordered. Unfortunately, the project was scrapped when Chrysler determined that the initial production of cars and the subsequent implementation of a service network around the country would be too costly. Meanwhile, the body designed for the new turbine car, sporting a new grille and taillights, was introduced as the 1966 Dodge Charger.

300 Perhaps NASCAR's most infamous car, Junior Johnson's *Yellow Banana* pushed the rules to the limit in 1966. The car, a 1966 Ford Galaxie, debuted at Atlanta International Raceway on August 7, immediately drawing the attention of the garage. With its sloping nose and upswept rear quarter panels, chopped top and laid back windshield, the low-slung, yellow car closely resembled a banana, and obviously wasn't a stock Ford Galaxie by any stretch of the imagination. Despite protests, Bill France Sr. allowed the car to clear tech and driver Fred Lorenzen qualified it third in a field of 44. Just past the halfway point of the race, with Lorenzen leading, a right-front suspension failure catapulted the car into the wall and out of the race. The Dixie 400 was the only time the *Yellow Banana* raced; NASCAR informed Johnson to never bring it to the track again.

301 Fred Lorenzen won the 1966 Old Dominion 500 at Martinsville Speedway, later having the victory taken away after NASCAR determined his Ford's gas tank held a whopping 23.1 gallons of fuel instead of the legal 22-gallon amount. NASCAR restored the win to Lorenzen three days later after clearing his Holman-Moody

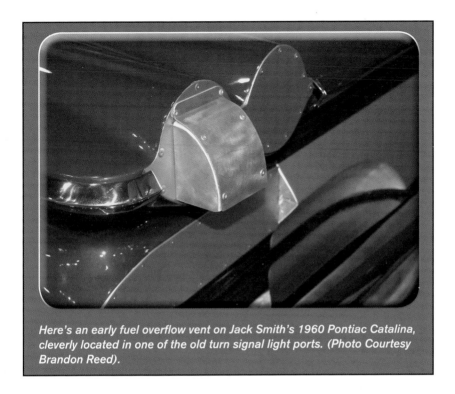

Here's an early fuel overflow vent on Jack Smith's 1960 Pontiac Catalina, cleverly located in one of the old turn signal light ports. (Photo Courtesy Brandon Reed).

team of any wrongdoing; they purchased the unaltered stock fuel tank from an authorized Firestone retailer.

302 Junior Johnson wasn't the only one to enter a creatively engineered car in the 1966 Dixie 400 at Atlanta International Raceway. Smokey Yunick fielded a 1966 Chevrolet Chevelle SS for the event that, rumor has it, was a scaled-down Grand National stock car. In actuality, the body was to scale, but had been moved back on the chassis for better weight distribution. In addition, the front bumper was pulled back for better aerodynamics. The imaginative design was most noticeable underneath, where Yunick had modified the stock floor pan by creating tunnels, bringing components including engine headers and exhaust pipes into the car instead of riding air underneath it. Surprisingly, the car cleared tech and driver Curtis Turner put it on the pole for the race. Turner led 60 laps before a broken distributor on Lap 130 saddled both him and Smokey's creation with a 24th-place finish. NASCAR banned the car after the race and Yunick appealed. On October 6, 1966, the NASCAR Commission issued a press release specifically detailing changes required before the car could return to competition. Instead, Yunick built a more radical 1966 Chevelle for the 1967 Daytona 500.

303 Given the stock nature of NASCAR in its early years, little attention was given to the body of the race car when it came to passing technical inspection. Thanks to higher speeds in the 1960s and a wave of creative engineering that produced several questionable stock-bodied cars throughout the 1966 season, NASCAR introduced its first body templates in 1967.

304 Richard Petty set an all-time NASCAR record of 10-straight victories in 1967. The streak began with a win in the Myers Brothers 250 at the half-mile paved Bowman Gray Stadium August 12. The final victory in Petty's monumental run came at the Speedway Wilkes 400 at North Wilkesboro, South Carolina on October 1.

305 NASCAR mandated cubic inch to weight rules, limiting the Chrysler Hemi to one 4-barrel carburetor. In 1967, Richard Petty ran a destroked 404-ci Hemi, 200 pounds less than the 426 Hemi, for most events that season.

306 After being synonymous with Chrysler products, Richard Petty switched to Ford for the 1969 season and promptly gave the brand a win in the third race of the season, the Motor Trend 500 at Riverside Raceway, February 1, 1969.

307 With competition fierce at the manufacturers' level, Cale Yarborough managed to score big, driving his Mercury to a crushing win in the 1969 Atlanta 500 at Atlanta International Raceway. Yarborough led 308 of the 334 laps run in the March 30 event, powered for the first time by Ford's new engine, the Blue Crescent Boss 429.

308 Before Chrysler introduced the "winged cars" late in the 1969 season, Ford cleaned up with its redesigned Ford Torino

From the mid-1950s through the end of the 1960s, the rooflines of Ford products went from rounded and square to flat and aerodynamic as illustrated by this Mercury, Thunderbird, and Torino trio (left to right). (John Close Photo)

Talladega and Mercury Cyclone. Both cars featured longer, sloped front nose extensions giving them more downforce than their Dodge and Plymouth counterparts. They produced wins for Ford in every superspeedway race that season until Richard Brickhouse and his new winged Dodge Charger Daytona won at Talladega in September of that year.

309 Dodge took its NASCAR program to a different level with the development of the 1969 Dodge Daytona. Specifically engineered for Grand National racing, the Dodge Charger R/T–based car featured a sloped bullet nose and a 2-foot-tall wing on the rear deck. Commissioned specifically to compete on NASCAR's superspeedways, the new Daytona had a drag coefficient of just .28. That number is still below the .30 to .35 average coefficients of today's modern cars.

310 The original plans for the 1969 Daytona had the rear wing positioned at a height of 12 inches. Unfortunately, the trunk couldn't be opened at that height, so engineers raised the wing to 23 inches to allow for trunk clearance. In doing so, they unwittingly gave the car much needed, and useful, rear downforce.

311 Plymouth, the standard bearer for Chrysler Corporation in NASCAR for most of the 1960s, wanted its own winged superspeedway warrior. Chrysler chose the Plymouth Belvedere as its donor vehicle, outfitting it with a Coronet hood and front fenders to accommodate the nosepiece developed for the Daytona. The Belvedere also got a back window plug similar to the Daytona's while the newly-dubbed Superbird featured a rear wing mounted on 40 percent bigger vertical side mounts.

312 The shelf life of the Dodge and Plymouth winged cars proved to be short. The two cars won a total of 14 Grand National events over two seasons, 1969–1970: Richard Petty (5 victories), Pete Hamilton (3), Charlie Glotzbach (2), Bobby Allison (1), Richard Brickhouse (1), Buddy Baker (1), and Bobby Isaac (1), together made the Daytona and Superbird winged winners.

TRACKS

313 The largest crash in NASCAR history occurred February 13, 1960, when 37 cars wrecked on Lap 2 of the 250-mile NASCAR Modified Sportsman Race at Daytona International Speedway. In all, eight drivers were transported to the hospital while 24 cars (12 of them rollovers) were eventually eliminated. Bubba Farr won the event in a 1956 Ford.

314 The World 600 NASCAR Grand National event at Charlotte takes off June 19, 1960, 11 years to the day after the first NASCAR Strictly Stock race was held at Charlotte Speedway. Drivers Buck Baker, Curtis Turner, Lee Petty, and Jack Smith have the distinction of competing in both events.

315 Nearly a decade before Bill France Sr. turned an old Air Force base into Alabama International Motor Speedway (Talladega), NASCAR competed at Stewart Air Force Base near Montgomery, New York. The 1.85-mile triangle-shaped road course was rudimentary at best, being made up of three runways connected by extremely sharp turns. The only retaining walls were hay bales that marked

With road graders still clearing the infield of the incomplete Atlanta International Raceway, Jack Smith and his 1960 Pontiac Catalina took the first laps on the 1.5-mile track prior to its 1960 opening. (Photo Courtesy Ed Samples Jr.)

chicanes on two of the straights. The track had no pit paddock, permanent bathrooms, or grandstand. Despite the primitive conditions, NASCAR held the 1960 Empire State 200 at SAFB, which was won by Rex White, who lapped the 19-car field in front of an estimated crowd of 5,000. Most of the fans stood in the tall grass surrounding the air base while a select few sat in a portable grandstand lent by NASCAR for the race.

316 Original investors Garland Bagley, Walker Jackson, Lloyd Smith, Ralph Sceiano, and Ike Supporter couldn't have envisioned their fate when hatching the idea for Atlanta International Raceway in 1958. One year later, with the 1.5-mile paved track far from completion and way over the original budget, all but Bagley had bailed on the project. Fortunately, Bagley engaged investors Dr. Warren Gremmel, Bill Boyd, Jack Black, and Art Lester to help him complete the project. Originally scheduled to open in November 1959, the track finally debuted with the Dixie 300 NASCAR Grand National event on July 31, 1960. An estimated 25,000 fans turned out for the opening of the $1.8 million facility to see Fireball

Roberts drive Smokey Yunick's 1960 Pontiac to victory over Cotton Owens, Jack Smith, Bobby Johns, and Fred Lorenzen.

317 Most NASCAR regulars decided to skip the June 12, 1960 Grand National event at Marchbanks Speedway in Hanford, California, largely due to its light purse. In all, 33 mostly West Coast drivers started the California 250 in sweltering 104-degree heat. Only 7,000 fans braved the heat to watch Marvin Porter score the second of his two career NASCAR victories.

318 Fred Lorenzen scored his first career NASCAR win driving a Holman-Moody Ford to Victory Lane in the 1961 Virginia 500 at Martinsville Speedway April 9, 1961. In Lorenzen's 10th career Grand National start, the race is red-flagged and made official after the completion of just 149 of the 500 scheduled laps.

319 Two weeks after sailing his way to a rain-induced, significantly shortened victory at Martinsville, Fred Lorenzen proves his mettle by winning the Rebel 300 at Darlington Raceway. Lorenzen and his Holman-Moody Ford win the pole for the May 6, 1961, NASCAR race and take the win after a torrid late-race battle with veteran Curtis Turner.

320 Oppressive summer heat greeted more than 25,000 fans for the opening of Bristol International Speedway (Tennessee) at the inaugural Volunteer 500 July 29, 1961. The high temperature and the new half-mile asphalt oval, featuring 22-degree banking in the corners, took its toll on leader Jack Smith, who eventually gave way to relief driver Johnny Allen on lap 292 of the 500-circuit event. Allen never surrenders and rolls to a two-lap victory over Fireball Roberts, Ned Jarrett, Richard Petty, and Buddy Baker.

321 Considered the first great NASCAR superspeedway racer, Fireball Roberts earned much of that praise after sweeping Daytona Speedweeks in 1962. Roberts opened the Daytona festivities by driving his No. 22 Jim Stephens'–owned Pontiac to the pole with a lap of 156.999 mph. Roberts then took the American

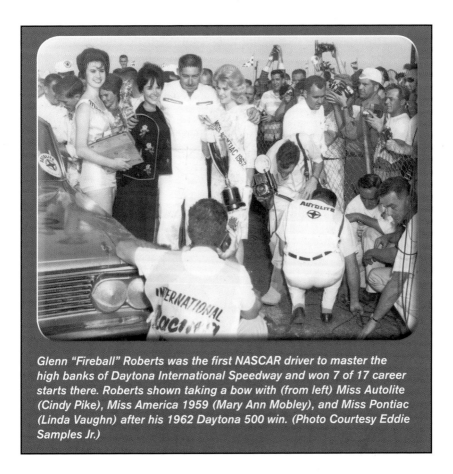

Glenn "Fireball" Roberts was the first NASCAR driver to master the high banks of Daytona International Speedway and won 7 of 17 career starts there. Roberts shown taking a bow with (from left) Miss Autolite (Cindy Pike), Miss America 1959 (Mary Ann Mobley), and Miss Pontiac (Linda Vaughn) after his 1962 Daytona 500 win. (Photo Courtesy Eddie Samples Jr.)

Challenge Invitational, a special event for 1961 GN winners, easily capturing the 100-mile qualifying clash. On February 18, Roberts completed his Daytona sweep by dominating the Daytona 500, leading 144 of the 200 laps contested.

322 Plenty of strange things happened at Bowman Gray Stadium long before television made the Winston-Salem, North Carolina, bullring "the Madhouse." After scoring his first NASCAR Grand National victory in the Myers Brothers Memorial June 16, 1962, Johnny Allen loses control and crashes over the first turn wall destroying his Fred Lovette–owned 1961 Pontiac. Allen wins $580, just $80 more than runner-up Rex White, who didn't crash. A crowd of 14,000 witnesses the event.

323 Chrysler's new Hemi engines are billed as advertised when Richard Petty dominates the 1964 Daytona 500 by leading 184 of 200 laps on 2.5-mile oval. Petty's Hemi Plymouth qualified nearly 20 mph faster than a conventional V-8 engine at Daytona in 1963. This day, the car performed flawlessly giving Petty his first Daytona 500 and superspeedway victories. Petty led the 1-2-3 Hemi Plymouth finish in the 500 with Jimmy Pardue second and pole qualifier Paul Goldsmith third.

324 LeeRoy Yarbrough scored his first NASCAR victory in just his 29th start May 1, 1964, running a 1963 Plymouth owned by Louis Weathersbee at Savannah Speedway (Georgia). Just 12 cars start the Savannah 200 on the dirt half-mile with only 7 left running at the finish.

325 When property owner Bill Land and Darlington Raceway builder Harold Brassington decided to construct North Carolina Motor Speedway in 1964, they offered shares to Rockingham, North Carolina, area residents and eventually sold about 1,000 shares at $1 each.

326 It was an all-Ford show as the carmaker swept the top 13 positions in the 1965 Daytona 500 at Daytona International Speedway. With the powerful Chrysler Hemi cars on the sidelines thanks to an early-season NASCAR boycott, Fred Lorenzen's Ford and Darel Dieringer's Mercury take first and second in the epic FoMoCo sweep.

327 Valdosta 75 Speedway (Georgia) hosted three Grand National events from 1962 to 1965. The last one (a 200-lapper on the half-mile dirt oval) was won by Cale Yarborough in a Kenny Myler–owned 1964 Ford. It's the first of what will turn out to be 83 NASCAR career victories for the Timmonsville, South Carolina, driver.

328 From 1962 to 1966, Dog Track Speedway in Moyock, North Carolina, was Ned Jarrett's personal playground, winning four of the seven events contested there. Jarrett's biggest moment

Jarrett drove this 1962 Chevrolet to a win at Dog Track Speedway in Moyock, North Carolina, on September 11, 1962. Jarrett sold the car to Wendell Scott who campaigned it on the NASCAR trail in 1963. (Photo Courtesy Jack Walker)

on the tiny .250-mile dirt oval was the final race of the 1965 season when he won the Tidewater 300. His victory in the 55th and final race of the season secured him the 1965 NASCAR Grand National championship.

329 Darlington Raceway provided free admission to 5,000 Boy Scouts at its 1966 spring event, the Rebel 400. The Scouts were the majority of the crowd due to Ford's NASCAR boycott, which kept fans home in droves; only 7,000 attending the April 30 event. The race is an all-Chrysler product showcase as Richard Petty, Paul Goldsmith, David Pearson, Bunkie Blackburn, G. C. Spencer, and Jim Paschal lead a 1–6 Mopar parade under the checkered flag.

330 The fans were back in full force as 94,250 jammed into Daytona International Speedway for the 1967 Daytona 500. The giant crowd was treated to a Ford-Chrysler factory showdown as each was back in the NASCAR garage area that season. More than 80 cars showed up for 50 starting spots. In the end, Mario Andretti scored his first NASCAR victory with Fred Lorenzen taking second. The Holman-Moody Fords ruled the day as six Mopars and four Fords sweep the top-10 finishing positions.

331 With the GM factory types still on the sidelines for the 1967 NASCAR Grand National season, drivers continuing to race their brand were often outgunned. In the 1967 Daytona 500, 11 Chevys started the event. Donnie Allison was the highest-finishing Bowtie, coming in 11th. Seven of 11 Chevy starters finished 41st or worse in the 50-car starting field.

332 GM's refusal to field factory-backed teams in the 1960s led to a NASCAR Grand National winless streak that lasted nearly three years. On October 13, 1963, Junior Johnson piloted a Chevy to victory in the National 400 at Charlotte Motor Speedway. Chevy then went on an epic 197 Grand National event losing streak before Bobby Allison corrected the skid by wheeling a Chevelle to victory in the 300-lap Maine 100 at Oxford Plains Speedway July 12, 1966. Allison's Chevy was just 1 of 5 GM entries in the 27-car starting field.

333 Jimmy Clark, the 1963 and 1965 Formula 1 world driving champion, made his one and only NASCAR Grand National start in the 1967 American 500 at North Carolina Motor Speedway in Rockingham. The "Flying Scot" started 24th in the 44-car field and finished 30th when the engine in his No. 66 Holman-Moody Ford expired.

334 Richard Petty smashed several records during his 27-win 1967 Grand National season. Included is season win number 19 at Bowman Gray Stadium August 12. The win broke Tim Flock's all-time record of 18 wins in a single season. Flock set the record 12 years earlier in 1955.

335 Peach County, Georgia, authorities made an amazing discovery at the conclusion of the 1968 NASCAR season opener at Middle Georgia Raceway in Macon. While Bobby Allison was celebrating in Victory Lane, county sheriff's deputies find a large illegal moonshine operation beneath the track.

336 Occoneechee Speedway hosted the third-ever NASCAR Strictly Stock race August 7, 1949. Bob Flock won the event in an Oldsmobile. On September 15, 1968, the Hillsboro, North Carolina, raceway (now Orange Speedway), hosted the last of 32 Strictly Stock/Grand National races. Richard Petty dominated the 150-mile GN final bow on the Hillsboro .900-mile dirt oval, winning by seven laps over James Hylton. The Hillsboro race date becomes the date for the inaugural 1969 event at the track we now call Talladega (Alabama) Superspeedway.

337 It took more than three years for the Melvin L. Joseph Construction Company to build Dover Downs International Speedway. The 1-mile, high-banked asphalt oval opened with the Mason-Dixon 300 July 6, 1969. Richard Petty and his 1969 Ford Torino won the track's lid-lifter by six laps over Sonny Hutchens. Since then, Dover has hosted more than 200 NASCAR GN/Cup, Xfinity, Truck, North Tour, and Pro East events. The track, nicknamed the Monster Mile, was repaved with concrete in 1995.

338 Track owner Larry Carrier increased the banking at Bristol International Raceway from 22 to 36 degrees and increased the length from 2,640 feet to 2,814 feet (.533-miles) prior to the running of the Volunteer 500 Grand National race on July 20, 1969. The new high-banked asphalt oval produced a 15-mph average increase over previous speeds there and proved to be a car eater as only 10 of 30 starters survive the 500-lap test. Winner David Pearson nabs the victory by three laps over Bobby Isaac with 10th-place finisher Roy Tyner (the last car running) 97 laps down at the finish.

339 Built by Bill France Sr. on 2,000 acres off Interstate 20 east of Birmingham, construction of the Alabama International Motor Speedway began May 23, 1968. Larger than France's first super track (Daytona International Speedway), Talladega features a giant 2.66-mile layout on the former Anniston Army Air Force base. The 4,300-foot curved front straight and 4,000-foot back straight are both longer than 20 other tracks that hosted 1969 Grand National events. The speedway opened September 13, 1969, with the Bama 300, a Grand Touring car event won by Ken Rush in a 1969 Camaro. A day later, NASCAR staged its first Grand National race at the track despite a boycott by the Professional Driver's Association over tire safety. Richard Brickhouse won the race in front of 62,000 fans. Since then, Talladega Superspeedway (renamed in 1989) has hosted more than 130 NASCAR Cup, Xfinity, and Truck Series races and remains the biggest and fastest oval track on the NASCAR circuit.

340 From the very beginning, the buzz about the new Alabama International Motor Speedway wasn't good. Bobby Allison was the first to criticize the giant track, noting how rough it was after driving a passenger car on it. After recording epic speeds of more than 193 mph in a Ford test, Donnie Allison suggested the track be repaved. Later, after Cale Yarborough and Bobby Isaac expressed concern about the rough conditions and excessive tire wear, 59-year-old Bill France Sr. took to the track himself in a Holman-Moody Ford in late August. The former driver turned in a best lap in excess of 170-mph and exited the car stating the track was fit for competition and the Talladega 500 was slated for the next month. To prove it, France filed an entry for himself the week before the race.

341 The Professional Driver's Association call to order came just prior to the race at Michigan Speedway, which was completed without incident. One week later at South Boston Speedway (Virginia), Hoss Ellington, Ed Negre, and Pete Hazelwood all parked their cars in protest of NASCAR's prize money distribution ($1,000 to win, $200 to start). The next day, Hazelwood and Ellington were joined by Bill Seifert, Earl Brooks, Wayne Gillette, and Cecil Gordon in a protest and they all quit at various points during the Myers Brothers Stock Car Spectacle at Bowman Gray Stadium. Ellington turned in his third-straight "start and park" protest along with Gillette as Henly Gray was ruled out as a "Quit" later in the event. Three weeks later, tire issues at Alabama International Motor Speedway lit the match for more drastic action by NASCAR Grand National drivers.

342 When 32 teams vacated the garage area at Alabama International Motor Speedway in support of the Professional Driver's Association boycott, Bill France Sr. had to scramble to fill the field for the next day's Talladega 500. Not all teams joined the PDA action and 13 GN cars started the race. Those starting included Bobby Isaac, Jim Vandiver, Jim Hurtubise, Don Tarr, Dick Brooks, Coo Coo Marlin, Toy Tyner, Homer Newland, Richard Brickhouse, Les Snow, Ramo Stott, and Earl Brooks, with Tiny Lund piloting the entry fielded by Bill France Sr. The rest of the field was filled out by NASCAR Grand Touring vehicles that had competed at the track on Saturday.

343 Real estate developer Larry LoPatin tried to take on Bill France Sr. in the late 1960s and found out just how tough that could be. LoPatin raised $3 million to form American Raceways Incorporated (ARI) and for seed money to build Michigan Speedway. France quickly awarded LoPatin two Michigan NASCAR dates annually over the next 10 years, finally getting the track he coveted in the Big Three's backyard. He also promised LoPatin the final 1969 NASCAR Grand National season event at ARI's new track, still under construction in College Station, Texas.

France, however, became suspicious of LoPatin when he acquired nearly half the interest in Riverside Raceway and a 19 percent share in Atlanta with an option to control up to 71 percent of the track's stock. LoPatin confirmed France's concerns when he announced ARI's plan to build a track in southern New Jersey with an ultimate goal of a dozen tracks nationwide holding two events at each. After LoPatin made a grandstand play to NASCAR drivers, stating that if he had been in charge, he would have postponed the Talladega 500 and avoided the PDA boycott, France had seen enough. France quickly pulled the final Texas race off the schedule despite it being two months away. The race was eventually restored after LoPatin agreed to increase the purse. Meanwhile, ARI was a sinking ship awash in debit and when France omitted all ARI tracks from the 1970 ABC television agreement; the writing was on the wall.

LoPatin somehow managed to stay afloat despite canceling ARI's June NASCAR event at Texas World Speedway. After ARI couldn't make the purse for the Dixie 500 at Atlanta in August, investors removed LoPatin as president of ARI. LoPatin never worked in racing again, returning to real estate development until his death in 1993.

PIT PASS

344 Bill France Sr. dreamed of the day when NASCAR would take center stage in Atlanta, Georgia, the major southern economic hub in the mid-20th Century. When that day came on July 31, 1960, France missed the race after getting caught in a massive traffic jam for the Dixie 300. Arriving late, he stayed outside and helped direct traffic into the parking lot.

345 During the inaugural Dixie 300 at Atlanta International Raceway, NASCAR official starter Ernie Moore was hit by a piece of metal while in the flag stand. A lengthy caution period ensued as an ambulance was dispatched onto the track to transport him to a local hospital. Moore, one of the original founders of the National Stock Car Racing Association (NSCRA) in the 1940s, began flagging NASCAR races at the inaugural 1950 Southern 500 at Darlington Raceway. Moore eventually recovered from the incident. Meanwhile, assistant starter Roby Combs finished the Atlanta race in Moore's absence.

Cotton Owens (6) and Fireball Roberts (22) lead the field to the start in the first of two 100-mile qualifying races for the Daytona 500 at Daytona International Speedway. (Photo Courtesy Georgia Racing Hall of Fame)

346 After a caution-free inaugural Daytona 500 in 1959, the second-annual 500-mile racing classic saw the yellow flag fly four times for a total of 32 laps. Junior Johnson started the 1960 Valentine's Day race ninth in a field of 68 cars and led on four occasions for 67 laps, including the final 9, to win the race. Johnson's Daytona Kennel Club 1959 Chevrolet averaged 124.740 mph over the 500-mile test, a full 10 mph slower than Lee Petty's 135.521 all-green-flag Daytona-winning run the year before.

347 In 1958, motorsports enthusiast and writer Denise McCluggage joined fellow racing scribes Don Stewart and Tom Swantek to launch *Competition Press*, a bi-weekly racing newspaper that eventually evolved into *Autoweek*. McCluggage was also a race driver of note who had competed in two NASCAR events: both 1960 NASCAR Compact Car races at Daytona International Speedway. Piloting a 1960 Volvo, McCluggage finished 11th in the initial 10-lap road race. In the nightcap, she finished 9th in the 20-lap event on Daytona's 2.5-mile oval.

348 Charlotte Motor Speedway opened June 19, 1960, with the NASCAR Grand National World 600. The race featured a 60-car starting field (the largest ever to start a top division NASCAR race at Charlotte), with only 18 finishing the grueling 600-mile test. Unheralded Chattanooga, Tennessee, driver Joe Lee Johnson won by four laps over Johnny Beauchamp, Bobby Johns, Gerald Due, and Buck Baker in a race, which took 5:34.06 hours to complete.

349 Prior to the start of the 1960 World 600, NASCAR officials warned drivers that entering pit road improperly at Charlotte Motor Speedway could result in penalties. A few days after the race, NASCAR announced that six drivers were disqualified for improper entrance into the pits. Richard Petty, Lee Petty, Bob Welborn, Paul Lewis, Junior Johnson, and Lennie Page were officially scored 55th through 60th in the final running order.

350 NASCAR team radio communications were sketchy during the 1960s. Communication between drivers and their crews was in large part still done with hand signals and a pit board. For instance, drivers reached out and tapped the roof of their car while passing their pit on the front straight to indicate the car was pushing. If the car was loose, the driver touched the outside of the door. Meanwhile, crews communicated by holding up a chalkboard as the driver sped by. Simple messages such as "Pit," "EZ," and "$" were used to keep the driver informed during a race.

351 As the designer of classic American cars, Harley Earl is credited as the first to use clay modeling in car designs employing modern features such as the wraparound windshield, hardtop sedan, two-tone paint, and rocket-like tail fins. His most famous designs are the Buick Y-Job (the first American concept car introduced in 1939) and the 1953 Chevrolet Corvette. Earl was the second NASCAR National Commissioner, serving from 1960 to 1969. Today, a model of his Firebird 1 concept car sits atop the Harley J. Earl annual trophy that is presented to the winner of the Daytona 500.

352 September 5, 1960, remains one of the darkest days in NASCAR history due to a pair of accidents. NASCAR official Joe Taylor and crewmen Paul McDuffie and Charles Sweatlund were killed when contact between Bobby Johns and Roy Tyner sent Johns' 1960 Pontiac into an unprotected area of the Darlington back straight. Three others on McDuffie's team (Joe Lee Johnson's No. 89) were also injured in the incident. The crash was the second of the day resulting in serious injury as earlier, Elmo Langley crashed into the front pit area; crewman Ankrum "Spook" Crawford was injured after being struck by crash debris.

353 NASCAR fans can tell you that Lee Petty had a devastating wreck in the second of two Daytona qualifying races February 24, 1961 at Daytona International Speedway. The incident left the two-time NASCAR champion with multiple fractures, as well as internal and head injuries. What is usually lost in the story is that Richard Petty's car also flew out of the speedway in the first qualifying race of the day. In that crash, Richard suffered a cut hand and a pair of black eyes after contact with Junior Johnson rocketed Richard's Plymouth out of the park, just as his father's did later that day.

354 On July 30, 1961, the Volunteer 500 (Bristol International Speedway's first race) featured three brothers; Sherman, Dub, and Layman Utsman. Sherman Utsman earned bragging rights by finishing 10th while Dub rolled in 29th. Layman Utsman had the distinction of finishing last (42nd) when his Dodge retired on Lap 35. The race marks the first time that three brothers competed in a NASCAR race since the Flock brothers (Tim, Fonty, and Bob) in the 1950s.

355 In the 1960s, the Teamsters Union was expanding its unionization of American professional sports, including auto racing. On August 7, 1961, the Teamsters held a meeting in Chicago at which NASCAR stars Curtis Turner, Fireball Roberts, and Tim Flock, along with drivers from other divisions, formed the Federation of Professional Athletes. When Turner publicly announced that several NASCAR drivers had joined the association, Bill France Sr. vowed to fight any unionization in NASCAR with a gun, and suspends Turner, Roberts, and Flock for life. Within days, Roberts renounces his Teamsters Union membership and is immediately reinstated by France. Rex White and Ned Jarrett follow suit, and France opens the pit back to them as well. Meanwhile, Turner and Flock refuse to abandon the union. Turner's lifetime ban lasts five years, while Flock quits NASCAR for good.

356 Curtis Turner and Tim Flock eventually took their grievances with Bill France Sr. and NASCAR to court, filing several lawsuits. Their petitions, including one for reinstatement to drive and another for $300,000 in punitive damages, were dismissed by Circuit Judge Robert E. Wingfield on January 13, 1962.

357 One of the reasons Bill France Sr. resisted NASCAR unionization was due to organized gambling. Curtis Turner had stated publically that pari-mutuel betting on auto races could be a reality

Wendell Scott's team (Scott at far right) unhook the No. 34 Chevy from its Packard "tow car" in the pits prior to a 1963 Grand National event at Rambi Raceway in Myrtle Beach, South Carolina. (Photo Courtesy Jack Walker)

if an agreement could be reached with NASCAR. France responded, stating that organized gambling "would be bad for our sport and would spill innocent blood on the racetrack."

358 Although the Teamster's effort failed in NASCAR, it led to some meaningful discussion about increased purses, driver pensions, death benefits, and safety. It also led to the formation of the Grand National Advisory Board. This board was composed of two drivers (Ned Jarrett and Rex White), two car owners (Rex Lovette and Lee Petty), two promoters (Enoch Staley and Clay Earles), and two NASCAR executives (Pat Purcell and Ed Otto). The group quickly introduced measures for the 1961 season including a revamped purse structure and increased death and dismemberment coverage. It proved to be the forerunner of today's National Stock Car Commission.

359 The Zellwood Mud Hens lost a great pitcher when Edward Glenn "Fireball" Roberts became a racer instead of a baseball player. Roberts, a Tavares, Florida, native proved to be an ace behind the wheel of a stock car, and won 33 NASCAR Grand

National events in his 15-year career. Considered by many as NASCAR's first superstar, Roberts was extremely effective on the superspeedways. He won at Daytona seven times from 1959 to 1963, also winning twice at the Southern 500 (1958 and 1962). Roberts was considering retirement to become a spokesperson for Falstaff Beer, when he was involved in a fiery wreck at the 1964 World 600 at Charlotte Motor Speedway. He died two weeks later at the age of 35.

360 When Fireball Roberts won the 1962 Daytona 500, he and car owner Jim Stephens collected $24,190. That's not bad, especially considering that 10th-place finisher Bob Welborn made $750 and 21st through 48th received $400 each.

361 Tiny Lund, subbing for the injured Marvin Panch, drove to his first Grand National career victory, capturing the Daytona 500 on February 24, 1963. Lund and his No. 21 Wood Brothers' Ford won the race by 24 seconds over Fred Lorenzen. Lund ran the entire 500 miles on a single set of Firestone Racing Tires.

362 In 1962, Joe Weatherly and Fireball Roberts led a Pontiac assault on the NASCAR record book. One year later with Ford now the hot brand, the pair bailed on the Chief mid-season and secured FoMoCo rides instead, with Weatherly in a Bud Moore Mercury and Roberts as a teammate to Fred Lorenzen at Holman-Moody. In his first race with the team, Roberts beat Lorenzen in a 1-2 finish at Bristol. Roberts later won the now-Firecracker 400 at Daytona and the Southern 500 at Darlington for Ford in 1963.

363 Darlington Raceway replaced the traditional spring NAS-CAR Convertible race in 1963 with a new format for what's now the NASCAR Grand National Rebel 300. The May 11 race was run in two parts: the first of two 150-mile events was won by Joe Weatherly in a 1963 Pontiac. Richard Petty's 1963 Plymouth then nipped Weatherly for the win in the second race. Using an aggregate scoring system that averaged the finishes of both races, Weatherly earned the overall race victory with a total of 197.8 points. Fireball Roberts, third in both races, finished second overall with 191.7 points while Petty was declared third with 187.9 points. After the event, NASCAR voices its displeasure with the convoluted scoring system to Darlington president, Bob Colvin. Not surprisingly, the scoring system is never used again.

364 The 1964 Grand National schedule featured a whopping 62 races, the most ever in NASCAR history. Two days short of one calendar year in length, the 1964 championship chase began at Concord Speedway November 10, 1963, and ended November 8, 1964, at Jacksonville Speedway (North Carolina). Coincidentally, Ned Jarrett won both races.

365 Joe Weatherly, the "Clown Prince of NASCAR," was killed on January 19, 1964, in a crash at Riverside Raceway, making him one of three drivers to perish in 1964. Fireball Roberts died due to burns suffered in a wreck at Charlotte in May, while Jimmy Pardue perished in a tire-test crash at Charlotte in September. Collectively, the three drivers won 60 NASCAR Grand National races.

366 Fred Lorenzen scored eight wins in just 16 starts in the 1964 NASCAR Grand National season. The most improbable victory came when Lorenzen, three laps down with just four remaining, rallied to win the Volunteer 500 at Bristol International Speedway. Lorenzen was almost certainly a runner-up to Richard Petty when Petty's Plymouth blew up on Lap 496 of the 500-lap contest. Petty coasted around the half-mile three times before slowing to a stop on pit road one circuit short of the finish. Lorenzen continued and won the race as Petty watched from the pits.

367 Curtis Turner was 41, overweight, and suffering a bad shoulder when his NASCAR lifetime suspension was lifted in 1965. Turner made his first start since the 1961 World 600 at Charlotte, rolling off 8th and finishing 35th (wheel bearing) in the September 6, 1965, Southern 500 at Darlington. After two disappointing finishes driving for Junior Johnson, Turner hooked up with the Wood

Before he was NASCAR's "Golden Boy," Fred Lorenzen (left) captured two consecutive United States Auto Club (USAC) stock car championships. (Photo Courtesy Russ Lake)

Brothers and won the American 500 (the first race held at North Carolina Motor Speedway in Rockingham) October 31, 1965. It was the 17th and last victory of Turner's NASCAR career.

368 Richard Petty won the first of his seven Grand National/Winston Cup championships in 1964. He earned 40,252 points to outdistance Ned Jarrett (34,950) and David Pearson (32,146) for the title. Petty won nine times, and scored 37 top-5 finishes, second in both categories behind Jarrett (15 wins and 40 top-5s). Petty captured the championship by competing in 61 of the 62 scheduled races with Jarrett competing in just 59 that year.

369 Rising Indy star Mario Andretti stunned the NASCAR world when he won the 1967 Daytona 500 at Daytona International Speedway. Prior to the race, Andretti insisted that his Holman-Moody team install an unconventional "loose" chassis in his Ford Fairlane stocker. The results have an immediate effect; Andretti rocketed from a 12th starting position to the lead by Lap 55. Andretti led eight times in 97 laps, including the final 33 to win his first and only NASCAR Grand National race.

370 Independent driver James Hylton capped off his 1966 NAS-CAR rookie season with a 10th-place finish in the American 500 at Rockingham, North Carolina. The finish secured him second place in the 1966 point championship behind David Pearson. To date, Hylton's runner-up championship effort is the highest finish for a rookie in the top division of NASCAR.

371 After seven Grand National races in 1956 produced no better than a 20th-place finish, Fred Lorenzen returned to Elmhurst, Illinois, to compete in the United States Auto Club (USAC) stock car series, winning the championship in both 1958 and 1959. A move back to NASCAR in 1961 to drive for Holman-Moody proved profitable as he captured 26 Grand National events over the next seven seasons. In 1963, he won six times, becoming the first driver to eclipse $100,000 in earnings in a single GN season. One year later, Lorenzen took eight Grand National checkered flags, and followed up with a victory in the 1965 Daytona 500. After a particularly hard crash in the 1967 Atlanta 500 at Atlanta International Raceway, Lorenzen, just 33 years old, surprised everyone by announcing his retirement. Lorenzen returned to NASCAR in 1970 with 29 starts over the next three seasons, with his best finish a second at Dover in 1971 in a Ray Nichels Dodge. Lorenzen was inducted into the NASCAR Hall of Fame in 2015.

372 David Pearson scored 36 top-5 finishes in 48 races to win the 1968 NASCAR Grand National championship. Pearson scored 16 wins, but his grinding streak of 18 consecutive top-5 performances garnered the most attention. The string began in June and ended September 13 at Beltsville Speedway (Maryland) when his runner-up finish was disallowed after his car failed post-race tech. Back in his Holman-Moody Ford for the final seven races of the season, Pearson finished no lower than sixth in six events, winning the 1968 Grand National championship by 126 points over Bobby Isaac.

373 David Pearson became the fourth driver in Grand National history to win back-to-back championships after wheeling a Holman-Moody Ford to the 1968 and 1969 titles. He competed in 51 of 54 events in 1969, winning 11 times and posting an impressive 44 top-10 finishes.

374 On August 14, 1969, 11 NASCAR drivers met secretly in a hotel room in Ann Arbor, Michigan, to form the Professional Drivers Association. The PDA elected Richard Petty as president, with Cale Yarborough and Elmo Langley tabbed as vice-presidents. The Board of Directors included James Hylton, Buddy Baker, Pete Hamilton, LeeRoy Yarbrough, Bobby Allison, Donnie Allison, Charlie Glotzbach, and David Pearson. The association retained Lawrence Fleisher, a New York-based sports attorney who helped found the National Basketball Association Player's Association in 1960. The PDA was open to all Grand National, Grand Touring, Sportsman, and Modified drivers. A $200 initiation fee was required for membership.

375 One of the most legendary throttle stompers of NASCAR's big-block era, LeeRoy Yarbrough scored 13 Grand National victories from 1964 through 1969. A product of the Sportsman and Modified ranks, Yarbrough's best season was in 1969 after he captured seven GN races including the 500 and Firecracker 400 at Daytona International Speedway and both the Rebel 400 and Southern 500 at Darlington. Yarbrough and his Junior Johnson/Herb Nab–built Fords and Mercurys won the World 600 at Charlotte Motor Speedway and the American 500 at North Carolina Motor Speedway that same year. This remains one of the greatest superspeedway seasons by any driver in the history of NASCAR. A practice crash at Texas Motor Speedway in late 1970 limited Yarbrough's starts to just seven in 1971. That same year he suffered another hard impact while practicing for his fourth career Indianapolis 500 start. The Jacksonville, Florida, driver was never the same physically after the two crashes and dropped out of the NASCAR scene by 1973. In and out of hospitals for the next decade, Yarbrough died in Jacksonville on December 7, 1984, at the age of 46, after suffering a seizure and brain injuries in a subsequent fall.

376 Speeds approaching 200 mph in practice and qualifying had Goodyear and Firestone scrambling to fix tires that were blistering and coming apart after just a few laps at Talledega in 1969. Both companies flew in new tires with different compounds hoping for better performance, but they were no match for the high speed and rough Talladega surface. In a Saturday morning meeting, Professional Drivers Association president Richard Petty met with Bill France Sr. and informed him the PDA had determined the tire situation was unsafe and, as such, the group would not compete in Sunday's Talladega 500. Petty suggested rescheduling until the tire companies had time to develop a new product, but France insisted that the race would go on with or without the PDA. Drivers promptly loaded their cars and equipment and later that evening, Petty led a parade of 32 competitors out of the garage area, creating the first driver boycott of a NASCAR Grand National event.

377 Richard Brickhouse almost didn't compete in the inaugural Talladega 500 at Alabama International Motor Speedway. A PDA member, Brickhouse was offered the No. 99 Nichels Engineering Dodge Daytona on Saturday. The unheralded Rocky Point, North Carolina, driver decided he couldn't pass up the opportunity and tried to contact PDA president Richard Petty to resign from the group. When Brickhouse couldn't connect with Petty, he resigned from the PDA over the speedway's public address system prior to the event. Brickhouse then went out and won the 1969 Talladega 500, his lone victory in 39 career GN events.

MILESTONES

378 Between 1960 and 1970, America's inner city populations shrank as the suburbs exploded, accounting for nearly 70 percent of the country's growth. The change was fueled by a massive road and interstate highway-building program that made the automobile a necessity for everyday driving and commuting. These changes to an even more automobile-centric society helped fuel the growth of NASCAR as interest in cars, especially high-performance models, peaks during the decade.

379 The first live television broadcast of a NASCAR event was January 31, 1960, when CBS broadcast two 25-mile NASCAR Grand National qualifying events, the Daytona 500 and the 10-lap NASCAR Compact Car Road Course Race, from Daytona International Speedway. The races were telecast as part of a CBS sports anthology show, *CBS Sports Spectacular,* and drew an estimated 17 million viewers.

380 One event on the 1960 Daytona Speedweeks racing card was the Air Lift Challenge. Sponsored by the automotive suspension company, drivers took a single lap around Daytona International Speedway in a 1960 Oldsmobile. The car's speedometer was covered and each driver was given a speed to match prior to his lap. Buck Baker won the "Blind Bogey" event by matching his target speed of 136 mph with a lap of 136.612.

381 Richard Petty won his first Grand National victory February 28, 1960, beating Rex White, Doug Yates, and Junior Johnson to the checkered flag at Southern States Fairgrounds in Charlotte, North Carolina. The win comes in Petty's 35th career start. His 1959 Plymouth competes the 200-lap distance on the half-mile clay oval in 1:52:21, with a winning average speed of 53.404 mph, and earning him $800 in prize money.

382 The Wood Brothers competed in 62 Grand National events from 1953 through 1960 without a win. That changed when the Stuart, Virginia, family team captured the National 400 at Charlotte Motor Speedway October 16, 1960. Speedy Thompson wheeled the No. 21 Wood Brothers 1960 Ford into the lead with 35 laps remaining and never looked back, scoring his 19th career win, and his first on a superspeedway. Thompson took the lead 35 laps from the finish after leader Fireball Roberts blew a tire and crashed. The $12,710 first-place prize money was twice the highest amount ever won by the team in a single season.

383 Beginning in the middle 1950s and through the early 1960s, Pontiac was regarded as the performance brand of General

Jim Paschal, a pair of race officials, and Paschal's crew conduct post-race tech after a second-place finish at a 1961 Grand National event at Rambi Raceway in Myrtle Beach, South Carolina. (Photo Courtesy Jack Walker)

Motors. That was especially true in NASCAR as Pontiacs won 60 Grand National events from 1960 to 1963. *The Chief* began its run of Victory Lane visits when Fireball Roberts won a 100-mile qualifying race for the 1960 Daytona 500. The streak ended with Joe Weatherly capturing his third win of the season in the second-to-last race of the 1963 season at Orange Speedway (Hillsboro, North Carolina). Roberts also won the 1962 Daytona 500 in a Pontiac, one of 30 victories the brand scored en route to its only NASCAR Manufacturers Championship.

384 Richard Petty's brother Maurice is best known for his work behind the scenes as crew chief for Petty Enterprises. Lesser known is that "Chief" took a turn behind the wheel making his NASCAR debut at Dixie Speedway (Birmingham, Alabama) August 3, 1960. He finished eighth in the 16-car field and went on to make 25 more starts through 1964; he earned seven top-5 and 16 top-10 finishes.

385 NASCAR drivers have been black flagged for every imaginable reason. That said, driver Herman Beam was the first driver to be black-flagged at Daytona International Speedway for forgetting to put on his helmet at a 1960 Twin 100-mile qualifying race. Beam completed eight laps before acknowledging the flag and pulling into the pits. NASCAR immediately parked Beam for the rest of the event, and he is credited with 37th out of 40 cars.

386 Others may have had more press, but Rex White was quietly the dominant force and NASCAR's most consistent driver in the early 1960s. White captured his first and only NASCAR championship after six wins and a whopping 35 top-10 finishes in 40 events on his run to the 1960 GN title. White won 36 poles and scored 28 victories in 233 NASCAR career starts. His last ride was in 1964 at Atlanta Motor Speedway; he finished fifth in the Dixie 400. White was named one of NASCAR's top-50 drivers in 1998 and inducted into the NASCAR Hall of Fame in 2015.

Event winner Junior Johnson (in his No. 26 Ford Galaxie) leads the field in the 1965 Old Dominion 500 at Martinsville Speedway. (Photo Courtesy Ed Samples Jr. Collection)

387 NASCAR's first all-star race, the 1961 American Challenge Cup, February 19, 1961, featured 11 drivers in a 10-lap dash for cash at Daytona International Speedway. The event was open to all 17 Grand National race winners, with 6 choosing not to compete. Joe Weatherly wheeled a Pontiac to the win and $1,000 in an event taking just 9 minutes 41 seconds to complete. Fireball Roberts, Junior Johnson, Cotton Owens, and Richard Petty round out the top-5.

388 David Pearson notched the first of his 101 Grand National Cup career wins wheeling a Pontiac to victory in the World 600 at Charlotte Motor Speedway May 28, 1961. And when I say he wheeled, I mean it, as Pearson completed the race on three wheels after blowing a tire with just two laps remaining. Pearson banks $24,280 for the win, the first of four career wins at the 1.5-mile Charlotte oval.

389 Network television's interest in NASCAR continued to grow as the American Broadcasting Company (ABC) featured the 1961 Firecracker 250. The July 4 race at Daytona International Speedway was one of several Grand National events the popular sports program highlighted in 1961 and throughout the decade. This gave NASCAR its greatest mainstream visibility prior to Grand National races on live network television in the 1970s and 1980s.

390 After taking a beating with no victories in the first part of the 1962 season, FoMoCo president Henry Ford II announces that Ford will reject the 1957 Automobile Manufacturers Association NASCAR participation edict and return to big-time stock car racing. The Blue Oval brand goes on to win 6 of the 53 races on the 1962 schedule with the highlights coming at Darlington. Nelson Stacy wins the Rebel 300 and Larry Frank captures the Southern 500 in a couple of stunning upsets.

391 The seed for today's Rolex 24 road course race at Daytona International Speedway was planted when the inaugural Daytona Continental flew the green flag February 11, 1962. Dan Gurney

Wilbur Rakestraw and his 1959 Ford convertible racer are shown during the 1959 season. This was the final year NASCAR-sanctioned the drop tops as a regular division. (Photo Courtesy Ed Samples Jr. Collection)

won the 3-hour time limit race on the 3.81-mile DIS road course, completing 82 laps and averaging 104.101 mph. Two years later, the event is extended to 2,000 kilometers (1,243 miles) becoming the longest sports car endurance event in the country. In 1966, the race is expanded again to the current 24-hour format.

392 Citing safety concerns, NASCAR put the tops up for good in the NASCAR Convertible Series. What started as a novelty in 1956 and survived the lack of factory support later in the decade took its last breath May 12, 1962, after Nelson Stacy won the Rebel 300 at Darlington Raceway. Stacy's Holman-Moody Ford ragtop topped a 43-car all-convertible field in a race that counted as one of the 53 points events on the 1962 Grand National tour.

393 Wendell Scott made history during the 1962 NASCAR season being the first African-American driver to win pole position for a GN race. Scott accomplished the milestone on Friday July 20, 1962, turning in a qualifying lap of 71.627 mph on the half-mile Savannah Speedway (Georgia) dirt oval. Scott finished eighth behind race winner Joe Weatherly, earning $175.

394 The 1963 Southern 500 at Darlington Raceway represents two significant milestones. On the track, Fireball Roberts captured his second and final Southern 500 victory, a caution-free run and the only non-stop race in the history of the event. Second, Fred Lorenzen makes news off the track when his $6,550 third-place prize money in the Southern 500 makes him the first driver in NASCAR history to eclipse $100,000 in earnings in a single season.

395 Joe Weatherly captured the 1963 NASCAR Grand National championship after scoring three wins in 53 starts. Amazingly, Weatherly drove for nine different owners that season: Bud Moore, Floyd Powell, Pete Stewart, Major Melton, Cliff Stewart, Worth McMillion, Petty Enterprises, Possum Jones, and Wade Younts.

396 History is made December 1, 1963, when Wendell Scott, a 42-year-old auto mechanic from Danville, Virginia, becomes the first African-American to win a Grand National race. Scott captured the Jacksonville 200 at Speedway Park in Jacksonville, Florida, only to have runner-up Buck Baker flag the victor two laps after Scott completed the race. Scott protested the decision and was eventually credited with the victory. He was presented with a replica trophy and a first-place check of $1,000 at the next race, the Sunshine 200 at Savannah Speedway December 29.

397 Upcoming star LeeRoy Yarbrough won his second-straight NASCAR Modified Sportsman race at Daytona International Speedway in 1963. He drove a 1953 Studebaker Hawk Modified to victory over Bobby Johns' 1957 Chevy. Yarbrough captured the 1962 Daytona Modified Sportsman 250-mile test in a 1956 Ford, beating Cale Yarborough to the finish.

398 On Friday July 10, 1964, Billy Wade wins the Fireball Roberts 200 Grand National race at Old Bridge Stadium (New Jersey). His win on the half-mile paved oval began a string of four-straight wins for the Houston, Texas, driver. His Bud Moore Mercury visited Victory Lane at Bridgehampton Raceway (New York), Islip Speedway (New York), and Watkins Glen International (New York). Wade became the first driver in NASCAR Grand National history to win four consecutive races.

399 Nomex fire suits, especially those made by safety guru, Bill Simpson, were being used extensively in NASCAR by the end of the 1960s. Simpson learned of the fire retardant Nomex material while working with NASA on another racing-related project, the invention of safety parachutes to stop drag cars. In all, Simpson developed more than 200 racing-related safety products including suits, gloves, helmets, shoes, and belt restraints in his 50-plus year racing career.

400 Two pieces of government legislation impacted NASCAR in the 1960s. They were the Clean Air Act of 1963 and the Vehicle Air Pollution and Control Act of 1965. The Clean Air Act was the first to address pollution control by establishing a U.S. Public Health Services branch to study air pollution, perceived to be a byproduct of auto emissions. As a result, the 1965 vehicle pollution legislation mandated that emissions controls be installed on all cars manufactured in American beginning with the 1968 model year. Tighter exhaust emissions rules and restrictions eventually helped reduce the number of high-performance vehicles produced and raced in NASCAR into the early 1970s.

401 Jonesboro, Tennessee, driver G. C. Spencer competed in 415 NASCAR Grand National events from 1958 to 1977. Spencer never won a GN race, but finished second seven times. One runner-up happened February 27, 1965, when Spencer piloted his own 1964 Ford in a 200-lapper at Piedmont State Fairgrounds to second place, an amazing 22 laps behind winner Ned Jarrett. Only seven of the 16 starting cars finished the 100-mile race at the Spartanburg, South Carolina, half-mile dirt oval.

402 Three months after hammering the field by 22 laps, Ned Jarrett did it again winning a 200-lap Thursday Night Grand National Special at Cleveland County Speedway in Shelby, North

Carolina. Jarrett and his Bondy Long Ford took the checkered flag a full 22 laps ahead of Bud Moore with Dick Hucherson and Doug Cooper third and fourth respectively, each 25 laps down at the finish.

403 Ned Jarrett puts the icing on a 1965 championship by winning the Southern 500 at Darlington Raceway. The victory is another stomping for "Gentleman Ned" who wins by 14 laps (a record 19.25 miles) over Buck Baker. In all, Jarrett scored 13 wins during the 1965 title march, lapping the field in all but three.

404 Venerable NASCAR driver and mechanic Cotton Owens guided David Pearson to his first GN championship in 1966. Pearson assumed the points lead early in the season with four-straight short-track wins at Hickory Speedway (North Carolina), Columbia Speedway (South Carolina), Greenville-Pickens Speedway (South Carolina), and Bowman Gray Stadium in Winston-Salem (North Carolina). He and his Dodge won 15 times, with 33 top-10 finishes in just 42 starts.

Thanks to Chrysler Corporation's 1965 NASCAR walkout, David Pearson found himself competing in events such as this United States Auto Club (USAC) race at the Milwaukee Mile. (Photo Courtesy Russ Lake)

405 Junior Johnson surprised many by announcing his retirement after a fifth-place finish in the American 500 at North Carolina Motor Speedway October 30, 1966. The move comes one year after Johnson, just 35 at the time, posted his finest season of 13 wins. Johnson finished his career with 50 GN wins in 313 starts over 14 seasons.

406 Richard Petty has been "The King" of NASCAR since May 13, 1967, when he captured the Rebel 400 at Darlington Raceway. His one-lap victory over David Pearson, a fresh replacement for Fred Lorenzen at Holman-Moody, was the 55th Grand National triumph of his career. It also pushed King Richard past his father, Lee, as NASCAR's all-time race winner. Petty went on to win another 145 times before retiring in 1992, as the first with 200 NASCAR Grand National Cup victories. It's a mark that will likely never be broken.

407 NASCAR fans will debate any "greatest-ever" fact pertaining to their sport except one: Richard Petty's 1967 Grand National campaign. Petty and his blue No. 43 Plymouth posted the most prolific season ever in Grand National history by winning a staggering 27 times in 48 events. That total includes 10-straight victories midway through the season, with both the number of wins and victories in a row still NASCAR single-season records. Petty's 2.1 average starting position and 5.0 season finishing average earned him his second Grand National championship by a massive 6,028-point margin over James Hylton.

408 Despite winning 31 of 49 NASCAR GN events, Plymouth did not win the 1967 NASCAR Manufacturers' Championship. That honor went to Ford, which scored just 10 wins on the season.

409 *Sports Illustrated*, an icon of the American magazine industry, featured NASCAR driver Curtis Turner in its February 29, 1968 issue in a story titled *"King of the Wild Road."* The story, written by Kim Chapin, details Turner's exploits as a moonshine runner and bootlegger during his teenage years and his rise to racing legend. The photo of Turner on the front cover (a low-angle shot of him in a hot red cockpit) marks the first time a stock car driver is featured on the cover.

410 ABC Television dabbled in NASCAR coverage beginning in 1962 with coverage of the Daytona 500 on Wide World of Sports. Just days before the close of the decade, the network announced that it reached a contract with NASCAR to telecast 9 Grand National races in 1970 with an option for 26 more in 1971. The $1.5 million contract tops the $1 million deal reached between the United States Auto Club and independent television network TVS for 10 championship races in 1970.

411 After Ford Motor Company showed up at Atlanta in March 1969 with its new, more aerodynamic Ford Torino and Mercury Cyclone models, Dodge shifted its NASCAR program into high gear with the development of the Dodge Daytona winged car. By April 13, Dodge engineers and Creative Industries (a design firm long associated with Chrysler Corporation concept cars) unveiled a prototype of the Dodge Daytona and announced that the car would debut at Talladega in September. That meant Creative Industries had to convert 500 Dodge Charger R/Ts into Daytona models by September 1 to be eligible for NASCAR competition. Creative Designs met the deadline and the Daytona was introduced as planned, winning the first time out in the Talladega 500 September 14, 1969, just six months after the launch of the project.

412 Bobby Isaac closed the decade on a high note by winning 20 Grand National pole positions in 1969. A total of 14 of Isaac's poles came on paved tracks with three each on superspeedways and dirt tracks. This includes the pole at Alabama International Motor Speedway despite the fact that Isaac only qualified seventh for the first Talladega 500. The pole was awarded to Isaac after the first six qualifiers withdrew from the race as part of the PDA boycott. Isaac finished fourth in the race.

413 Greenville, South Carolina, driver Jimmy Vaughn drove his 1968 Chevy Camaro to a 14th-place finish in the Bama 400 Grand Touring Series race at Alabama International Motor Speedway September 13, 1969. He was down 25 laps, earning $600 for the finish. The next day, Vaughn drove the same Camaro to a seventh-place finish in the Talladega 500 Grand National race. Vaughn was the highest finishing GT replacement entry in the race. He was 29 laps behind winner Richard Brickhouse at the finish, earning $2,000 in prize money. Afterward, Vaughn indicated he had run all 281 laps (747.46 miles) over two days on the same set of tires.

414 Just six years after Fred Lorenzen became the first Grand National driver to win $100,000 in a season, David Pearson was the first to bank more than $200,000 in a single GN year. Pearson collected $229,670 for winning the 1969 Grand National title (nearly triple the amount he earned for his first GN championship in 1966) and nearly $100,000 more than Richard Petty earned for his runner-up finish in the 1969 season points race.

Chapter 5

The 1970s: Birth of the Modern Era

If you fell asleep in 1968 and woke up four years later in 1972, you were greeted by a very different world than the one you left.

Man had walked on the moon not once, but so many times that NASA was shutting down the program. More incredibly, the Beatles had broken up (a couple of years prior) and worse, all your Fab Four record albums had been rendered somewhat obsolete with the wide-spread acceptance of eight-track and cassette tapes. The first "pay television" cable station, HBO, was launched in 1972. Meanwhile, typewriters were quickly being replaced at work and home as computers showed significant integration into everyday life, especially after the first "electronic mail" messages were transmitted in 1972.

There was a dark side to this progressive new decade. America was in a financial and philosophical funk in the early 1970s. The average worker grossed just under $9,500 a year. Meanwhile, the seemingly unending Vietnam conflict early in the decade polarized popular opinion while the Watergate scandal and subsequent resignation of President Richard Nixon divided ranks of the populace in the latter half.

The uneasy financial and political times, and growth of government watchdog scrutiny of all things, including American business, had a massive impact on U.S. automakers.

Cale Yarborough (11) and Benny Parsons (72) lead the field to a restart during the 1978 Daytona 500. (Photo Courtesy of General Motors)

When you dozed off in 1968, Detroit was drunk with horsepower as a wide array of muscle cars sped along American highways. The Hemi 'Cuda, Challenger, Road Runner and Charger, along with the Chevelle, Camaro, Mustang, Firebird, and GTO big-block asphalt-eaters ruled the day. When you came to in 1972, they were all but dead, on life support thanks to government intervention in automobile safety and pollution.

With crusading politicians such as Ralph Nader, and new government entities including the Environmental Protection Agency leading the way, the automobile industry was the target of a very public battle for environmental and safety accountability. Detroit's response was to ditch the high-horsepower flashy muscle of the 1960s in favor of drab, quirky, and safer low-performance cars including the Chevy Vega, Ford Pinto, and AMC's Gremlin and Pacer.

The public hated the lackluster offerings. Combined with low pay and the subsequent energy embargo in 1974, American car sales dropped from 10 to 12 million annually in 1970 to 1973 to less than 9 million in both 1974 and 1975.

None of this was good news for an aging Bill France Sr. and NASCAR. His sport was under financial duress before Ford and Chrysler joined General Motors in cutting team factory support programs prior to the start of 1971 season. Financially strapped teams started dropping out. Top stars were on the sidelines too. NASCAR was in trouble. Fortunately, so was the tobacco industry.

The U.S. government watchdogs had their eye on the smokes folks for a long time. In the late 1960s, the government required all cigarette manufacturers to post warning labels on their packaging as medical science began discovering the link between tobacco products and cancer. In the 1970s, additional steps were taken against the tobacco industry, the harshest being the banning of all television and radio advertising of tobacco products and requiring minnimum-age purchase restrictions.

While seemingly unrelated, government intervention of the American car and tobacco industries converged to present an opportunity for NASCAR. Searching for new ways to sell its products to the public after the media ban, the R.J. Reynolds Tobacco Company redistributed some of its more-than-$500 million annual marketing/advertising budget to NASCAR in 1971. With Winston cigarettes as its first "title" sponsor, the NASCAR Winston Cup Series was born.

A year later, NASCAR retooled its product with a reduction in races, a new point system, and a significant increase in prize money as Winston's full-blown investment and influence changed the sport of American stock car racing forever.

Amazingly, NASCAR had again dodged The Big One. It not only survived what U.S. historians refer to as the Decade of Malaise, but also managed to grow in national scope and secure its financial future for decades to come.

Somehow, NASCAR managed to take a hard left out of hard times at the corner of Luck and Opportunity Streets in the 1970s.

It was the birth of the Modern Era.

CARS

415 Few individuals had a greater impact on the rules that govern NASCAR vehicles than Bill Gazaway. A former USMC member, Gazaway was instrumental in writing the car and race rules for NASCAR's Winston Cup division as the Competition Director from 1969 through 1987. Among his accomplishments were the stabilization of engine rules in the early 1970s and later, approval

For nearly 20 years, Bill Gazaway served as NASCAR's top official, setting and enforcing the rules. (Photo Courtesy Ed Samples Jr. Collection)

of a single engine (Chevy) for all General Motors NASCAR teams regardless of nameplate. Gazaway also ran events from the tower and had the final say on any post-race technical rules violations. Among his stiffest penalties was a 12-week suspension of driver Keith Davis in 1978 for having a nitrous bottle in his car. Gazaway, who oversaw the downsizing of Winston Cup cars in the early 1980s, instituted restrictor plates on Cup cars at superspeedways prior to his retirement at the end of the 1987 season. He passed away in 2006 at the age of 76.

416 In an effort to ensure the public could continue to purchase the more purpose-built, race-specific cars on the track, NASCAR increased the number of cars needed for homologation to one car for every two dealers for the 1970 season. That meant a brand such as Plymouth, with 3,840 dealers in 1969, had to build and provide 1,920 of Superbirds to meet the edict and have the car remain eligible for Grand National competition. Plymouth responded by building 1,935 of the iconic cars in 1969 with just 93 of them featuring Mopar's famed 426 Hemi engine.

417 With attention to detail and craftsmanship superior to any other chassis manufacturer of the era, Edwin Keith "Banjo" Matthews was NASCAR's premier car builder in the 1970s and 1980s. The former Modified and Cup Series driver fashioned the cars that won 262 of 362 Winston Cup races from 1974 through 1985 and four-straight Cup championships from 1975 through 1978. During the 1978 season, Matthews' cars achieved an unequalled sweep capturing all 30 Winston Cup events. Matthews was inducted into the International Motorsports Hall of Fame at Talladega in 1998, two years after he passed away at the age of 64 from heart disease.

418 After the tire debacle resulting in the Professional Drivers Association (PDA) boycott of the 1969 race at Alabama International Motor Speedway, Goodyear introduced NASCAR's first "slick" at the 1970 Alabama 500. Goodyear had been researching the concept since the mid-1960s and off-season testing at Talladega proved the tires worthy of use in competition.

419 More than a third of the field (14 of 40 starters) in the 1970 World 600 at Charlotte Motor Speedway were Chrysler winged cars. Donnie Allison spoiled the Mopar party by winning the race in his No. 27 Banjo Matthews–tooled Ford Torino.

420 Prior to the Grand National race at Michigan International Speedway, August 16, 1970, NASCAR announced it would employ carburetor restrictor plates for the event. The plates, installed between the carburetor and intake manifold, reduced the venturi opening on a 4-barrel from $1\tfrac{11}{16}$ to $1\tfrac{1}{4}$ inches. Speeds at Michigan dropped more than 5 mph while Talladega saw a dramatic decrease of 13 mph in pole speed (199.658 to 186.834) from the 1970 spring race to the fall event.

421 As stock car racing sped into the 1970s, the United States Auto Club (USAC) was still a threat to NASCAR's goal to be the top sanctioning organization in America. Like NASCAR, USAC had its own star power as Indy Car drivers A. J. Foyt, Johnny Rutherford, Mario Andretti, Bobby and Al Unser, and Parnelli Jones

The Dodge and Plymouth winged cars were raced extensively in the Automobile Racing Club of America (ARCA) and the United States Auto Club (USAC) ranks. Here, Roger McClusky (1) and Don White (3) battle for the lead in the 1970 Miller 200 USAC event at The Milwaukee Mile. (Photo Courtesy Russ Lake)

regularly competed in USAC events at big-league tracks including the Milwaukee Mile and Langhorne Speedway. Similar in specifications to NASCAR stock cars at the time, USAC drivers regularly competed in top NASCAR events, especially at Daytona and Talladega. The battle for managerial control of the Indy Car division between USAC and Championship Auto Racing Teams (CART) all but ended USAC's bid for Stock Car sanctioning supremacy in the late 1970s. The USAC Stock Car division limped through the early 1980s until folding after the 1984 season.

422 The 1970 season proved to be the most successful for Chrysler's winged Dodge Charger Daytona and Plymouth Superbird. The cars combined to win 11 of 18 superspeedway races that season. Petty Enterprises driver Pete Hamilton led the way winning the Daytona 500 and the Alabama and Talladega 500s at Alabama International Motor Speedway.

423 NASCAR's fluctuating engine rules and the costly conversion to the small-block forced Ford and Chrysler to alter their factory-supported Winston Cup team lineups in 1971. Just two Mopars (the Petty Enterprise Plymouths of Richard Petty and Buddy Baker) received factory assistance. Left out were Pete Hamilton, the 1970 Daytona 500 winner, and Bobby Isaac, the 1970 Grand National champion, in addition to several team owners including Cotton Owens and Nord Krauskopf. Ford pulled out completely, financially crippling teams run by the Wood Brothers, Holman-Moody, Junior Johnson, and Banjo Matthews, while sending drivers including Cale Yarborough and Donnie Allison to find rides in the Indy Car ranks.

424 In 1971, the Chrysler winged cars faded from the NASCAR scene nearly as fast as they joined it. The Winged Warriors last appearance was at the 1971 Daytona 500 when Dick Brooks piloted a 305-ci Dodge Charger Daytona to a seventh-place finish.

425 Chrysler's winged cars posted a total of 239 Grand National/ Winston Cup starts (32 drivers) during their brief time in NASCAR. Bobby Allison and Bobby Isaac made the most starts (22 each) with each winning one race. Meanwhile, Richard Petty was the biggest winner, posting 5 victories in 17 starts in Mopar's winged cars.

426 Due to various boycotts and disagreements with NASCAR, the Chevrolet brand was absent from the winner's circle for 207 consecutive races. That winless streak ended July 11, 1971, when Charlie Glotzbach and relief driver Friday Hassler teamed up and drove Richard Howard's 1971 Monte Carlo to victory in the Volunteer 500 at Bristol International Speedway. They led 411 of 500 laps, breaking the streak that started after Bobby Allison's July 11, 1967 victory at the Maine 200 at Oxford Plains Speedway (Maine).

427 On October 13, 1963, Junior Johnson and his Chevrolet drove to a dominating victory in the National 400 at Charlotte Motor Speedway. Little did anyone know that would be Chevrolet's last win on a superspeedway until March 26, 1972, when Bobby Allison captured the Atlanta 500. Allison's 1972 Monte Carlo nipped A. J. Foyt's Wood Brothers Mercury in a photo finish, taking the win by a scant .16 second.

David Pearson's Ford Mustang looks a bit used up after a hard Grand American Series outing. (Photo Courtesy Ed Samples Jr. Collection)

428 Despite a name change to Grand American from the Grand Touring Series, NASCAR's pony car division was all but out of business by the middle of the 1971 season. In an effort to have more race dates, NASCAR allowed the Mustangs, Camaros, Firebirds, and Javelins to compete in all Winston Cup short-track events for the remainder of the season. In his first outing August 6, 1971, Bobby Allison drove a 1970 Mustang to victory in the Myers Brothers Memorial 250-lap event at Bowman Gray Stadium in Winston-Salem, North Carolina. Richard Petty's Plymouth was the only full-size Cup car in the top-7, finishing second as Jim Paschal (Javelin), Buck Baker (Firebird), Dave Marcis (Camaro), Tiny Lund (Camaro), and Wayne Anderson (Mustang) rounded out the pony car club.

429 Window nets made their appearance in the mid 1960s, but they were optional starting with the 1970 season. That changed when Richard Petty crashed on the 176th-lap of the May 9 Rebel 400 at Darlington Raceway. His Plymouth ran head-on into the front-stretch retaining wall, flipping several times. The car came to a rest upside down with Petty's arm and head hanging outside of the car. Almost immediately, NASCAR added window nets to rulebook as a mandatory item.

430 American Motors had a storied history in NASCAR due to its Hudson and Nash roots; however, the company had not fielded a NASCAR winner since the brands merged in 1954. That changed January 21, 1973, when second-year team owner Roger Penske and driver Mark Donohue put an AMC Matador in Victory Lane in the Western 500 at Riverside International Raceway. Donohue dominated the race, leading 138 of the 191. This was due in part to being outfitted with four-wheel disc brakes, a first in a Winston Cup race.

431 Chevrolet drivers had the hot setup for the March 1974, Southeastern 500 at Bristol International Speedway. Cale Yarborough won in a Monte Carlo while Bobby Isaac, Benny Parsons, Bobby Allison, Donnie Allison, Cecil Gordon, Joe Mihalic, James Hylton, Alton Jones, and Coo Coo Marlin took the top-10, all in

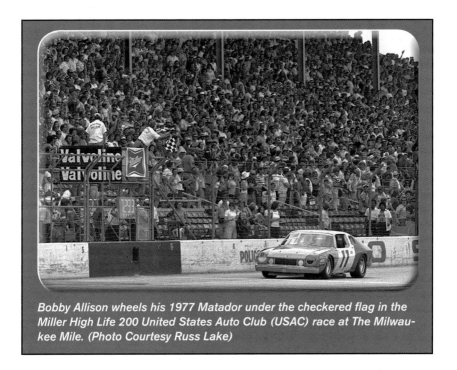

Bobby Allison wheels his 1977 Matador under the checkered flag in the Miller High Life 200 United States Auto Club (USAC) race at The Milwaukee Mile. (Photo Courtesy Russ Lake)

Chevys. The sweep marks the first time a single brand earned the first 10 positions in the 26-year history of NASCAR's top division.

432 After several seasons of changing engine rules, NASCAR said good-bye to the big block for good in 1975 by restricting them to a maximum of 358-ci. The new engines allowed NASCAR to standardize carburetors and remove restrictor plates, for the time being.

433 In an effort to keep costs in check, Goodyear gave free tires to the top qualifiers at all 1975 Winston Cup events. The top-4 qualifiers got five free sets (20 total), with 5th through 8th getting three sets; 9th through 12th earned one set of fresh Goodyear racing tires for a total of 144 on the big tracks. On the short-tracks, the top-5 qualifiers got two sets of tires while 6th through 10th received one set.

434 Ransom E. Olds was one of America's earliest racers and his cars revolutionized stock car racing with the Rocket 88 V-8 engine. Unfortunately, the brand was absent from Victory Lane for nearly 20 seasons before Cale Yarborough won the Western 500 at Riverside International Raceway January 22, 1978. Oldsmobile had not won since May 22, 1959, when Lee Petty wheeled his 1957 Olds to a victory at Southern States Speedway in Charlotte.

435 Winning 16 races and eight pole positions from 1977 through 1979, *Buckshot Bertha* was one of the most iconic cars of the decade. Built by Banjo Matthews and fielded by DiGard Racing, the Monte Carlo is remembered more as a cheat than for its on-track accomplishments. *Bertha* was often equipped with up to 80 pounds of buckshot in the left-side frame rail. Because NASCAR didn't have a mandatory post-race weigh-in, driver Darrell Waltrip just loosened a bolt to opening a hole in the frame, thus allowing the buckshot to drain out of the jack post. The lighter car handled and cornered better, which made things easier on the brakes and tires. It is unclear how many times it was done; the team ceased the practice after nearly getting caught after the Volunteer 500 at Bristol in August 1978. A week later, NASCAR added mandatory weigh-ins to its post-race technical inspections.

436 The 1970s were a bonanza for the Chevrolet, winning 7 of 10 Manufacturers' Championships. Chevy earned the award on the strength of its individual titles in 1972, 1973, 1974, 1976, 1977, 1978, and 1979. Dodge had two Manufacturers' wins in 1970 and 1975, while Plymouth took one in 1971. Ford, which captured seven-straight Manufacturers' crowns from 1963 through 1969, was shut out of battle throughout the 1970s, waiting until the 1992 season to earn its title.

TRACKS

437 In an effort to stave off another strike by the PDA, Bill France Sr. scheduled an Automobile Racing Club of America (ARC) race at Talladega for April 11, 1970. The 50-lap, 133-mile qualifying race was won by Ramo Stott. A total of 19 cars entered the race, assuring France enough cars for the following day's Alabama 500 GN just in case the PDA pulled out as they had in September 1969.

438 A state-of-the-art facility when it opened in 1970, Ontario Motor Speedway played brief but important role in the history of NASCAR by hosting nine Winston Cup events from 1971 through 1980. The track (40 miles east of Los Angeles) broke new ground by introducing many of today's modern amenities such as corporate suites, impact absorbing safety walls and fences, computerized timing and scoring, and enclosed garage areas. It also gave NASCAR, which first raced there February 28, 1971, an extra foothold in the coveted southern California market. A. J. Foyt (1971–1972), Bobby Allison (1974, 1978), and Benny Parsons (1979, 1980) each won two Winston Cup events on the 2.5-mile Ontario Motor Speedway oval. In late 1980, the 800-acre facility was sold to Chevron Land Company, a branch of Chevron Oil Company, for a fraction of its value and was demolished in 1981 at a cost of more than $3 million. Today, the OMS site is bordered by Interstate 10 and a mixed-use commercial and residential development.

439 The 1970 Alabama 500 at Alabama International Motor Speedway drew a crowd estimated at around 36,000. With no exact numbers available, some of the crowd was admitted free; their tickets honored in a special "two-for-one" deal given after 1969's PDA-strike at the Talladega 500 opener.

440 Driving a 1969 Plymouth, Richard Petty won the Home State 200 event at the North Carolina State Fairgrounds Speedway in Raleigh September 30, 1970. Neil Castles, Bobby Isaac, James Hylton, and Cecil Gordon fill in the top-5 of what proves to be the last dirt-track race in the history of the division.

441 Bobby Isaac was all smiles in Victory Lane after piloting his K&K Insurance-sponsored Dodge to a dominating win in the Greenville 200 at Greenville-Pickens Speedway April 10, 1971. Isaac led 181 of 200 laps, beating David Person by 2 laps. The Greenville,

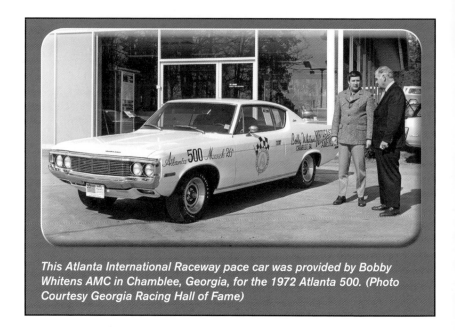

This Atlanta International Raceway pace car was provided by Bobby Whitens AMC in Chamblee, Georgia, for the 1972 Atlanta 500. (Photo Courtesy Georgia Racing Hall of Fame)

South Carolina, half-mile oval event is the first Winston Cup race televised live flag to flag by ABC Sports.

442 On July 11, 1971, Charlie Glotzbach and relief driver Friday Hassler won the Volunteer 500 race at Bristol International Speedway. The event took a record time of 2 hours 38 minutes with a record average speed of 101.074 mph. It is the first time (and to date the only time) a 500-lap race at Bristol is run caution-free.

443 After staging 48 events in 1971, NASCAR announced the 1972 season would have just 30 events (31 were actually run). For the first time no dirt tracks or tracks less than a half-mile are on the schedule. In addition, all races are a minimum of 250 miles or more with the two 125-mile qualifying races at Daytona no longer part of the points race. The schedule reduction, as part of the new NASCAR's new sponsorship by R.J. Reynolds Tobacco Company, is hailed as the birth of NASCAR's Modern Era.

444 Even before the 1972 schedule "rollback," smaller tracks and those with short-distance races saw the handwriting on the wall in 1971. That year, no races of 250 miles or less in length were officially on the schedule although all events were awarded championship points toward the title. The move came as part of Winston's desire to concentrate on high-profile events in major markets and set the stage for the schedule overhaul and the disenfranchisement of the dirt and smaller paved ovals from stock car racing's top series in 1972.

445 Located in Malta, New York, the Albany-Saratoga Speedway was a prime example of the type of short-track "spun out" of the scheduling mix in 1972. The .362-mile paved bullring hosted Grand National events in 1970 and 1971, with Richard Petty winning both. While NASCAR was concentrating on superspeedway racing, the Empire State track continued, hosting local and regional short-track events. This tradition continues today on the now-4/10-mile dirt oval running weekly Modified, Sportsman, Pro Stock, Street Stock, and 4-cylinder Division racing.

446 Despite hosting just three top-level NASCAR races (the last July 9, 1970) Thompson Speedway (Connecticut) has earned a place as one of NASCAR's busiest tracks. In all, more than 160 NASCAR-sanctioned races have been held at the .625-mile oval. The track was billed as the first paved auto-racing oval when constructed in the late 1930s. It has been a part of the Whelan Modified Tour since the inception of the series in 1985, hosting more than 130 ground-pounding events. Over the last 50 years, nearly every Modified driver has participated in its most-noted events: the Spring Icebreaker and the Fall World Series of Speedway Racing, a weekend of competition hosting up to 15 different divisions.

447 Prior to the 1973 season, Nashville Fairgrounds Speedway underwent its second major renovation in four years by reducing the banking from a steep 36 degrees to a more manageable 18. The adjustment, along with expansion of the track to .596-miles in length, gave the facility (originally opened in 1904) the layout that exists today. Cale Yarborough dominated the first Winston Cup event on that new layout by leading all but 4 of 420 laps in the 1973

Music City 420. The Richard Howard-owned Chevy coasted home two laps ahead of runner-up Benny Parsons.

448 The first "big one" at Alabama International Motor Speedway occurred on Lap 9 of the May 6, 1973, Winston 500 when Ramo Stott's 1972 Mercury blew an engine and 21 cars wrecked behind him on the oil-slick track. Wendell Scott was the most seriously injured with broken ribs and a cracked pelvis while Earl Brooks was treated for a broken arm. David Pearson and his Wood Brothers Mercury won the race as only 17 of the 60 starters completed the 188-lap event on the 2.66-mile oval.

449 With parent company American Raceways, Inc. (ARI) on the brink of financial failure, Michigan International Speedway was saved when Roger Penske purchased the 2.0-mile oval in the

Bobby Allison's crew chief Herb Nab (second from left) gets a hug from the trophy girl after leading Allison's team to the pit stop contest victory prior to the American 500 at Rockingham. (T. Taylor Warren Photo Courtesy of J. Murrey Atkins Library Special Collections and University Archives, the University of North Carolina at Charlotte)

spring of 1973 for $2 million. Over the next 25 years, Penske invested millions in the "new" Michigan Speedway with seating expanded from 25,000 to 125,000, new garages, terrace seating, hospitality suites, and several administrative and maintenance buildings.

450 Three days before the August 12, 1973, Talladega 500 at Alabama International Motor Speedway, Dick Brooks didn't have a ride. But when NASCAR questioned Jimmy Crawford's experience to compete at Talladega, Crawford and his brother Peter tagged Brooks to pilot the family-owned Mickey Mouse-sponsored No. 22 Plymouth. Brooks started 24th in the 50-car field and went on to win by 7.2 seconds over Buddy Baker and his K&K Insurance Dodge Charger. The victory is Brooks' only Winston Cup win in 358 career starts. The win stands as the only triumph for the College Park, Georgia–based team in 23 Winston Cup races.

451 David Pearson scored 101 Grand National/Winston Cup career wins, but none more dominating than his April 15, 1973, win in the Rebel 500 at Darlington Raceway. Pearson dominated the 40-car field winning by a staggering 13 laps over runner-up Benny Parsons. The margin of victory ranks as the second most lopsided finish in Darlington history, just one lap behind Ned Jarrett's 14-lap win over the field in the 1965 Southern 500.

452 When the Organization of Petroleum Exporting Countries (OPEC) restricted oil sales/exports to the United States in 1974, NASCAR and other professional sports organizations were challenged by the Federal Energy Office to voluntarily reduce energy consumption by 25 percent. Bill France Sr. "suggested" that all NASCAR tracks look to reduce the length of their events by 10 percent. In response, the first 15 races, through the June 16 Motor State 400 at Michigan, complied. NASCAR then went back to full-length races beginning with the July Firecracker 400 at Daytona and throughout the remainder of the season.

453 In an effort to appease the U.S. government and show an effort to combat the energy crisis, NASCAR reduced practice for the

1974 Daytona from eight to five days while limiting each entry to 30 gallons of fuel for each practice. Meanwhile, both 125-mile Daytona 500 qualifying events were cut by five laps to 112.5-miles in length. Finally, NASCAR cut the first 50 miles (the initial 20 laps) to reduce fuel consumption during the event. Despite the reduction to a 450-mile race NASCAR still referred to it as the Daytona 500. Richard Petty captured his fifth Daytona 500 victory as Richard Childress finished last falling out on the second lap of the 1974 "Daytona 450."

454 The energy crisis had a chilling effect on attendance for the 1974 Daytona 500. A crowd estimated at 85,000 watched the race, down from over 103,000 the previous year. Considering that the price of gas had more than doubled and the government had ordered the nationwide closing of gas stations on Sundays, it was still considered to be a good turnout.

455 Opened in 1969 and plagued with financial woes since starting construction, Texas World Speedway fell victim to the 1974 energy crisis. The track, which previously hosted seven NASCAR events (Five Grand National/Cup and two NASCAR West), was closed for two years due to the gas shortage before reopening with the Texas 150, a USAC Indy Car event, August 1, 1976. NASCAR returned for the College Station oval in 1979 with Darrell Waltrip winning the Texas 400. Benny Parsons captured the final Winston Cup race at the track on June 7, 1981. The track has remained open for testing and is scheduled for development as a housing tract.

456 The entire state of Wisconsin let out a cheer when Wausau, Wisconsin, native Dave Marcis scored his first Winston Cup victory September 28, 1975. Driving the K&K Insurance Dodge, Marcis battled brake problems throughout the race but was took the lead for good with 40 laps remaining in the Old Dominion 500 at Martinsville Speedway. The victory, which earned Marcis $14,500, was his 223rd career NASCAR start.

457 NASCAR's return to Texas World Speedway in 1979 was met with indifference from the ticket-buying public as only 11,500 fans watched Darrell Waltrip beat Bobby Allison, Buddy Baker, Cale Yarborough, and rookie Terry Labonte to the checkered flag. The track had 23,000 numbered seats with an additional 10,000 general-admission seats in the lower grandstand, hillside turn areas, and an infield that was twice the size of the 65,615-seat Texas Stadium, home of the Dallas Cowboys.

458 Opened in 1971 with a USAC IndyCar race won by Mark Donohue, Pocono International Raceway (Pennsylvania) hosted its first Winston Cup event August 4, 1974. The Purolator 500, won by Richard Petty, marked the beginning of a relationship that has seen it host at least one top-division race every year (two races each season since 1982). Billed "the Tricky Triangle" soon after it opened, the 2.5-mile paved oval featured three distinct turns, each modeled after those at Trenton Speedway (Turn 1), Indianapolis Motor Speedway (Turn 2, or the Tunnel Turn), and the Milwaukee Mile (Turn 3).

459 In one of the greatest comebacks in Winston Cup history, Richard Petty rallies from six laps down to win the 1975 Delaware 500 at Dover Downs International Speedway. Petty's "miracle" was aided in part when Buddy Arrington (more than 50 laps down at the time) intentionally stopped his car on the track in an effort to bring out a late-race caution flag. NASCAR refuses to throw the yellow flag and Arrington drives to the pits, only to return to the track and park in Turn 3. This time, NASCAR puts the race under caution allowing Petty to motor by leader Dick Brooks and Benny Parsons on the restart, (the only other two cars on the lead lap) with less than 10 laps remaining. Meanwhile, Arrington (who had purchased a used race hauler from Petty during the week of the race) drove his car back to the pits where he was greeted by NASCAR officials and promptly parked for the day. Arrington is credited with 18th in the final running order, 61 laps behind Petty.

460 In his 37th Winston Cup race, Neil Bonnett scored his first career victory September 11, 1977, out-dueling Richard Petty in the Capital City 400 at Richmond Fairgrounds Raceway. This is a first for new team owner Jim Stacy. Afterward, Bonnett gives much of the credit to crew chief Harry Hyde for coaching him over the radio lap-by-lap throughout the final circuits of the 400-lap event on the .542-mile paved oval.

461 A win at the 1978 Talladega 500 at Alabama International Motor Speedway provided a pair of firsts for team owner Harry Ranier and his driver, Lenny Pond. The victory gave Ranier, fielding just 36 Winston Cup entries in the past 11 seasons, the first of 24 career division wins as an owner. Meanwhile, Pond (who led nine times for 22 laps) took the lead with just 5 laps remaining, beating Bobby Allison to the checkered flag by less than two car lengths. It was the first and only victory for Pond in 234 Cup division career starts.

462 On Lap 166 of the 1978 Southern 500 at Darlington Raceway, a violent crash took out the cars of Grant Adcox, D. K. Ulrich, David Pearson, and Coo Coo Marlin. While all drivers are uninjured, the same could not be said for their cars, particularly Ulrich's, shedding nearly one whole side of the body. The damage revealed a nitrous oxide bottle and earned Ulrich a $2,000 fine and suspension for the final eight races of the 1978 season.

463 Today's "Clash Unlimited at Daytona" debuted as the "Busch Clash" February 11, 1979. The cash-rich event featured nine pole winners from the 1978 Winston Cup season and was televised live on CBS. The field was set by blind draw with Benny Parsons selecting the lucky pole position pill for the 20-lap race. Buddy Baker, driving a Harry Ranier Oldsmobile, took the lead late in the race and rolled to a $50,000 first-place payday. The 50-mile event ran caution-free taking just 15 minutes 26 seconds to complete. J. D. McDuffie, who captured the pole for the second 1978 Dover event to qualify for the 1979 Busch Clash, finished ninth (last) in the event. McDuffie's $10,000 payout is nearly double the amount he banked in any of his 30 starts during the regular 1978 Cup season.

464 CBS Television couldn't have dreamed up a better outcome when it broadcast the first flag-to-flag coverage of the Daytona 500 at Daytona International Speedway. The February 18, 1979 race drew a staggering Nielsen rating of 10.5 (approximately 16 million viewers). This was due in large part to a large snowstorm hitting the northern part of the United States. The race, punctuated by a battle for the lead between Cale Yarborough and Donnie Allison culminated in a crash on the final lap and a fist fight between the two afterward. The Nielsen meter pegged a 13.5 rating in the final half hour of the telecast. The epic television numbers, and the buzz generated by among the public and media proved to be a giant boost for NASCAR and its efforts to gain widespread acceptance in the mainstream sports world.

465 Veteran short-track racer Dave Watson (a 33-year-old NASCAR rookie in 1979) was leading the Atlanta 500 at Atlanta International Raceway until he ran out of gas on Lap 123. As Watson coasted toward pit road, tragedy struck. While trying to restart the car, the rear end of the car broke and sent his Chevrolet spinning into the pit box striking 18-year-old jack man Dennis Wade, who later died at an Atlanta hospital. Watson immediately parked the car, finishing 32nd in the race. The Milton, Wisconsin, driver continued his Midwest short-track career, later racing in the SCCA Trans-Am Series, but never ran another NASCAR race after that fatal day.

466 Twenty years prior to the opening of Las Vegas Motor Speedway in 1996, Craig Road Speedway was the place to race in "Sin City". The quarter-mile paved oval was a NASCAR staple hosting nine Winston West events from 1971 through 1979. The track, which fueled interest in NASCAR on the West Coast, was a proving ground for many NASCAR drivers including Ernie Irvan, Derrike Cope, and Ron Hornaday Jr. Craig Road Speedway closed in 1982 and now sits empty in the Nevada desert.

467 Neil Bonnett captured the pole for the 1979 National 500 at Charlotte Motor Speedway with a lap of 164.304 mph. His effort marked the 13th-straight Cup Series pole position won by the Wood Brothers team at Charlotte. The streak began when David Pearson grabbed the top spot for the 1973 National 500. The 13-consecutive poles by a team at a single track stands as an all-time milestone and is considered one of NASCAR's most unbreakable records.

PIT PASS

468 On November 30, 1969, driver Charlie Glotzbach was shot twice by a former employee of his construction firm. Doctors removed the bullet from Glotzbach's stomach but left the slug in his shoulder as it presented no danger. Glotzbach returned to NASCAR competition the following February and won his 125-mile qualifying race for the 1970 Daytona 500.

469 Richard Howard was a self-made man who at one time or another had interests in a furniture company, hardware store, bowling establishments, a restaurant chain, and supply business. He was also an original investor in Charlotte Motor Speedway. When the facility declared bankruptcy in December 1961, Howard helped reorganize the track's finances and was named general manager in 1964, holding the position until 1976. Howard, who served as the Chairman of the NASCAR Television Committee in the early 1970s, was instrumental in arranging early sponsorship discussions with R.J. Reynolds Tobacco Company. Howard played a large part in bringing Chevrolet back to NASCAR by fielding non-factory-supported BowTie entries for Charlie Gloztbach in both 1971 Winston Cup events at Charlotte. Howard posted 111 Cup starts as an owner, winning 21 times from 1970 through 1981.

470 Inman, South Carolina, driver James Hylton won his first career Grand National event March 1, 1970, at Richmond Fairgrounds Raceway. Hylton rallied his Ford from six laps down to the lead when pacesetter Richard Petty's car suffered electrical problems. Back on track, Petty made up three laps, but ultimately finished 15 seconds behind Hylton at the checkered flag. The Richmond 500 victory was Hylton's 187th career Grand National start, paying $5,195 in prize money.

471 After driving a Ford throughout the 1969 season, Richard Petty returned to the Plymouth camp for the 1970 season. The first victory back in his No. 43 Petty Blue Mopar was the sixth race of the season in the Carolina 500 at North Carolina Motor Speedway. Petty won by three laps despite spinning out twice during the 492-circuit event on the 1.017-mile Rockingham oval.

472 Minutes after taking off from Dubous-Jefferson Airport in Reynoldsville, Pennsylvania, Curtis Turner, piloting the Aero Commander 500 airplane, crashed into a mountainside.

En route to Roanoke, Virginia, both Turner and professional golfer, Clarence King were killed instantly in the October 4, 1970, crash. One of NASCAR's greatest early legends, Turner was just 46. He was enshrined in the NASCAR Hall of Fame in 2016.

473 Unlike today's championship bonuses that are paid at the end of the season, the first Winston Cup points fund in 1971 was

In an effort to contain the driver in the cockpit during a violent wreck, window nets became common in NASCAR during the 1980s. Shown is an early version of the device on one of Richard Petty's Winston Cup cars. (John Close Photo)

parceled out in three installments. The $100,000 kitty paid $25,000 to the top-10 drivers in the championship standings after the World 600 at Charlotte Motor Speedway in May. Another $25,000 was then paid after the Southern 500 Labor Day classic at Darlington Raceway. The lion's share ($50,000) was distributed to the top-20 drivers in the final season standings. Richard Petty, the 1971 Winston Cup champion, took home the bulk of the money, pocketing $40,000.

474 In his first five races at Riverside International Raceway, Ray Elder posted a less-than-impressive average 23rd-place finish. That all changed for the Carruthers, California, driver January 10, 1971, after qualifying third in his family-owned Dodge and winning the 1971 season-opening Motor Trend 500 at RIR. Elder made 19 of his 31 career starts at Riverside, capturing his second (and only other Cup victory), in the 1972 Golden State 400.

475 A field of just 17 cars took the green flag for the Asheville 300 at New Asheville Speedway May 21, 1971. That number thinned out on Lap 1 after James Hylton and Neil Castles parked their cars protesting NASCAR's purse and appearance money structure for non-factory backed (independent) teams. By Lap 125, independents John Sears, Bill Shirley, Frank Warren, and Earl Brooks had also parked in protest. When Dick May rolled in at Lap 155, just five cars were on the track to run the final 145 laps. May is credited with sixth in the final running order while Richard Petty won two laps ahead of Elmo Langley.

476 Since the early 1970s, NASCAR has protected its series and sponsors by granting exclusive rights to those supporting the sport. The practice of not allowing sponsorship from direct competitors began in 1972 after British tobacco company Viceroy began sponsoring teams. Marlboro immediately ended its sponsorship of the United States Auto Club Championship Car Series (Indy). This practice is often referred to as the "Viceroy Rules."

477 NASCAR introduced a new points system for the 1972 season, rewarding both winning and completed laps. The system gave 100 points to the winner of each race, dropping two points for each following position. In addition, fractions of points were awarded based on laps and on track size. For example, competitors were awarded .25 points for each lap completed on tracks under 1 mile, while receiving .50 for each lap completed on a 1-mile oval. Darlington, at 1.3 miles, had its own scale (0.70 per lap) while the 2-mile Michigan and Texas World Speedways awarded 1.0 points per lap. Tracks 1.5 miles in length earned .75 points per circuit, with Daytona and Talladega (each 2.5-miles or longer) garnered 1.25 points per lap. The convoluted system lasted just two seasons before being overhauled prior to the 1974 Winston Cup.

478 Ten-year NASCAR veteran Friday Hassler was killed on Lap 19 of the first of two qualifying races for the 1972 Daytona 500. The February 17 multi-car accident on Daytona's back straight resulted in the 17th fatality in NASCAR history. Hassler, (an independent driver with 135 career NASCAR top-tier division starts from 1960 through 1971), was extremely well liked and highly regarded by his fellow competitors. Hassler was 36.

479 After a disappointing 33rd-place finish in the 1973 Daytona 500 due to engine failure, David Pearson won the next five Winston Cup Series races (Rockingham, Atlanta, Darlington, Martinsville, and Talladega) that season. Pearson later drove the No. 21 Wood Brothers Mercury to four consecutive wins (Dover, Michigan, Daytona, and Atlanta) and his 1973 win total of 11 was 5 more than any other driver and a 10 more than 1973 Cup champion Benny Parsons. Pearson, however, finished 13th in the final standings, competing in just 18 of the 28 races that year.

480 Cale Yarborough competed in 11 United States Auto Club IndyCar events in 1971 and 1972 before returning to the Winston Cup ranks in 1973. In his fifth race back, Yarborough steered his Kar-Kare Chevrolet to the pole and a win in the Southeastern 500 at Bristol International Raceway. Yarborough led all 500 laps, scoring his 15th career Winston Cup victory. Yarborough's wire-to-wire win was the first time a driver led every lap in a top-tier

With virtually no Detroit Big Three factory support of NASCAR in the early 1970s, top drivers, including Donnie Allison, turned to Indy cars. Here is Allison and his No. 81 Ford Coyote T/C after qualifying 20th for the May 29, 1971, Indy 500. Allison finished sixth. (Photo Courtesy Russ Lake)

event since Darel Dieringer's domination of the Gwyn Staley 400 at North Wilkesboro Speedway (North Carolina) April 16, 1967.

481 After two years of tabulating points based on finishing positions and completed laps, NASCAR re-engineered its points system for the fourth time in eight seasons. The new 1974 system awarded points based on prize money. With a formula even more convoluted than prior system, a driver's total season winnings were multiplied by the number of races started and divided by 1,000 to determine the final tally. Not only was it a math nightmare, but it produced unexpected consequences; winning or finishing well in a big-money race totally skewed the championship battle. Not surprisingly, Richard Petty and Cale Yarborough (first and second in the cash-heavy season-opening Daytona 500) led the chase all year and finished 1–2 in points. The system was dropped after the 1974 season for yet another new points program for 1975.

482 An administrative assistant who joined R.J. Reynolds Tobacco Company in 1971, T. Wayne Robertson's first duty for the company's new Winston Cup program was as a show-car driver. Robertson rose through the ranks, becoming president of the Sports Marketing Enterprises (SME) division, managing multiple marketing and sponsorship programs, including NASCAR, for the tobacco giant. While the creation of "The Winston" All-Star race in 1985 is most visible contribution to NASCAR, his efforts as a lobbyist helped keep the government at bay in its attempt to further restrict tobacco sports sponsorship during the 1970s and 1980s. On January 14, 1998, Robertson was one of six people killed when their 28-foot aluminum boat collided with an oilrig vessel near the Vermillion Parish Intracoastal Waterway 110-miles west of New Orleans. Robertson was 47.

483 Prior to the start of the 1973 season, Richard Petty announced he would no longer be a member of the Professional Driver's Association (PDA). Petty, as the first president of the group in 1969, led the famed Talladega boycott that season. With a dwindling membership of approximately 30 drivers over several divisions and its brightest star no longer associated with the group, the PDA shut down soon after Petty's resignation.

484 On April 29, 1973, David Pearson rallied his Wood Brothers Mercury from two laps down to a win in the Virginia 500 at Martinsville Speedway. Cale Yarborough's pit stop under a green flag conditions allowed Pearson to get back on the lead lap. Moments later, NASCAR is forced to throw a yellow flag to allow an ambulance to transport an infield spectator suffering a heart attack. During the caution, Pearson pits for fresh rubber and outruns Yarborough over the final 60 laps to win the event by 12 seconds.

485 After years of tearing up the southern Sportsman Late Model Stock Car ranks, 33-year old Harry Gant made his Winston Cup debut October 7, 1973, in a Junie Donlevy–owned Ford, taking an 11th-place finish in the National 500 at Charlotte Motor Speedway. Gant made just 12 starts in six seasons (1973–1978) before getting his first full-time shot in Cup in 1979. Driving for team owner Jack Beebe, Gant posted five top-10 efforts, finishing fourth in the 1979 NASCAR Rookie of the Year standings behind Dale Earnhardt, Joe Millikan, and Terry Labonte.

486 Northeast Modified and Sprint Car legend Dick "Toby" Tobias is said to have won hundreds of open-wheel races and is credited as one of the first to construct a tubular, non-production car-based chassis for the Modified division. Tobias made his first and only Winston Cup start in the Delaware 500 at Dover Downs International Speedway September 16, 1973. Driving for Norris Reed, Tobias' 1971 Mercury suffered an engine failure on Lap 50 saddling the Lebanon, Pennsylvania, driver with a 38th-place finish. On June 23, 1978, Tobias was killed in a USAC Sprint Car race when his car flipped and landed cage down on top of the concrete retaining wall.

487 The worst instance of tampering in the garage area occurred prior to the August 11, 1974, Talladega 500 at Alabama International Motor Speedway. The morning of the race, crews discovered more than two-dozen cars had been sabotaged during the night. Tires, fan belts, hoses, brake, and oil lines had been cut while gas tanks were contaminated with lead pellets and sand. In addition, suspension pieces were purposely loosened. NASCAR allowed teams to fix their cars before the race and scheduled two competition cautions that allowed crews to re-check their vehicles. No one was ever caught.

488 Bobby Allison was supposed to take home $15,125 for driving his AMC Matador to a win in the *Los Angeles Times* 500 at Ontario Motor Speedway November 24, 1974. After the race, his Roger Penske mount was found to have illegal roller tappets. Allison was allowed to keep the win, but NASCAR issued a record fine of $9,100 leaving Allison just $6,025 for the victory.

489 Prior to the 1975 season, Bob Latford, longtime publicist and statistician at Daytona International Speedway, suggested a new points system in which equal points are awarded for each event

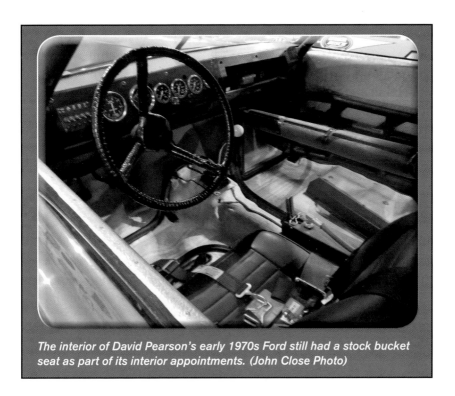

The interior of David Pearson's early 1970s Ford still had a stock bucket seat as part of its interior appointments. (John Close Photo)

regardless of track size or race purse. Latford detailed the new points system (the fourth in five years) to public relations director Joe Whitlock on a stack of cocktail napkins at the Boot Hill Saloon in Daytona. The plan would award 175 points to the winner of each race, dropping five points per position through 5th place, four points per position from 6th to 10th-place, and three points per position throughout the remainder of the field. With Whitlock's encouragement, Latford presents the plan to NASCAR and sponsor Winston who implement it. Latford's plan proves to be viable, ending years of revisions to determine a champion. It remained in place until the 2010.

490 With NASCAR's biggest team owners awash in red ink, the sanctioning body institutes an Awards and Achievement Plan for each top-4 team by brand for the 1975 season. What is basically appearance money and the birth of today's "Winner's Circle" program, NASCAR offers to pay Petty Enterprises (Richard Petty Plymouth), Bud Moore Racing (Buddy Baker Ford), K&K

Insurance Team (Dave Marcus Dodge), and Junior Johnson Racing (Cale Yarborough Chevrolet) $3,000 in bonus cash for each super-speedway appearance and $2,000 for short-track events. In return, the four organizations must guarantee they'll enter all 30 Cup races that season. Both Petty and K&K agree, but the sponsor-less teams of Johnson and Moore decline. Any teams and drivers outside the top-4 and A&A plan are left to work their best deal with track promoters to remain financially solvent throughout the season.

491 In 16 seasons, Ed Negre fielded 294 Winston Cup entries as a car owner. On May 25, 1975, the Kelso, Washington, native gave unheralded driver Dale Earnhardt a seat for the World 600 at Charlotte Motor Speedway. Earnhardt, the son of local racing legend Ralph Earnhardt, started his 10,000 RPM Speed Equipment Dodge 33rd and finished 22nd, still running at the finish but 45 laps behind winner Richard Petty.

492 August 16, 1975, became one of the saddest days in NASCAR history when one of its most likable drivers, DeWayne "Tiny" Lund, died in an accident in the Talladega 500 at Alabama International Motor Speedway. His first Winston Cup event since the 1973 World 600 at Charlotte, Lund lost control of his Dodge on Lap 7, and was T-boned in the driver's door by rookie Terry Link. Minutes after the wreck in the track's infield care center, Lund was pronounced dead of massive internal injuries.

493 Who finished third in the inaugural 1959 Daytona 500 behind Lee Petty and Johnny Beauchamp? The answer to this trivia question is driver Charlie Griffith. The Daytona finish was the best of his career, which ended on Lap 46 of the September 21, 1975, Wilkes 400 at North Wilkesboro Speedway when the Chattanooga, Tennessee, driver was black-flagged for being too slow.

494 Janet Guthrie ran her first Winston Cup event, the World 600 at Charlotte Motor Speedway on May 30, 1976, having made her Indy Car debut in Rolla Volstedt's Bryant Cooling Offenhauser at Trenton Speedway just three weeks earlier. Guthrie stomped the

Lynda Ferreri–owned Chevy to a 15th-place finish. Guthrie, who went on to make 33 Cup Series starts through the 1980 season, is the first woman to compete in a Winston Cup race since Goldie Parsons finished 14th in the Tidewater 300 at Dog Track Speedway in Moyock, North Carolina, November 7, 1965.

495 After Charlotte Motor Speedway general manager Humpy Wheeler arranges for Janet Guthrie to compete in the 1976 World 600, he swings a deal for Lynda Ferreri to become Guthrie's car owner. Ferreri, Vice-President at First Union Bank in Charlotte, paid $21,000 via cashier's check to secure ownership of a Hoss Ellington–tooled Chevrolet. Over the next three seasons, Ferreri is listed as the car owner for Guthrie in 31 Winston Cup events. Their best finish together is the 1977 Volunteer 500 at Bristol International Speedway (Virginia) when Guthrie and the No. 68 Kelly Girl Chevrolet arrive home sixth.

496 When A. J. Foyt, Darrell Waltrip, and Dave Marcis captured the top-3 spots for the 1976 Daytona 500 running nearly 10 mph faster than the rest of the field, NASCAR figured something was up and they were right. Foyt's Hoss Ellington–owned Chevrolet and Waltrip's DiGard Chevrolet had been outfitted with fuel lines suspected of containing nitrous oxide while Marcis' Dodge had an illegal radiator incorporating a moveable air deflector. Their qualifying efforts were nullified, but they were allowed to compete in the event. Foyt posted the best finish of the trio at 22nd with a blown engine; Waltrip was 32nd, also suffering engine failure. Marcis was the only one running at the end, at a distant 27th, 88 laps off the pace set by winner David Pearson.

497 O. Bruton Smith made countless decisions throughout his NASCAR Hall of Fame career, but perhaps the most important one was in January 1976 when he hired Howard Augustus "Humpy" Wheeler as the general manager of Charlotte Motor Speedway. The choice paid massive dividends for Smith and the track as, over the next four decades, Wheeler became a top promoter in all professional sports, not just auto racing.

498 The movie *Jaws* (a giant killer shark terrorizing an oceanfront resort town) became a cultural sensation when it premiered in 1975. After the 1977 Southern 500 at Darlington, Cale Yarborough hung the moniker "Jaws" on Darrell Waltrip, a snide reference to Waltrip's constant banter with competitors and the media. Charlotte Motor Speedway master showman Humpy Wheeler pounced on the feud between the drivers and to promote interest in the upcoming National 500 event, purchased a dead shark and put a chicken in its mouth (At the time, Yarborough's sponsor was Holly Farms Chicken). The dead animals were loaded on a flatbed trailer and paraded around the Charlotte track. The publicity stunt drummed up huge interest in the race and forever solidified Wheeler's position as NASCAR's most creative showman.

499 One year before his Winston Cup debut in the 1979 Daytona 500, Geoff Bodine dominated the NASCAR Modified ranks. Bodine raced his way to 55 victories including the Race of Champions at Pocono Raceway (Pennsylvania), the Spring Sizzler at Stafford Speedway (Connecticut), the Thompson 300 at Thompson Speedway (Connecticut), the Budweiser 200 at Oswego Speedway (New York), and both races at Martinsville Speedway. The Chemung, New York, driver started 84 events and his division record of 55 victories earned him a spot in the *Guinness Book of World Records.*

500 From 1971 through 1976, Zanesville, Ohio, driver Larry "Butch" Hartman dominated the USAC Stock Car ranks, winning five championships in six seasons. However, Hartman's success on the USAC circuit didn't carry over to NASCAR. He posted just one top-5 finish in 20 career starts by wheeling a Junie Donlevy Ford to fifth–place in the 1972 National 500 at Charlotte Motor Speedway. Hartman's best season was 1977, starting 11 Winston Cup events and posting a pair of top-10 finishes (Michigan and Pocono). Hartman ended his USAC career with 29 wins and was one of eight 2015 inductees into the USAC Hall of Fame in Indianapolis, Indiana.

501 It became apparent that NASCAR was fed up with drivers concealing nitrous oxide bottles in their cars by the 1978

Winston 500 at Alabama International Motor Speedway. Team owner Harold Miller and driver Keith Davis were suspended for 12 weeks after the illegal device was discovered in their car during pre-race inspections. The suspension short-circuited what would have been Davis' first Winston Cup start.

502 The NASCAR record book indicates team owner Will Cronkite fielded 14 Winston Cup entries from 1978 through 1983. None was more interesting than his first attempt. Charlotte Motor Speedway promoter Humpy Wheeler convinced him to let Willy T. Ribbs drive his car in the 1978 World 600. It was a Winston Cup first for Ribbs, America's top African-American race driver at the time. Unfortunately, a series of incidents prior to the race, including an arrest at local Queens College after a high-speed chase while driving a speedway pace car, put Ribbs on ice, opening the seat in Cronkite's car. Cronkite put an unknown short-track racer, Dale Earnhardt, in his No. 96 Carolina Tractor Ford. It's the first of four Winston Cup starts Earnhardt made for Cronkite in 1978 and opened the door for the future seven-time NASCAR champion to join the sport full-time in 1979.

503 Few drivers hold the iconic status accorded to Richie Evans. Considered the greatest of all NASCAR Modified drivers, Evans won nine Mod titles, the first in 1973, and the final eight all in a row from 1978 through 1985. Winning hundreds of races (37 in 1979 and 52 in 1980), Evans also captured a staggering 30 track championships throughout his 20-year career. His final title came in the first Whelan Modified Tour championship season in 1985. Evans won 12 of 28 races before he perished in a practice accident prior to the final race at Martinsville Speedway (Virginia), at the age of 44. Evans, crowned the Modified Tour's Most Popular Driver nine times, was named one of NASCAR's Greatest 50 Drivers of All Time in 1998. He was the first non-Cup Series driver inducted into the Hall of Fame in 2012.

504 After amassing a fortune in the coal mining business, Jim Stacy burst onto the NASCAR scene after purchasing the financially struggling K&K Insurance team from Nord Kroskopf in May 1977. From the start, Stacy's efforts were plagued by a string of bad debts and lawsuits that forced him from the sport for a short time. Stacy returned to NASCAR prior to the 1981 season when he acquired the 1980 Winston Cup championship–winning team of Rod Osterlund and Dale Earnhardt for $1.7 million. Two-thirds through the year, driver Earnhardt left the team when Stacy again ran afoul with financial problems. Undaunted, Stacy continued throwing money at the sport by fielding and/or sponsoring multiple cars in one race, including seven in the 1982 Daytona 500. Stacy's ownership ride came to an end after the 1983 season after fielding cars for Rodney Combs, Mark Martin, and Morgan Shepherd. While his cars won 4 of 121 NASCAR Winston Cup starts, his legacy will remain tinged with the smell of Cuban cigars and bad debt.

505 You won't see Red Farmer's name all over the NASCAR Cup record book, but he's an important figure stock car racing just the same. The patriarch of the "Alabama Gang," Farmer started his racing career in 1948, making his first top-tier division start at the Daytona Beach-Road Course in 1953. His first championship came in 1956 when he won the Modified title. Farmer competed primarily in the Sportsman Division throughout the 1960s and 1970s, winning the title three straight years from 1969 to 1971. The last of his 36 starts came at Talladega, where, in 1975, he finished 44th after engine failure sidelined his Ford just eight laps in. At age 59, Farmer wheeled a Davey Allison–owned car to a 17th-place finish in the 1992 Kroger 200 at Indianapolis Raceway Park, his final Busch Series event. Farmer, whose win total is estimated as high as 900, continued to race after his career ended.

Now in his 80s, he has defied Father Time and continues to compete on a regular basis in the Late Model division at the Talladega Short Track in Eastaboga, Alabama. Farmer, a member of no less than five racing Halls of Fame, was named one of the 50 Greatest Drivers in NASCAR History in 1998.

506 One of the top competitors of the 1970s NASCAR Sportsman Series (now Xfinity), Clyde "Butch" Lindley Jr. captured Series championships in 1977 and 1978 and finished second in the points in 1979 capping a string of six-straight top-3 division title finishes starting in 1974. One of America's top short-track racers, Lindley won more than 500 feature events in his career. On April 13, 1985, the Greenville, South Carolina, driver was leading in an All-Pro Late Model race at DeSoto Speedway in Bradenton, Florida, when he crashed late in the race. He suffered a severe head injury and lapsed into a coma from which he never woke up. He passed away June 6, 1990 at an assisted-care facility in Greer, South Carolina.

507 After posting a victory in NASCAR's top series for 18-straight seasons, Richard Petty was winless in the 1978 season. With the Dodge Charger no longer eligible for Winston Cup competition, Petty's 1978 Dodge Magnum, a clone of Chrysler's boxy Cordoba model, proved totally non-competitive. This forced Petty to switch to Chevrolet 20 races into the season, making his Bowtie debut August 20 in a Monte Carlo purchased from Cecil Gordon. Petty finished 14th in the Champion Spark Plug 400 at Michigan International Speedway.

508 Nobody was more surprised to see Richard Petty in Victory Lane in the February 18, 1979, Daytona 500 than his doctors. After they surgically removed 40 percent of Petty's ulcerated stomach in December 1978 during the off-season, he was given strict instructions not to race for at least three months afterward. Petty defied the doctor's orders and not only raced, but won after leaders Cale Yarborough and Donnie Allison crashed on the final lap.

509 After 43 victories in eight seasons behind the wheel of the No. 21 Wood Brothers car, the wheels came off the association between David Pearson and the Stuart, Virginia, team in the 1979 Rebel 500 at Darlington Raceway. After pitting on Lap 302, Pearson sped out of the pits only to have both driver-side tires fall off the car, and finished 22nd. The following week, Glen Wood announces both Pearson's release from the team and his replacement by Neil Bonnett.

In the early 1970s, few combinations were tougher to beat than David Pearson and the Wood Brothers. Shown is one of their famed No. 21 Mercury racers on display at the NASCAR Hall of Fame in Charlotte, North Carolina. (John Close Photo)

510 Throughout 60-plus years of NASCAR history, Petty Enterprises has fielded more than 2,800 top-tier division entries. Two of those came on August 5, 1979, with Richard Petty driving a family-owned Oldsmobile to a fourth-place finish in the Talladega 500 at Alabama International Motor Speedway. The second entry in the race, a 1979 Dodge Magnum, was piloted by Kyle Petty in his first career Cup start. Only 19 at the time, Petty and his No. 42 STP-sponsored Mopar roll off 18th in the 41-car starting grid and finish 9th, seven laps behind race winner Darrell Waltrip.

511 After a 48th-place finish in the 1970 Talladega 500 at Alabama International Motor Speedway, having won the inaugural Winston Cup race at Talladega just a year earlier, Richard Brickhouse faded from the NASCAR scene. Brickhouse returned to the cockpit October 7, 1979, more than nine years after the 1970 Talladega race, wheeling the No. 16 Jimmy Edwards–owned Oldsmobile in the NAPA National 500 at Charlotte Motor Speedway. Engine failure sidelined the Rocky Point, North Carolina, pilot after just 15 laps, leaving him 39th in the 40-car field. After two more Cup starts

Alabama car dealer Sonny King (left) sponsored many NASCAR drivers over the years, including fellow Anniston, Alabama, native Charlie Roberts during the 1973 Winston Cup season. (Photo Courtesy Ed Samples Jr. Collection)

in 1982, Brickhouse retired for good with a reputation as one of NASCAR greatest "one-hit wonders."

512 Just weeks after winning the final race at Atlanta's famed Lakewood Speedway, Buck Simmons made his Winston Cup debut November 4, 1979, in the Dixie 500 at Atlanta Motor Speedway. The Georgia dirt-track legend finished 14th, a Cup career-best that lasted only eight starts.

MILESTONES

513 Seeing the success of the Universal Racing Network (URN) in the late 1960s, Bill France Sr. and Ken Squire (track announcer at Daytona International Speedway since 1959) launched the Motor

Racing Network (MRN) prior to the start of the 1970 NASCAR season. The network, fully owned by NASCAR and promoted as "The Voice of NASCAR," opened with a broadcast of the 1970 Daytona 500. Today, MRN has more than 400 affiliates nationwide and broadcasts all Cup and Xfinity Series events at International Speedway Corporation (ISC) tracks in addition to NASCAR Camping World events regardless of venue.

514 Pete Hamilton had just 19 career Grand National starts (two of them at Daytona International Speedway) before taking over the No. 40 Petty Enterprises Plymouth Superbird for the 1970 season. The 27-year-old driver was an instant hit in his first race for the team, passing David Pearson with less than 10 laps remaining to win the 1970 Daytona 500. Hamilton earned $44,800 for the victory, the first of four career Winston Cup victories for the Dedham, Massachusetts, native.

515 Driving Test Car No. 88 (a non-descript 1969 Dodge Charger Daytona powered by a 426-Hemi engine) Buddy Baker became the first to average more than 200 mph on a closed course on March 24, 1970. He turned the 200.447-mph lap on the 30th circuit of a test run on the giant 2.66-mile Alabama International Motor Speedway (Talladega). Chief NASCAR Timer and Scorer Joe Epton verified the lap with the sanctioning body's electronic timing equipment, leaving no doubt that Baker had broken the record. Just to make sure, Baker returned to the track and clicked off laps at 200.330 and 200.447 mph, both recorded and verified by Epton.

516 Signed into law April 1, 1970, by President Richard Nixon, the Public Health Cigarette Smoking Act required cigarette manufacturing companies to cease all television and radio advertising by the end of the year. The government edict forced the tobacco industry, which collectively spent a reported $220 million in TV and radio advertising, to find other ways to market their products. The law opened the door for NASCAR to secure the R.J. Reynolds Tobacco Company and its Winston cigarettes as the first title sponsor of the national stock car racing series in 1971.

517 With Ford, Chrysler, Chevrolet, and Firestone on the sidelines in the early 1970s, NASCAR's financial picture was bleak. That changed in December 1970 when R.J. Reynolds Tobacco Company announced its Winston brand of cigarettes as the title sponsor of NASCAR's Grand National Series and the spring race at Talladega, Alabama. As part of the deal, the company dedicated $100,000 to NASCAR's 1971 championship points fund and awarded the first Winston Cup to the division titlist at season's end. Thus began a 33-year association between Winston and NASCAR; the cigarette company poured millions of dollars into the sport from the grass-roots level all the way to the Cup Series.

518 On February 21, 1971, saw the NASCAR Winston Cup Series wave the green flag at the inaugural event at Ontario Motor Speedway (California). While it's a red-letter day for race fans, it's also a major milestone for NASCAR: the Miller Lite 500 marks the 1,000th race in Strictly Stock/Grand National/Winston Cup history.

519 One of the largest marketing partnerships in the history of sports is created when STP (Scientifically Treated Petroleum) and its president Andy Granatelli agree to sponsor Richard Petty's Plymouth for the 1972 Winston Cup season. The deal, to pay the team $250,000 in sponsorship money and $50,000 more if Petty wins the 1972 Winston Cup title, is originally rejected because Granatelli wants the car painted in the company's signature "STP Red." Petty, who had never driven a car not painted the family's iconic "Petty Blue," eventually agrees to a paint scheme featuring both colors. Today, more than 50 years later, the relationship between STP and the Pettys is the longest-running sponsorship association in the history of NASCAR.

520 Just three drivers, A. J. Foyt, Richard Petty, and Bobby Allison, led the 1972 Daytona 500. It is still the fewest number of drivers to lead NASCAR's premiere event. Foyt crushed the competition, leading 168 out of 200 laps, including the final 119 on the 2.5-mile Daytona International Speedway, beating out runner-up Charlie Glotzbach by nearly two laps.

521 To say that Richard Petty was consistent during the 1971 and 1972 seasons would be an understatement. Beginning on June 26, 1971, at Greenville Pickens Speedway through January 23, 1972, at Riverside Raceway, Petty never finished lower than fifth, amassing a string of 23-consecutive top-5 finishes. Petty took 13 wins during the amazing stretch.

522 For the second time in his career, Richard Petty scored more than 20 NASCAR top division victories in a season, taking 21 Cup wins in 1971. Petty, who notched 27 NASCAR GN triumphs in 1967, is the only driver to win more than 20 races in a single year. He had 18 victories in 1970, in a tie with Tim Flock (1955), for third most wins in a single Cup season. In all, 92 of Petty's 200 career NASCAR Cup victories were won over five seasons, from 1967 through 1971.

523 After guiding NASCAR from its infancy to a sport of national consequence, Bill France Sr. retired as president on January 11, 1972, naming his son, Bill France Jr., as new president. Among his last acts as president, France Sr. hammered out a deal with R.J. Reynolds Tobacco Company and its Winston cigarettes. He retooled the 1972 schedule by cutting the number of events, abandoned the dirt tracks in favor of modern paved speedways, and ushered in NASCAR's Modern Era.

524 Nashville Fairgrounds (Tennessee) Late Model Stock Car ace Darrell Waltrip made his first Winston Cup career start on March 26, 1972, in the Winston 500 at Alabama International Motor Speedway. He entered a 1971 Mercury Cyclone, a former Holman-Moody car constructed in 1966 (the same chassis that Mario Andretti drove as a Ford Fairlane to a win in the 1967 Daytona 500). Waltrip started 25th in the 50-car Talladega field and finished 38th, falling out with engine failure on Lap 69.

525 Cale Yarborough nearly doubled his biggest 1973 single-race payout when he won the National 500 at Charlotte Motor Speedway. Yarborough's $45,425 victory booty dwarfed his second-best total of $23,140 for winning the Southern 500 at Darlington

Raceway earlier that year. Yarborough's big payday was boosted an additional $25,800; that was $100 for each lap led.

526 Benny Parsons, who once worked as a cab driver, won the 1973 Winston Cup championship on the strength of one victory and immeasurable determination. Driving for team owner L. G. DeWitt, Parsons won his single event at Bristol International Raceway (with relief help from John Utsman) in his unsponsored Chevy to a seven-lap victory over runner-up L. D. Ottinger. Parsons had a comfortable 200-point plus lead over Petty and Yarborough when starting the final race of the season, the American 500 at North Carolina Motor Speedway in Rockingham. Parsons' title hopes suffered a crushing blow early on in Lap 13 after a crash destroyed the passenger's side of his car.

Undaunted, Parsons, with help from several teams in the garage, got his car repaired and returned to the race, 136 laps down. With no sheet metal on the right of his car, Parsons soldiered on to complete 308 laps. Parsons eventually parked the badly vibrating car on Lap 394 (of 492), knowing his 28th-place finish was enough to edge Yarborough for the title. In the end, Yarborough finished third in the race, but second in the season standings, while Parsons rolled to his only NASCAR crown by 67.15 points.

527 On September 29, 1974, Earl Ross became the first Canadian driver to win a Winston Cup, after capturing the Old Dominion 500 at Martinsville Speedway. The 32-year-old rookie qualified his No. 52 Junior Johnson Chevrolet 11th in the 30-car field and led the final 78 laps, beating Buddy Baker by just three seconds to earn the victory. Ross, after winning the 1974 NASCAR Rookie of the Year Award, started just five more Winston Cup races. After a failed attempt to qualify for the 1978 Daytona 500, he quietly faded from the NASCAR scene.

528 After winning numerous races at Nashville Fairgrounds Speedway, and the track's 1970 and 1973 Late Model Stock Car titles, it came as no surprise when Darrell Waltrip notched his first Winston Cup victory at the half-mile track. The win came May

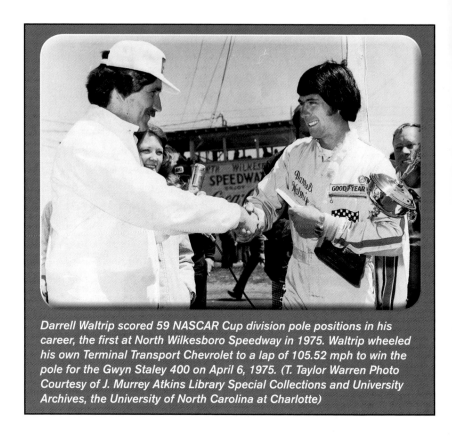

Darrell Waltrip scored 59 NASCAR Cup division pole positions in his career, the first at North Wilkesboro Speedway in 1975. Waltrip wheeled his own Terminal Transport Chevrolet to a lap of 105.52 mph to win the pole for the Gwyn Staley 400 on April 6, 1975. (T. Taylor Warren Photo Courtesy of J. Murrey Atkins Library Special Collections and University Archives, the University of North Carolina at Charlotte)

10, 1975, when Waltrip won the pole, later thumping the remainder of the 28-car Music City USA 420 by two laps.

529 Two future NASCAR superstars made their first imprint on the sport with Sportsman Stock Car victories in the 1974 racing season. On July 19, a 22-year-old Dale Earnhardt scored his first career Sportsman triumph, outdistancing veteran Tommy Houston to win a 55-lap feature at Metrolina Speedway in Charlotte, North Carolina. On September 7, Dawsonville, Georgia, driver Bill Elliott took his first career Sportsman victory at Dixie Speedway in Woodstock, Georgia. Elliott was 18 at the time.

530 NASCAR sponsorship in the early 1970s was considered a "tobacco, beer, and motor oil" proposition. That changed when Gatorade, partnered with DiGard Racing and driver Darrell Waltrip for the 1976 Winston Cup season. The deal is one of the first non-automotive–related sponsorships in NASCAR and helped open the door for other companies to form NASCAR marketing associations.

531 David Pearson and his Wood Brothers Mercury served notice that they would be the team to beat in 1976 after surviving a last-lap battle against Richard Petty to win the Daytona 500. The team proved it after capturing both the World 600 at Charlotte Motor Speedway and the Southern 500 at Darlington Raceway, a triple crown of victories, in NASCAR's three largest events that season.

532 On July 4, 1977, Janet Guthrie, Christine Beckers, and Lella Lombardi took the green flag in the Firecracker 400 at Daytona International Speedway. This is the first time three women start a Winston Cup race since September 11, 1949, when Ethel Mobley, Sara Christian, and Louise Smith competed in the Strictly Stock race at Langhorne Speedway. Lombardi posts the best finish with 31st, (rear-end failure) while Belgian-born Beckers and her Junie Donlevy Ford call it a day on Lap 23 with brake failure. Guthrie fares the worst when the engine in her Chevrolet expires 15 laps into the race.

533 From 1976 through 1978, Cale Yarborough started all 90 events on the Winston Cup schedule. In Chevrolets and Oldsmobiles fielded by Junior Johnson, Yarborough won 28 races, finishing in the top-5 a staggering 70 times in a three-year span. The impressive record earned Yarborough the distinction of being the first driver in NASCAR history to win three-consecutive Winston Cup championships, a mark that stood for more than 30 years until Jimmie Johnson became the first to win four consecutive titles from 2006 to 2009.

534 Richie Evans celebrated the 30th anniversary of the Modified Series by winning the 1978 division title. The division (NASCAR's first in 1948) held 19 events in 1978 including a season-opening 80-lap clash at the 2.5-mile Daytona International

Speedway (won by Darrell Waltrip). Evans, finishing second behind Waltrip, goes on to win seven more division events including five in a row midway through the season. Despite Evans' stellar season, the championship battle goes down to the final race of the year, the Cardinal 500 at Martinsville Speedway. After rival Jerry Cook finishes 28th with an engine failure, Evans grabs his second Modified title by a margin of 4,331 to 4,221.

535 After fielding 99 Winston Cup entries over six seasons, Roger Penske quit the team-owner ranks after the 1977 season. Frustrated with back-to-back winless seasons in 1976 and 1977, Penske parked his AMC Matadors in favor of concentrating on his Indy-Car ownership efforts. He eventually returned to NASCAR in 1980 fielding a Chevrolet for Rusty Wallace in the Atlanta 500. Amazingly, Wallace wheeled to a second-place finish in his first Winston Cup start. Penske returned for the 1981 season as a full-time NASCAR car owner, which began a run of more than 1,500 NASCAR top-division entries that continues today.

536 Guided by legendary crew chief Jake "Suitcase" Elder, Dale Earnhardt notched his first Winston Cup victory on April 1, 1979, in the Southeastern 500 at Bristol International Speedway. The Rod Osterlund-owned No. 2 Monte Carlo starts ninth and Earnhardt leads three times, including the final 27 laps, beating Bobby Allison and Darrell Waltrip to the checkered flag by three seconds. The win comes in Earnhardt's 16th career Winston Cup start.

537 On May 28, 1978, Darrell Waltrip scored the first of his record five victories in the World 600 (now Coca Cola 600) at Charlotte Motor Speedway. Waltrip made it two wins in a row in the longest event on the NASCAR Winston Cup tour on May 20, 1979, beating Richard Petty to the checkered flag by nearly six seconds. One day earlier, Waltrip doubled his pleasure on the 1.5-mile Charlotte oval winning the Sundrop 300 NASCAR Sportsman/Grand American race in front of John Anderson, Rusty Wallace, Dave Marcis, and Morgan Shepherd.

538 In one of NASCAR's most epic championship battles, Richard Petty won his seventh and final Winston Cup title after he edges Darrell Waltrip by a mere 11 points. Waltrip led the championship battle by two points heading into the 31st race of the 1979 season. The tussle came down to the final race at Ontario Motor Speedway when Petty finished fifth, just three positions in front of Waltrip.

539 In 2016, NASCAR Modified legend Jerry Cook was inducted into the NASCAR Hall of Fame. The honor was well deserved for the Rome, New York, driver who dominated the Modified division by winning six championships in seven years (1971, 1972, 1974, 1975, 1976 and 1977). Cook retired in 1982 with a total of 342 modified victories. He stayed connected to the division, helping launch the NASCAR Whelen Modified Tour in 1985 and serving as its first series director.

Chapter 6

The 1980s: Million Dollar Decade

When Bill Elliott took the checkered flag to win the 1985 Southern 500 at Darlington Raceway, he forever became "Million Dollar Bill" capturing a special $1 million bonus prize posted by the R.J. Reynolds Tobacco Company, the sponsor of the NASCAR Winston Cup Series. Every moment of the spectacle was broadcast live on ESPN. Thanks in large part to ESPN and cable television, Elliott wasn't the only one in NASCAR making big bank by September 1985.

Cable television was the in-thing to have in the early 1980s. Instead of having a handful of local television stations with affiliations to one of the "Big Three Networks," homes could now have dozens of stations in markets across the country providing a wide array of programming. One of those ideas, a 24-hour sports and news network, was now a possibility as long as you could fill the time with something people would pay to watch.

So it was that ESPN (Entertainment Sports Programming Network) was launched on September 7, 1979. ESPN looked for inexpensive sports events to broadcast and its initial program log was an eclectic mix of kick boxing, Australian Rules football, volleyball, and pool tournaments. Also among the network's most popular early programming was live, dirt-track Open Wheel Sprint Car racing.

Bill Elliott's million-dollar payday at Darlington became a recurring event for NASCAR in the 1980s as big money found its way into the pockets of many in the sport. (John Close Photo)

Initially an oddity with limited distribution and viewership, ESPN went viral in 1980 when it broadcast every game of the NCAA Men's Basketball Tournament not covered by network giant NBC. Three weeks of seemingly unending "March Madness," along with the first live telecast of the National Football League Draft a month later, grew ESPN by 250 percent and viewership to 6 million subscribers after its second year of operation.

Cable became a great opportunity for NASCAR, which partnered with ESPN for the first time in 1981. ESPN broadcast the March 1 Carolina 500 Winston Cup race at North Carolina Speedway on a taped-delayed basis, and followed up with three more delayed telecasts before airing its first live flag-to-flag Winston Cup telecast on November 8, 1981, from Atlanta.

More live Winston Cup races followed on ESPN in 1982 while TBS joined the NASCAR live cable television parade with a live broadcast of the final race of the year at Riverside Raceway.

Both ESPN and TBS added more Winston Cup events plus new Busch Grand National Series races to the broadcast mix over the next two years, which fueled a burst of growth nationally for both racing and the cable television industry.

By the time the fake photo opportunity money rained down on Elliott in Victory Lane at Darlington in 1985, ESPN and TBS, along with network players ABC and CBS, were now telecasting all NASCAR Winston Cup season events.

In the meantime, real money was raining down on everyone associated with the sport. By the end of the 1980s, Elliott and the other top drivers and team owners were millionaires. Fueled by truckloads of dough from mainstream Fortune 500 companies looking to cash in on the cable marketing opportunity, the sport's top personalities morphed into the first-generation of high-profile, celebrity product spokespersons populating NASCAR today.

NASCAR's logo was a valuable, widely recognized brand in a rapidly growing fan base of millions. That allowed NASCAR to capture the deep Fortune-500 pockets. The worries about money problems, or maintaining superiority as the top sanctioning organization, were over. Bill France Sr.'s dreams had been realized; to millions everywhere, NASCAR *was* stock car racing.

And ESPN? The 1980s worked well for it also. Cable television revolutionized how, and what, Americans watched on television. ESPN led the charge and by the end of the decade, 6 out of 10 American households were wired for cable and ESPN had more than 58 million subscribers.

Thanks to cable television, it was truly the "Million-Dollar Decade" for everybody.

CARS

540 As in the late 1970s, Chevrolet dominated the 1980 Winston Cup Manufacturers' Championship with its Monte Carlo, winning 22 of 31 races contested. Meanwhile, Oldsmobile, Ford, and Mercury managed just three wins, allowing Chevy to win its fifth-straight and 12th-overall constructor title.

541 In an attempt to reflect current American passenger cars, NAS-CAR mandated a reduction in the minimum wheelbase from 115 inches to 110 inches prior to the 1981 season. Models eligible for competition included the Buick Regal, Chevrolet Monte Carlo and Malibu, Chrysler LeBaron, Dodge Mirada, Ford Thunderbird and Granada, Mercury Cougar XR7 and Monarch, Oldsmobile Cutlass Supreme and Pontiac Gran Prix and LeMans.

542 The new downsized 1981 GM car models approved by NAS-CAR had styling differences to make each aerodynamically unique. One thing that wasn't different was under the hood. Each Winston Cup entry was outfitted with a 358-ci small-block Chevrolet racing engine.

543 Chrysler Corporation hoped for a comeback in 1981 with the Dodge Mirada. One of the newer, smaller models eligible for competition, the car was extensively tested at Daytona in January. Unfortunately, the boxy racer wasn't up to the task posting speeds well below its GM and Ford counterparts. The test all but killed interest in racing the Miranda, if not for Buddy Arrington. He had the most success with the Mirada, wheeling to an 11th-place finish in the final 1981 standings and seventh in the 1982 championship chase. Dodge and the Mirada faded from the scene in 1984, not to return until 2000.

Here are Dale Earnhardt's Wrangler rig and several others parked at Bristol International Speedway in 1986. Note that all of the haulers were outside the track in Turns 1 and 2, as at the time, teams were not allowed to park transporters in the Bristol infield at the time.

544 NASCAR teams solved the problem of transporting their equipment across the continent by adopting the semi-truck and box trailer team hauler in the 1980s. Measuring up to 53-feet, the trailers ranged from bare-bones equipment haulers early in the decade to sophisticated transporters with amenities such as a crew lounge and food galley. By the end of the decade, open trailers were practically non-existent in the garage area, becoming a distant memory of simpler times.

545 Only one brand of car paced the Daytona 500 throughout the 1980s: Pontiac. Its 30-year run began in 1972 with actor James Garner driving a Pontiac LeMans pace car in "The Great American Race." The tradition continued throughout the 1970s, with the Pontiac Firebird Trans Am pacing the 500 from 1980 to 1987. A Grand Prix finished out the decade, with other models used until the promotional association ended in 2002.

546 Geoff Bodine was known for constructing "creative" race cars during his Modified career. While some of Bodine's technical enhancements didn't meet the approval of NASCAR, one that did was the introduction of power-assisted steering to the Winston Cup Series. Bodine first used the technology in his No. 01 Emanuel Zervakis Buick Regal at the 1981 Old Dominion 500 at Martinsville Speedway. By the 1982 season, virtually every car in the Winston Cup garage was outfitted with power steering.

547 While some of the downsized cars in the 1980s never made the grade, the same couldn't be said for the 1981–1982 Buick Regal. Due to a more aerodynamic sloped nose and grille, the Regal had better down force and superior handling in the corners than any of its counterparts. This resulted in Buick winning 47 of 62 Winston Cup races in 1981 and 1982, which in turn resulted in Buick's two NASCAR Manufacturers' Championships.

548 Buick's Winston Cup success in 1981 was due in large part to NASCAR's restriction of the Pontiac LeMans. The Buicks were fast, but the LeMans was faster, evidenced by Bobby Allison's pole-winning speed of 194.624 and a 125-mile qualifying victory prior to the Daytona 500. NASCAR immediately leveled the playing field by changing the height and total square inches of the spoiler for each brand. By the fifth race at Atlanta, Allison's LeMans had been limited to a 1.5-inch-high spoiler, all but eliminating the car as a winner. Allison threatened legal action against NASCAR, which recanted and allowed the car to race at Atlanta with a 2.5-inch-high spoiler. Allison finished fourth despite blistering his hands trying to drive the unpredictable car. NASCAR bumped the LeMan's spoiler height to 3 inches for the next two races at Bristol and North Wilkesboro where Allison finished third and second, respectively. One week later at Darlington, Allison and the Harry Ranier team parked the LeMans and its revolving rule changes for good and ran a Buick for the remainder of the season.

549 After Buick's domination of Winston Cup racing in 1981, it appeared everyone wanted one in 1982, evidenced by the fact that 27 of the 42 starters in the season-opening Daytona 500 were behind the wheel of a Buick Regal. Bobby Allison won the race in his DiGard Racing steed. Buick swept the first four places and seven of the top-8 spots in the final rundown.

550 Morgan Shepherd scored his first Winston Cup victory April 26, 1981, in the Virginia 500 at Martinsville Speedway. His Cliff Stewart-owned Pontiac broke a 27-year winless streak for the marque. A win by Joe Weatherly in a Bud Moore-owned Pontiac at Orange Speedway in Hillsboro, North Carolina, October 27, 1963, was the last win for Pontiac before Shepherd's triumph.

551 The introduction of the 1983 Thunderbird proved a game changer in NASCAR. Considered one of the first aerodynamic stock cars, the Thunderbird was significantly rounder than its boxy, square-nosed, slab-sided racing counterparts. The original low-drag 1983–1986 Thunderbird scored 26 wins while the 1987 model took 11.

552 An influx of sponsorship money helped create the Budweiser Late Model Sportsman Series in 1982. The series brought all of NASCAR's regional Late Model Sportsman Division stars together under a national touring series format with a 29-race national championship schedule. Dale Earnhardt won the first race for the new division (the Goody's 300 at DIS February 13, 1982) and Jack Ingram was its first champion after the final season race at Martinsville, Virginia. Today, we know it as the NASCAR Xfinity Series.

553 Richard Petty's 198th career Winston Cup victory in the 1983 National 500 at Charlotte Motor Speedway becomes tainted when both the tires and the engine of his Pontiac are deemed illegal in post-race inspection. The win stands, but the infractions cost Petty $35,000 in fines and 104 championship points. The incident, dubbed "Pettygate," frustrates Petty to the point that he leaves the family-owned and -run team at the end of the 1983 season. He makes good on the promise by joining Mike Curb Racing for the 1984 season.

In late 1985, Alan Kulwicki basically used one car, **Old Sirloin,** *in his run to the 1986 Rookie of the Year Award. Here is Kulwicki putting the car through its paces at Bristol that year. (John Close Photo)*

554 Alan Kulwicki was a NASCAR hopeful as he and his Thunderbird, nicknamed *Old Sirloin*, went after the 1986 Rookie of the Year title. Sponsored by Quincy's Steakhouse, Kulwicki and the former Bill Terry–owned Thunderbird competed in 22 events that season. The one car, two-engine, three-employee team scored a total of four top-10 finishes with a season-best fourth at Martinsville Speedway. Kulwicki was awarded the ROTY title at season's end.

555 Restrictor plates on superspeedways became a full-time reality after the Winston 500 at Talladega May 3, 1987. Bill Elliott established an all-time NASCAR qualifying record of 212.809 mph average to win the pole. During the race, Bobby Allison blew a tire at high speed, sending his Buick into the front-straight catch fence. Several fans were injured by flying debris and the event was delayed 3 hours for fence repair. After the race, NASCAR mandates restrictor plates at Talladega and Daytona to slow the cars.

556 After making tires for the NASCAR Sportsman Division, Hoosier Tire Company announced it would construct tires for the 1988 Winston Cup season. The move was a direct shot at NASCAR tire kingpin Goodyear. At the season-opening Daytona 500, Hoosier supplied 10 teams with tires, including fourth-place finisher Neil Bonnett. One week later, Bonnett gave Hoosier its first Winston Cup victory at Rockingham, North Carolina. At the time, Bob Newton's Lakewood, Indiana, racing tire company employed just 18 people, while Goodyear had over 350,000 associates.

557 Driver-safety gear improved in the 1980s with higher-quality thermal protection–driver's suits, gloves, and shoes finding their way into most cockpits by the end of the decade. Dave Marcis bucked the safety shoes portion of the uniform in exchange for his trusty black dress shoes. The footwear became his trademark and he was respectfully known as "Old Wingtips."

558 Davey Allison qualified on Hoosier Tires in the 1988 Miller High Life 400 at the all-new Richmond International Raceway. The first race on .75-mile, D-shaped oval proved too stressful for the Hoosier rubber, forcing Allison and several others to switch to Goodyear. Allison, who won the pole, made the change after just six laps and went on to win by 3.37 seconds over Dale Earnhardt.

559 You could say the numbers tumbled into alignment when Lake Speed won the 1988 TranSouth 500 at Darlington Raceway. The March 27 event saw Speed score his first and only Winston Cup career victory. It was also the only Cup win for Oldsmobile that season. In addition, Speed's triumph was the first time in NASCAR history that No. 83 graced the door of a Winston Cup winner.

560 The tire wars of the late 1980s had Goodyear and Hoosier testing the limits of what their tires could bear under extreme conditions. For 1989, Goodyear introduced its first radial-ply as a step forward in speed and safety. While test results were favorable, tire-related hard crashes by Bill Elliott and Dale Earnhardt during Daytona 500 practice forced Goodyear to pull the tires and leave the majority of the cars riding on Hoosier Tires.

561 Goodyear's commitment to NASCAR didn't end due to tire failure at the 1989 Daytona 500. Later that year, the company brought new, redeveloped radials to the First Union 400 at

Check out how sparse Darrell Waltrip's pit box was at this late 1980s race at Bristol. No giant war wagons here. (John Close Photo)

Martinsville Speedway. Dale Earnhardt promptly rode the new tires, which seemed to hold speed longer than bias-ply Hoosiers, to a win. Earnhardt's victory proved the value of the new technology, changing the sport forever. Meanwhile, Hoosier, with no radial tire production capability, announced that it would cease tire production for NASCAR at the conclusion of the season.

562 The American automobile industry entered the 1980s with more than 13 million units sold in 1979. General Motors owned a whopping 62.6 percent of the U.S. sales market while Ford produced 22.4 percent of the cars sold in the United States. Both companies continued using NASCAR as a marketing tool throughout the decade; the Chevy Monte Carlo, the Ford Thunderbird, and later the Taurus were mainstays in both the Winston Cup and Busch Series ranks. The Honda Accord became the nation's top selling car in 1989 with 362,707 units purchased. Foreign-brand cars zoomed to 31 percent of the market.

563 Despite its Strictly Stock beginnings and efforts to keep its vehicles stock appearing, NASCAR's connection to Detroit production vehicles had dissolved by 1989. By then, all GM mid-size cars rolling off the production line were front-wheel drive, with V-6 engines. NASCAR continued morphing its cars into V-8 rear-wheel-drive spec racers, retaining only a few stock body parts such as the hood, roof and deck lid through the 2003 season.

TRACKS

564 In 1980, more than half of the 31 races on the Winston Cup tour had no title sponsorship. With a handful of companies including Holly Farms Chicken, Busch Beer, Champion Spark Plug, Coca-Cola, Valleydale Meats, and, of course, Winston, serving as sponsors early in the decade, most races still had generic names: World 600, American 500, The Old Dominion 500, and the Firecracker 400. By the end of the 1989 season, all but one of the 29 events (the Daytona 500) had a corporate title partner. Companies including AC Delco, Goody's, Miller Beer, DieHard Batteries, Pepsi, First Union Bank, and GM Goodwrench were among those lending their names and financial resources to NASCAR race events.

565 Always a threat to win on the superspeedways, the Wood Brothers team finished last (42nd) in the 1989 Daytona 500. Their Ford made just two laps when an oil line failure cooked the team's and driver Neil Bonnett's hopes of victory. The team's worst-ever result at Daytona occurred in the 1961 Daytona 500 when Curtis Turner's No. 21 Wood Brothers Ford lost an engine, finishing 55th out of 58.

566 Lee Petty captured the inaugural 1959 Daytona 500 and walked away with $19,050 of the then-record total purse of $53,050. In 1985, the total purse for the 500 eclipsed $1 million for the first time with a total payout of $1,097,125. Bill Elliott, the winner of the 1985 Daytona 500, collected the lion's share of the kitty, taking home $185,500.

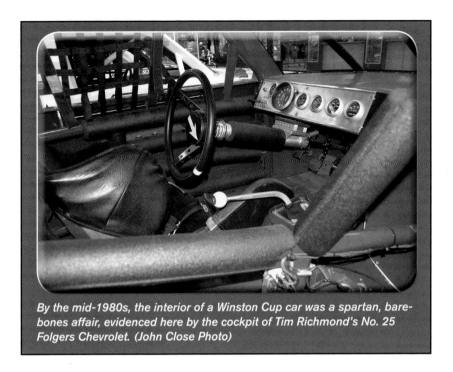

By the mid-1980s, the interior of a Winston Cup car was a spartan, bare-bones affair, evidenced here by the cockpit of Tim Richmond's No. 25 Folgers Chevrolet. (John Close Photo)

567 A clear indicator of which manufacturer built the fastest 1981 downsized Cup car was revealed during qualifying for the Daytona 500. Bobby Allison won the pole in a Pontiac LeMans (194.624 mph) leading a sweep of the top-8 spots for General Motors. Neil Bonnett qualified his Ford Thunderbird ninth, 2 mph slower than Allison, breaking the top-10 qualifying sweep by Pontiac, Buick, Oldsmobile, and Chevrolet.

568 Up and coming driver Terry Labonte scored an improbable Winston Cup victory (his first) when the leaders crashed on the second to last lap of the 1980 Southern 500 at Darlington Raceway. Labonte raced back to the white and yellow flag nipping at the wounded car of former leader David Pearson at the stripe. Initially, Pearson was declared the winner, but Labonte was later proclaimed the victor. Labonte, 23, earned $27,325 for the triumph.

569 Thanks to a call by crew chief Dale Inman to take gas only on the last pit stop, Richard Petty won his seventh and final

Daytona 500 in 1981. After the race, Inman was extremely emotional, hinting that his time at Petty Enterprises was limited. Two days later, Inman leaves the team he grew up in, taking a crew chief job for Dale Earnhardt and the No. 2 Rod Osterlund Chevrolet.

570 The 5th-Annual Busch Clash on February 14, 1983, resulted in an epic standoff between NASCAR and Dale Earnhardt. After being involved in a multiple-car wreck just laps from the finish, Earnhardt ignored NASCAR's black flag request to park his badly damaged and smoking Bud Moore Ford. At Lap 18 of the 20-circuit contest, NASCAR pulled Earnhardt's scorecard officially leaving him 12th at the finish. NASCAR fined Earnhardt $10,000, the amount he won for 12th-place; the fine was later reduced.

571 Crew chief Tim Brewer was fined $500 and driver Tim Richmond was held in the pits for five laps after a tire violation in the 1983 Virginia 500 at Martinsville Speedway. Brewer put a softer compound driver-side tire on the passenger's side of the Blue Max Pontiac on a late pit stop, a violation of safety rules at the time. Richmond finished in 15th.

572 International Speedway Corporation (ISC) expanded its track ownership in 1983 with the purchase of Darlington Raceway. Later that year, ISC acquired 50-percent ownership in Watkins Glen International. This put four tracks under the ISC umbrella joining Daytona International Speedway and Talladega Superspeedway. It was the company's first major acquisition since building and opening Talladega in 1968–1969.

573 Fans attending the 1985 Winn-Dixie Late Model Sportsman Division race at Charlotte Motor Speedway received a special treat: free admission to the inaugural Winston All-Star Race. The May 25, race came after Tim Richmond wheeled a Pontiac to a win over Neil Bonnett's Chevy in the 300-mile LMS opener.

574 The first 1985 Winston Cup featured 12 drivers, all winners from the 1984 season. Terry Labonte and Darrell Waltrip sat on the first row leading Harry Gant, Bill Elliott, Geoff Bodine, Cale Yarborough, Dale Earnhardt, Bobby Allison, Ricky Rudd, Tim Richmond, and Benny Parsons into a charge for the $200,000 prize. Labonte snared a $20,000 bonus for leading Lap 20, but it was Waltrip who passed Gant for the lead headed to the white flag of the 70-lap race to win. Gant, Labonte, Yarborough, and Richmond took second through fifth, respectively. Suspicious to some, Waltrip's Junior Johnson–owned Budweiser Chevrolet began billowing smoke from a blown engine just past the checkered flag.

575 The day after grabbing $200,000 for winning the 1985 Winston All-Star Race at Charlotte, Darrell Waltrip guns his No. 11 Budweiser Chevrolet to victory in the Coca-Col World 600 Winston Cup event. The winner's purse of $90,733 puts Waltrip's two-day take at $290,733. To put that into perspective, 1984 NASCAR titlist Terry Labonte banked just under $750,000 for his 30-race championship campaign.

576 Two weeks before the 1985 Firecracker 400 at Daytona, Greg Sacks was hired by DiGard Racing to drive a "research and development" car as a teammate to Bobby Allison. A former Ranier Racing/Cale Yarborough Chevrolet, Sacks' No. 10 unsponsored mount was wrenched by crew chief Gary Nelson and engine builder Robert Yates for the event. In one of the biggest upsets in NASCAR history, Sacks drove the car to a half-lap win over pole sitter and runner-up Bill Elliott. Allison was so upset over Sacks' victory that he quit the team after finishing 18th. Sacks was DiGard's primary driver for the rest of the season. Sacks, who had never posted a top-5 finish prior to the Daytona win, never won another race throughout his 263-start Cup career.

577 Although it never has and never will host a Sprint Cup Series race, Riverhead Raceway (New York) is one of the sanctioning body's most enduring raceways. That's because the .250-mile paved

Darrell Waltrip (11) and Dale Earnhardt (3) were unable to hold off Rusty Wallace (27) as he motors by en route to his first Winston Cup victory in the 1986 Valleydale 500 at Bristol International Speedway.

bullring has hosted at least one NASCAR Modified Tour race since the inception of the modern-era division in 1985.

578 Rusty Wallace won nine Winston Cup events at Bristol Motor Speedway, the most victories at a single track throughout his 26-year career. Wallace's first Bristol win (and the first of his Cup career) came in the Valleydale 500 April 6, 1986. Wallace and his Raymond Beadle–owned Alugard Pontiac took the lead with 101 laps left and won by 10.69 seconds over Ricky Rudd.

579 Dale Earnhardt was fined $5,000 and put on probation after triggering a massive wreck in the final laps of a 1986 Winston Cup race at the old Richmond Fairgrounds half-mile oval. NASCAR also required Earnhardt to post a $10,000 bond before he could compete in Winston Cup again. Earnhardt appealed, producing a letter of reference endorsed by more than 20 individuals employed in Winston Cup racing at the time. After a meeting, NASCAR reduced Earnhardt's fine and dropped the probation and bond requirement.

580 On July 8, 1965, Marvin Panch hammered a 1965 Wood Brothers Ford to victory over Ned Jarrett, Buddy Baker, Cale Yarborough, and Tiny Lund in The Glen 151.8. The race at the then 2.3-mile Watkins Glen International marked the last time NASCAR's top division raced there. On August 10, 1986, the Winston Cup returned to the now 2.428-mile track. Tim Richmond won the 90-lap, 219-mile contest before a sell-out crowd by 1.45 seconds over Darrell Waltrip.

581 In 1976, Davenport, Iowa, driver Terry Ryan became the first rookie to qualify on the front row for the Daytona 500. Eleven years later, Davey Allison was the second when he piloted the No. 28 Harry Ranier–owned Ford Thunderbird to the runner-up starting spot. Allison had some trouble in the race and finished 27th, 16 laps behind winner Bill Elliott.

Notice the cramped quarters and lack of safety gear on crewmembers in this Bobby Allison pit stop in the 1987 Daytona 500. (T. Taylor Warren Photo Courtesy of J. Murrey Atkins Library Special Collections and University Archives, the University of North Carolina at Charlotte)

582 Bill Elliott was fond of Michigan International Speedway; he won six out of eight races in the mid-1980s. Elliott's "Irish Hills" hot streak began with a win in the 1984 Miller High Life 400. After finishing third in the fall 1984 Michigan Cup event, Elliott and his No. 9 Coors Ford won four-straight Winston Cups, both the spring and fall races in 1985 and 1986. After starting third but finishing 34th because of engine failure in the 1987 spring race at Michigan, Elliott won for the sixth time at the August 16 Champion Spark Plug 400.

583 Phil Parsons had competed in 110 Winston Cup races before taking the green flag in the 1988 Winston 500 at Alabama International Motor Speedway. Despite qualifying third, Parsons was nearly a lap down after running out of fuel on Lap 48. Parsons rallied the Leo and Richard Jackson–owned Oldsmobile to the front, leading the final 15 of 188 laps to win his first and only Winston Cup race.

584 In late 1987, Calder Park Raceway, a road course facility in Melbourne, Australia, opened a 1.1-mile double-dogleg oval track modeled after Charlotte Motor Speedway. Nicknamed the "Thunderdome," the track featured 24-degree banking in the turns with modest 4- and 6-degree banking in the front and back straights respectively. Constructed over four years at a cost of $54 million ($41 million U.S.), NASCAR visited the track in 1988 for a pair of Exhibition Races. They proved to be the only NASCAR races held there. Calder Park Raceway is still open today, hosting occasional drag racing, drifting, and car club events. Meanwhile, the Thunderdome oval has not hosted any competitive events in more than a decade.

585 On April 26, 1987, NASCAR's 1,500th Strictly Stock/Grand National/Winston Cup event rolled off as the Sovran Bank 500 flew the green flag at Martinsville Speedway. The landmark race occurred just shy of the 40th anniversary of the December 1947 chartering and legal registration of the sanctioning organization. Dale Earnhardt won the race, his fourth win in a row on his way to a division-high 11 and the 1987 Winston Cup championship.

586 Charlotte Motor Speedway has hosted all but one All-Star Race since the concept started in 1985 with The Winston. The one all-star event not held at Charlotte took place May 11, 1986, at Atlanta International Raceway. Just 10 cars took the green flag in an 83-lap race that proved to be a landslide payday for Bill Elliott. Elliott led every lap, grabbing $240,000 in prize money and lap bonuses. Unfortunately, the event proved a financial bummer for NASCAR and the track as slightly more than 18,000 fans witnessed the race. In 1987, the All-Star race returned to Charlotte, where it has been held ever since.

587 The Budweiser 400 held on June 12, 1988, was the 48th, and last time NASCAR competed at Riverside International Raceway. In addition to staging its first NASCAR event on June 1, 1958 (the Crown America 500, won by Eddie Gray), RIR hosted multiple racing divisions, including IndyCars, SCCA Trans-Am, Can-Am, AMA Superbikes, and NHRA Drag Racing. Riverside also hosted the Formula 1 United States Grand Prix in 1960. In NASCAR's final 1988 RIR appearance, Rusty Wallace led three different times including the final 14 laps, beating Terry Labonte, Ricky Rudd, Dale Earnhardt, and Phil Parsons to the finish. The legendary California road course closed for good a year later as real estate developers continued their rapid growth of Los Angeles and its new "Inland Empire."

588 Pocono International Raceway's "Tricky Triangle" has had its share of bad accidents, but few worse than the one that ended Bobby Allison's illustrious driving career. Allison was critically injured on the first lap of the June 19, 1988, Miller High Life 500 at Pocono when he spun in the Tunnel Turn and was T-boned in the driver's door by Chauncey "Jocko" Maggiacomo. It took over an hour for crews to extricate Allison from his car. After spending six weeks in a coma at a local hospital, Allison eventually recovered from his injuries. He never raced again; he ended a 25-year driving career that included 85 victories, the 1983 championship, and 11 top-5 season title finishes.

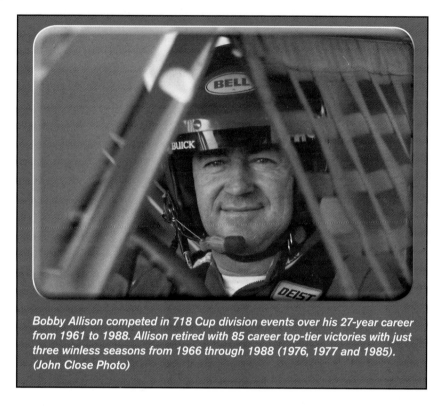

Bobby Allison competed in 718 Cup division events over his 27-year career from 1961 to 1988. Allison retired with 85 career top-tier victories with just three winless seasons from 1966 through 1988 (1976, 1977 and 1985). (John Close Photo)

589 NASCAR contested four Grand National events at the Arizona State Fairgrounds in Phoenix from 1951 to 1960. Nearly three decades later, the Winston Cup Series returned to the desert southwest November 11, 1988, at Phoenix International Raceway. The Checker 500 (312 miles on the 1-mile paved oval) was won by Alan Kulwicki as his Ford *Underbird* beat Terry Labonte's Chevrolet by 18.5 seconds in front of a crowd of 63,000 fans.

590 The record book shows that Bill Elliott won the 1988 Winston Cup Championship, but it was Rusty Wallace who captured everyone's imagination down the stretch. Elliott saw a commanding 124-point lead dwindle to just 24 markers. Wallace clicked off four wins of the remaining five races at Charlotte, North Wilkesboro, Rockingham, and the season-ender at Atlanta. Elliott was never a factor in Atlanta, finishing a lap down to Wallace in 11th, but still good enough to win the title.

591 On June 11, 1989, NASCAR made its first trip to Sears Point International Raceway (now Sonoma Raceway). The 74-lap race at the 2.520-mile Sonoma, California, road course replaced Riverside Raceway on the schedule. Ricky Rudd and his King Motorsports Buick dominated the event, leading all but 13 laps, only to stave off a hard-charging Rusty Wallace for the win. The event was decided three laps from the finish when Wallace went off the course in Turn 7 after contact with Rudd. Attendance for NASCAR's first race in the California wine country was estimated at 80,000 and the track has been a staple of the Sprint Cup schedule ever since.

592 The 1989 Valleydale 500 at Bristol International Speedway became the race of the decade regarding caution flags. The yellow flag waved 20 times in the April 9, 1989, race at Thunder Valley, more than at any other Winston Cup race in the 1980s. Rusty Wallace edged out Darrell Waltrip for the win in a 3½-hour event that featured 98 caution laps.

593 After 513 consecutive Winston Cup starts, Richard Petty saw the streak coming to a close when he failed to qualify for the

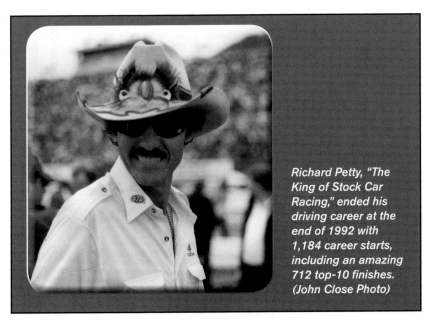

Richard Petty, "The King of Stock Car Racing," ended his driving career at the end of 1992 with 1,184 career starts, including an amazing 712 top-10 finishes. (John Close Photo)

1989 Pontiac Excitement 400 at Richmond International Raceway. The last time Petty had failed to make a race was November 7, 1971, when he sat out the Georgia 500 Winston Cup/Grand American race at Middle Georgia Speedway after he and the event promoter couldn't agree on appearance money. Petty's Richmond streak ended after wrecking his Pontiac in practice and his back-up car was too slow in qualifying.

PIT PASS

594 Cale Yarborough had a standout 1980 season. Driving the No. 11 Busch Beer Chevy for Junior Johnson, Yarborough posted a Cup division-high 14 pole positions in 1980. Yarborough won seven out of eight poles in a two-month period (May 10 to July 27). He won a pole on every kind of track with top qualifying efforts at Daytona (superspeedway), Bristol (short track), Riverside (road course), and Charlotte and Dover (1.5- and 1.0-mile intermediate).

595 In 1978, Semon "Bunkie" Knudsen became the fourth NASCAR National Commissioner succeeding South Carolina "Dixiecrat" politician L. Mendel Rivers. Unlike Rivers, Knudsen was a car guy first; he followed his father to General Motors where he became head of Pontiac in 1956, head of Chevrolet in 1961, and vice-president of General Motors in 1967. In 1968, Knudsen shocked the automobile world by leaving General Motors after 29 years to take the helm at rival Ford. Just 19 months later, Ford fired him. He retired as chairman of White Motor Company in 1980. Knudsen died in 1998 at the age of 85.

596 Bunkie Knudsen kept a low profile during his term as NASCAR National Commissioner from 1978 to 1998, sometimes being referred to as "The Wizard of Oz." Knudsen rarely left his Royal Oak, Michigan, home to attend races during his term and when he did, it was without fanfare. Knudsen believed that a final arbitrator needed to preserve objectivity.

NASCAR drivers often competed in special short-track events on week-nights between Cup races. Here are Rich Bickle, Ken Schrader, Kyle Petty, Bobby Allison, Alan Kulwicki, and Davey Allison prior to the 1988 Slinger Superspeedway (Wisconsin) Nationals in 1987. (Photo Courtesy Russ Lake)

597 It was a day of firsts and lasts for David Pearson in the April 13, 1980, Rebel 500 race at Darlington Raceway. Pearson made his first start for team owner Hoss Ellington memorable by winning the 258-mile rain-shortened event. Pearson's 105th trip to Victory Lane also was the last of his storied 574-race Winston Cup career.

598 Californian Doug Richert had never seen a live NASCAR race until moving to North Carolina to become a crew-member on Rod Osterlund's team in 1979. Tutored by crew chief "Suitcase" Jake Elder that year, Richert proves a quick learner and after Elder quit 13 races into the 1980 season, Richert (just 20 years old) was named crew chief for Dale Earnhardt and the No. 2 team. Earnhardt went on to win his first NASCAR Winston Cup championship that year while Richert, with a guiding hand from veteran crewman Roland Wlodyka, became the youngest crew chief to ever win a Winston Cup title.

599 Jack Ingram was a top star in the new Budweiser Late Model Sportsman Series launched in 1982. Nicknamed "The Iron Man," he won the title in its first year and again in what became now the Busch Series in 1985. Ingram never finished lower than fourth in the first six Sportsman/Busch seasons (1982–1987) and concluded his driving career in 1991 with 31 series wins and 164 top-10 finishes in 275 starts.

600 Regarded as the "Dean of American Motorsports Journalism," Chris Economaki wrote his first auto racing column, "Gas O Lines," as a teenager for *National Auto Racing News* (now *National Speed Sport News*) in the 1930s. Throughout the late 1940s and 1950s, the Brooklyn, New York, native served as track announcer at several Northeast raceways and in 1950, he became the editor of *Speed Sport*, a position he held for the next 60 years. Economaki became best known as a television pit reporter and commentator after Bill France Sr. insisted that he be a part of ABC's television broadcast of the 1961 Firecracker 400 at Daytona International Speedway.

Over the next 40 years, Economaki was television's busiest reporter, working NASCAR and IndyCar races, the 24 Hours of Le Mans, Formula 1, and the International Race of Champions for several different networks. In his later years, Economaki penned his autobiography *Let Them All Go*. He passed away at his home in Wyckoff, New Jersey, at the age of 91 in 2012.

601 Known for his rough and tumble driving and his fistfights in the pits after the races, "Terrible" Tommy Ellis was a standout driver during the 1970s and 1980s. The stocky Richmond, Virginia, native won the 1981 Late Model Sportsman title and the 1988 NASCAR Busch (now Xfinity) Series championship. In all, Ellis posted 235 career Busch Series starts from 1982 to 1995 with 22 wins. He also made 78 Winston Cup career starts and posted one top-5 finish at Charlotte in 1981. In 2010, Ellis was sentenced to 18 months in prison for income tax evasion.

After a promising first swing at the Winston Cup Series in the early 1980s, Mark Martin fought his way back to NASCAR's top division through success in the American Speed Association. (John Close Photo)

602 Driver Greg Sacks was seriously injured while testing one of NASCAR's new downsized models prior to the 1981 Daytona 500. In a Richard Childress–owned Pontiac Gran Prix, Sacks flipped end over end in Turn 4 at Daytona International Speedway, eventually coming to a rest in the tri-oval area. The accident ripped Sacks' helmet off, leaving him unconscious. He also suffered a broken cheekbone, leg, and collarbone. Sacks, who had not yet made his NASCAR racing debut, did not compete in the Cup Series for more than two years after the massive wreck.

603 Mark Martin, a 22-year-old driver from Batesville, Alaska, made five Winston Cup starts in 1981, driving for team owner Bud Reeder. In two of those races, veteran crew chief Harry Hyde was calling the shots. Martin promptly won pole position in both events; one was at Nashville and the other at Richmond Fairgrounds Speedways.

604 Victoria, British Columbia, driver Roy Smith never competed in more than three Winston Cup races in a single season, turning in just 26 starts from 1975 to 1989. His biggest payday came in the 1982 Daytona 500, finishing 10th after starting 38th. This, one of four career top-10 finishes, earned him and his Pride of Victoria–sponsored Pontiac $18,975 in prize money.

605 Sam Ard made just one Winston Cup start, completing just one lap, and finishing 31st in the 1984 Goody's 500 at Martinsville Speedway. However, many consider the Asheboro, North Carolina, native one of NASCAR's greatest drivers. Ard won countless Late Model races throughout the southeast in the 1970s, finishing second in the championship standings in NASCAR's new Budweiser Late Model Sportsman Series in 1982. The next two seasons, Ard and his No. 00 Thomas Country Ham stocker dominated

Sam Ard celebrates winning the 1984 Red Carpet Lanes 200 Busch Grand National race at The Milwaukee Mile. Alan Kulwicki, Dick Trickle, Bobby Allison, and Davey Allison filled out the top-five finishers. (Photo Courtesy Russ Lake)

the division with 17 wins, 17 pole positions, and 57 top-10 finishes on his way to two LMS championships. Ard crashed hard on Lap 14 of the 1984 Komfort Koach 200 at North Carolina Motor Speedway, suffering severe head injuries. Although he didn't race in the final event of the season, Ard won the by 426 points over Jack Ingram. Unfortunately, Ard never drove again.

606 The son of legendary NASCAR driver David Pearson, Larry Pearson was a fine driver in his own right, winning the 1986 and 1987 Busch Series championships. In 16 seasons, Pearson made 259 NBS starts, winning 15 times. He also took a shot at the Winston Cup Series competing in 57 events over seven seasons. Pearson's only full-time season was in 1989, wheeling a Buick owned by his father in 29 events and posting two top-10 finishes.

607 Race announcer Bob Jenkins grew up in Eastern Indiana in the 1960s. After earning a degree in Broadcast Journalism at Indiana University, Jenkins apprenticed at the Indianapolis Motor Speedway, joined its broadcast network in 1978, and began calling races for ESPN (at the time a fledgling cable network) one year later. In 1981, Jenkins was on call for the first NASCAR race televised on ESPN, a tape-delayed broadcast from North Carolina Motor Speedway. Jenkins was at the ESPN NASCAR microphone through 2003, also hosting "Speedweek," one of ESPN's first racing anthology shows. Jenkins stayed connected to his IndyCar roots by serving as both the radio (1990–1998) and television voice (1999–2006) of the event. Today, Jenkins is retired and works twice a year as the track announcer at the Indianapolis Motor Speedway for the Indy 500 and Brickyard 400. He lives in Crawfordsville, Indiana.

608 Long before he was a NASCAR Hall of Fame team owner, Richard Childress made 285 Winston Cup starts as an independent driver. Unable to break through and win, Childress turned his No. 3 Chevrolet over to an up-and-coming Dale Earnhardt after the 21st event of the 1981 season. Their debut proved to be successful as Earnhardt started 10th and finished ninth in the August 16, 1981, Champion Spark Plug 400 at Michigan International

Speedway. In all, Childress and Earnhardt scored 67 Cup victories and six championships together.

609 Dale Earnhardt made 272 of 676 career starts with Kirk Shelmerdine calling the shots as crew chief for Richard Childress Racing. Their best seasons came in 1986 and 1987 when Earnhardt won back-to-back championships by capturing 16 races. The pair reprised their championship double dip, winning both the 1990 and 1991 Cup crowns on the strength of 13 victories over two seasons. Shelmerdine's crew chief record lists 406 starts, producing 46 wins and 246 top-10 finishes. Shelmerdine was also an occasional driver, competing in 41 total Cup, Xfinity, and Truck Series events from 1981 through 2008. The Pittsburgh, Pennsylvania, native never posted a top-10 finish.

610 Richmond, Virginia, team owner Junie Donlavey fielded 863 NASCAR top division entries over 52 years. His first entry was with Runt Harris in 1950 and ended with Hermie Sadler in 2002. On May 17, 1981, Donlavey sent his one and only Winston Cup career winner to the post as Jody Ridley captured the Mason-Dixon 500 at Dover Downs International Speedway.

611 NASCAR's partnership with R.J. Reynolds Tobacco Company took the sponsorship program to the grassroots level with the creation of the Winston Racing Series in 1982. Muscatine, Iowa, Late Model Stock Car driver Tom Hearst captured 27 of 50 NASCAR-sanctioned events, taking the inaugural season's national title. Hearst was more dominant in his non-NASCAR events in the 1982 season, winning 15 times in 17 races.

612 Ricky Rudd won the Miller High Life 400 at Richmond Speedway On February 26, 1984. Rudd raced in spite of a concussion, rib cage injuries, and facial bruises so severe that his eyes were taped open so he could see. While heroic to a point, NASCAR determined that racing with those types of injuries should be regulated. Later that season, it was mandated that drivers who had been involved in accidents needed medical clearance from a doctor before being allowed to compete.

613 NASCAR hopeful Rusty Wallace suffered a concussion and eye abrasions after his No. 72 Easter Seals–sponsored, John Childs–owned Buick plowed into the soft backstretch mud, flipping multiple times in the 125-mile qualifying race for the 1983 Daytona 500. The Lap 26 accident put Wallace in the DNQ (Did Not Qualify) column of the final 500 rundown that year. Wallace did not attempt to qualify for another race that season, returning to the division full-time in 1984 with Cliff Stewart Racing.

614 The 1985 Winston All-Star race at Charlotte was held one day prior to the Indianapolis 500 at Indianapolis Motor Speedway. In an effort to make sure the national motorsports media didn't miss NASCAR's first All-Star event in more than 20 years, R.J. Reynolds Tobacco Company and Piedmont Airlines partnered to fly media members from Indianapolis to Charlotte for The Winston on Saturday and back in time for the 500 on Sunday.

615 NASCAR drivers have long been noted for their toughness. On March 17, 1985, Bill Elliott won the Coca Cola 500 at Atlanta International Raceway while competing with a compound fracture of his lower left leg. Elliott kept relief driver Jody Ridley on the sidelines all day and covered the 328-lap, 500-mile distance in a winning time of 3 hours 32 minutes 30 seconds.

616 Free-spirited Tim Richmond turned in the best performance of his Winston Cup career in 1986. The Ashland, Ohio, driver scored a division-high seven wins, with 6 of 10 events contested from June 8 through September 7. Richmond ended the season on a high note by winning at Riverside International Raceway, finishing third in the Winston Cup championship behind Dale Earnhardt and Darrell Waltrip. The 1986 campaign proved to be the high point of Richmond's career because he took ill shortly after Riverside. He died from AIDS less than three years later.

617 The 1981 Winston Cup season had one of the strongest freshman classes ever with Morgan Shepherd, Tim Richmond, Ron Bouchard, Mike Alexander, Joe Ruttman, Connie Saylor, Gary

Future star Tim Richmond finished ninth in the 1980 Indianapolis 500. It was his first IndyCar start of any kind. In all, Richmond made just three career IndyCar starts, posting a 21st-place finish in a 1980 event at Mid-Ohio Sports Car Course and 14th-place in the 1981 Indianapolis 500. (Photo Courtesy Russ Lake)

Balough, and Elliott Forbes-Robinson battling for Rookie of the Year honors. Shepherd won one race in 31 starts (the Virginia 500 at Martinsville Speedway), finishing 13th in the final standings. However, Bouchard edged out Shepherd for the award thanks in large part to his thrilling three-wide victory in the Talladega 500 and five top-5 finishes in just 22 starts. However, Talladega proved to be Bouchard's only victory in 160 career starts.

618 Patty Moise was the best female NASCAR driver to come out of the 1980s. A Jacksonville, Florida, native, Moise was 25 when she qualified third for her first NASCAR race, the 1986 Busch Series battle at Road Atlanta. A year later, Moise debuted in the Cup Series at Watkins Glen, making five top division starts by the end of the decade. Moise settled into the Busch Series in which she made 133 career starts before calling it a career after the 1998 season. Her best Busch Series finish was a seventh at Talladega in 1995.

619 Northeast NASCAR Modified driver Geoff Bodine is credited with being the first driver to regularly wear a full-face helmet in the Winston Cup division in the early 1980s. Despite the additional protection and safety advantage, few drivers switched from open-face helmets. Many drivers continued using open-face helmets until NASCAR mandates the use of a full-face model after Dale Earnhardt's death in 2001.

620 On July 27, 1986, Bobby Hillin Jr. became the youngest winner in NASCAR Winston Cup history by capturing the Talladega 500 at Talladega Superspeedway. Hillin (22 years and 52 days old) breaks the 26-year record set by Richard Petty. Petty was 22 years and 241 days old when he set the mark at Southern States Speedway in Charlotte, North Carolina, on February 28, 1960. Hillin's record lasted another 26 years before Joey Logano (22 years and 7 days) claimed the honor at Pocono in 2012.

621 Bill Elliott had the fastest Ford in qualifying for the 1987 Daytona 500 with a blistering lap of 210.364 mph, but it was Ken Schrader's Blue Oval that took the checkered flag in a head-to-head matchup in a Twin-125 qualifying race. Schrader inched ahead of Elliott off the final turn, winning by a foot and giving team owner Junie Donlavey a trip to Victory Lane.

622 Myrtle Beach, South Carolina, company MAXX Race Cards introduced a limited set of Winston Cup trading cards in 1987, following up with a full set in 1988. Generally considered the first company to concentrate its efforts on NASCAR, MAXX captured the market for several years before big "stick and ball" companies flooded stores with multiple racing card sets in the mid 1990s. One such company, Upper Deck, purchased MAXX in 1996. It discontinued the NASCAR collectible card line four years later.

623 In 1988, Winston Cup rookie Ken Bouchard competed in 22 Cup races, earning one top-10 finish and posting a 21.4 average finish. Despite his less than impressive stats, Bouchard was named 1988 Rookie of the Year over fellow first-year drivers Ernie

Dale Earnhardt went to the top of the General Motors food chain when he became the face of Mr. Goodwrench's dealership service entity in the late 1980s. (John Close Photo)

Irvan and Brad Noffsinger. Bouchard, with his brother Ron, are the only siblings to date to have won Rookie of the Year honors.

624 Dale Earnhardt was famous as "The Man in Blue Jeans" long before he became "The Man in Black." In the early 1980s, Earnhardt drove the No. 3 Blue and Yellow Wrangler Jeans Chevrolet to the top of the sport. In 1988, however, Earnhardt received an image makeover and a wardrobe change when GM Goodwrench took over as the primary sponsor of his Richard Childress–owned entry.

625 The advent of NASCAR races as a viable and regular television property created new opportunities for former drivers in the 1980s. Past Winston Cup champions Ned Jarrett and Benny Parsons were part of that group. Jarrett, the 1965 Cup titlist, joined ESPN full-time in 1986 while Parsons, the 1973 champion, first served as a booth analyst while remaining a part-time driver in the late 1980s. Along with Bob Jenkins, the trio quickly became one of the most highly regarded broadcast teams, opening the door for past drivers to advance to the media ranks after retirement.

626 Buddy Baker finished 10th in the DieHard 500 at Talladega Superspeedway on July 31, 1988. Two weeks later, Baker had emergency surgery to remove a blood clot from his brain. While Baker had intended to return to racing a month or so later, he chose instead to retire and sat out the remainder of 1988 and all of the 1989 season. He returned to the cockpit in Atlanta in 1991 and competed in 17 races throughout the next three seasons. Baker ended his career with 700 Winston Cup starts producing 19 wins plus 202 top-5 and 311 top-10 finishes.

627 Wisconsin's Dick Trickle was 28 years old when his made his Grand National (now Cup) debut in the 1970 Daytona 500. Nearly 20 years later, Trickle earned the 1989 Winston Cup Rookie of the Year Award, driving the Stavola Brothers Buick to six top-5 and nine top-10 finishes. Trickle, then 48, remains the oldest driver to win the title.

628 Like a Supreme Court Justice, the NASCAR National Commissioner position is iron-clad. Once someone is selected, he (or she) cannot be removed. The lifetime job pays $1 per year.

629 Kenny Wallace received the first Busch Series Rookie of the Year Award at the end of the 1989 season. Wallace beat a strong contingent of freshman drivers including Bobby Hamilton, Robert Pressley, and Jeff Burton with 16 top-10 finishes and three pole positions.

MILESTONES

630 Buddy Baker competed in 17 Daytona 500s before winning the Great American Race February 17, 1980. His Harry Ranier–owned Oldsmobile dominated the race; he led 129 of 200 laps averaging 177.602 mph. Baker's winning race speed is still an all-time record for the race.

631 In his first appearance at Daytona in 1960, Buddy Baker earned $100 for finishing 14th in a Twin 125 qualifying race. After winning the 1980 Daytona 500, Baker grabbed $102,175 in prize money, the first time a winner banked over $100,000 in a single NASCAR event.

632 Even before the creation of NASCAR, Bill France Sr. held a championship banquet in Daytona Beach, Florida. In 1981, decades after the halcyon days of the Streamline Hotel, NASCAR moved its annual awards ceremony from the Plaza Hotel in Daytona Beach to the famed Waldorf Astoria Hotel in New York City. The annual event remained in New York until it moved again in 2009, this time to Las Vegas.

633 After 10 runner-up finishes in the previous two seasons, Harry Gant scored his first Cup victory April 25, 1982, capturing the

Rising star Dale Jarrett carried the colors and logos of Busch Series division title sponsor on his Oldsmobile in 1985. The son of champion driver, Ned Jarrett, Dale managed nine top-10 finishes in NBS competition that year before scoring his first Busch Series victory in 1986 at the L. D. Swain 150 at Orange County Speedway in Rougemont, North Carolina. (Photo Courtesy Russ Lake)

Virginia National Band 500 at Martinsville Speedway. Gant and the No. 33 Hal Needham–owned Oldsmobile proved to be the best in the field, lapping all 30 starters in the event. The win comes in Gant's 107th career Winston Cup start.

634 In 1955, the Anheuser-Busch Brewing Company introduced Busch Bavarian Beer to its product mix. Nearly 30 years later, Busch Beer replaced Budweiser as the title sponsor of the Late Model Sportsman Series. The Busch Grand National Series debuted in 1984, and ran 739 races under the Busch flag until Nationwide Insurance took over sponsorship in 2008.

635 Benny Parsons must have been dejected after entering the final lap as leader only to finish third behind Darrell Waltrip and Terry Labonte. However, Parsons left the 1982 Winston 500 Alabama International Motor Speedway with something bigger than a win. Parsons' record pole qualifying run of 200.176 mph gave him the distinction of being the first driver in NASCAR history to post an official qualifying lap of more than 200 mph.

636 On September 6, 1982, Cale Yarborough won the Southern 500 at Darlington Raceway steering a Buick. His first win in the event was in 1969 driving a Mercury, while his 1972 and 1973 Southern 500 wins were in Chevrolets. In 1978, he won the race in an Oldsmobile. Yarborough's five wins in the Southern 500 are second only to Jeff Gordon's six, but he is the only driver to pilot four different makes to Victory Lane at NASCAR's oldest superspeedway event.

637 One lap after becoming the first to break 200 mph (200.550) in qualifying for the 1983 Daytona 500, Cale Yarborough destroyed his Chevrolet in Turn 4 of the 2.5-mile oval, flipping it at full speed. Because the car was too damaged to repair, Yarborough ran a back-up car. Based on current NASCAR rules, his record qualifying run was disallowed. One day later, in second-round qualifying, Yarborough drove a Harry Ranier–owned Pontiac to eighth. One week later, Yarborough drove the replacement Pontiac to win the Daytona 500, passing Buddy Baker on the final lap.

638 The 1983 Daytona 500 started off with a full field of 42. Nearly the same amount of drivers and cars (39) were on the sidelines after either withdrawing during practice or failing to qualify.

639 Listed as not running at the finish in the final eight races of the 1982 season, Dale Earnhardt was hoping for more with his Bud Moore Ford team in 1983. Unfortunately, his string of bad luck continued with 13 DNFs in 30 races, most of them engine-related failures. Somehow, Earnhardt managed to finish eighth in the final standings despite completing just 75.4-percent of laps run.

640 Everyone saw the potential in Bill Elliott and his family-owned, Dawsonville, Georgia–based Winston Cup team when they joined NASCAR in the late 1970s. The group waited through eight second-place finishes before Elliott scored his first victory in the 1983 Winston Western 500 at Riverside International Raceway. Elliott shook off his bridesmaid role in the final event of the season, beating Benny Parsons, Neil Bonnett, Dale Earnhardt, and Tim Richmond to the finish. Elliott, who went on to be "Million Dollar Bill," won $26,380 in his first Cup victory.

641 NASCAR and R.J. Reynolds introduced the competition performance index (CPI) into the lexicon of terms when they launched the Winston Racing Series in 1982. The complicated formula of wins, finishes, and bonus points was used to create a grassroots championship series. Open to virtually all dirt or pavement Modified, Sportsman, Super Stock, Pro, Late, and Super Late cars, it resulted in an infusion of bonus and prize money for both the tracks and their racers. It also provided a positive guilt-by-association boost by attracting local and regional sponsorship partners who wanted to ride the whirlwind of NASCAR's growing mass-market appeal. Still a staple of the NASCAR division mix, the Winston Racing Series lives on as the Whelan All-American Series, running at more than 60 short tracks across the United States.

642 Richard Petty, the "King of Stock Car Racing," scored his 200th and final Winston Cup victory in the Firecracker 400 at

Daytona on July 4, 1984. Petty took the landmark win under caution in front of Harry Gant, Cale Yarborough, Bobby Allison, Benny Parsons, and Bill Elliott, the only other drivers to complete all 160 laps. Joining the Independence Day crowd of more than 80,000 was President Ronald Reagan. After the race, the president joined Petty and his team at a picnic; the main course was Kentucky Fried Chicken and Tammy Wynette provided entertainment.

643 President Reagan's visit to the Firecracker 400 at Daytona was more than just a picnic and a concert. The president was touring the South campaigning for second-term votes when he headed to Daytona Beach on Independence Day. ABC broadcast Reagan's live call to start engines from Air Force One, parked just off the Daytona back straight at the airport, as well as an extended stint in the broadcast booth during the race. Meanwhile, photos of Petty and Reagan appeared the following day on the front pages in both the sports and news sections. The unprecedented print exposure, along with live television viewership provided a giant spike for both NASCAR and for Reagan, who was elected to a second term that year.

644 Any concerns about the financial stability of NASCAR were forgotten on December 6, 1984, when Jerry Long, president and CEO of R.J. Reynolds Tobacco Company, announced that it would provide $11.5 million in sponsorship money over the next five years.

645 R.J. Reynolds had a few more financial tricks up its sleeve when it announced its full-on, long-term sponsorship deal in 1984. The company funded a new event, an invitational, in 1985 called The Winston. The All-Star race was open to any driver who had won a 1984 NASCAR Winston Cup regular-season event. It was also the richest per mile event in racing history with a $500,000 total purse. $200,000 was spooned off the top to the winner of the 70-lap sprint at the 1.5-mile Charlotte Motor Speedway. The first event came off without a hitch on Saturday, May 25, when Darrell Waltrip topped a total field of 12 cars. The Winston is now known as the NASCAR All-Star race and is run the week prior to the Coca-Cola 600 at Charlotte.

646 Bill Elliott's victory in the 1985 Southern 500 at Darlington Speedway not only earned him a $1 million dollar bonus for his sweep of three of the top-5 superspeedway races that season, but pushed his season earnings to $2,433,186, the first time a driver eclipsed the $2 million mark in the history of NASCAR.

647 Prior to the 1985 season, David Pearson held the record for NASCAR superspeedway wins in a single season with 10 victories in 1973 behind the wheel of the No. 21 Wood Brothers Mercury. Bill Elliott went one race better in 1985, winning 11 races. This included both Daytona events, Atlanta, Darlington, Michigan, and Pocono. Only Cale Yarborough's victories at Talladega and Charlotte and Darrell Waltrip's Charlotte win prevented Elliott from winning all 14 races of the 1985 season.

648 You can argue about who is the best driver in NASCAR history. You can't argue about who is the fastest. Bill Elliott owns the top six fastest pole speeds in the history of NASCAR. Elliott's top qualifying mark of 212.809 mph at Talladega in April 1987 will probably stand for all time due to speeds slowing in deference to safety. Elliott's all-time top qualifying laps include 212.229 mph (Talladega, May 1986), 210.364 mph (Daytona, February 1987), 209.398 mph (Talladega, May 1985), 209.005 mph (Talladega, July 1986) and 207.578 mph (Talladega, July 1985).

649 Hall of Fame team owner Rick Hendrick fielded his first Winston Cup entry in 1984 and eight races into the season, scored its first win. Geoff Bodine was victorious in the April 29 Sovran Bank 500 at Martinsville Speedway, driving the No. 5 Northwest Securities Bank Monte Carlo to a 6-second win over Ron Bouchard. Since then, Hendrick has fielded more than 3,600 Sprint Cup entries producing nearly 250 victories.

650 Given the first NASCAR-sanctioned race was a Modified Stock Car race on the beach at Daytona; it seemed appropriate that NASCAR and R.J. Reynolds should create the Winston Modified Tour in 1985. As with the Winston Cup and Busch Series, NASCAR reformulated the Modified division to 29 non-competitive date events in 1985, a big change from the previous year when the championship required the physically and financially grueling demands of 60 to 70 races. The Modified Tour opened on March 31, 1985, at Thompson Speedway Motorsports Park (Connecticut) where Richie Evans scored the first of 12 victories that season. Evans also won the division's first championship that year. More than three decades later, the (now) Whelan Modified has traveled to dozens of historic short-tracks, contesting more than 600 races and crowning multiple champions.

651 Hard-charging Jimmy Spencer was one of the first major stars of the NASCAR Winston Modified Tour. The rowdy Berwick, Pennsylvania, driver scored four wins, finishing eighth in the 1985 inaugural season before scoring 10 victories and the first back-to-back championships in 1986 and 1987. Spencer blazed into the Busch Series full-time in 1988, becoming a Winston Cup regular by the 1990 season. Spencer's NASCAR Modified career totals include 15 victories and 46 top-5 finishes in just 90 starts.

652 To increase the prestige of the fledgling Late Model Sportsman Division, NASCAR dropped the term Grand National from the Winston Cup title, applying it solely to the LMS series for 1986. The new moniker, along with financial title support from Anheuser-Busch Brewing Company, creates the Busch Grand National Series, while NASCAR's top division becomes Winston Cup.

653 Bobby Allison started the 1988 Winston Cup season with his third Daytona 500 victory. The two-car-length victory over his son Davey marks the first time a father and son finish 1-2 in a top NASCAR division race since Lee and Richard Petty's 1-2 finish at Heidelberg Speedway (Pennsylvania) on July 10, 1960.

654 Two weeks after Bobby Allison won the 1988 Daytona 500, he and 31 other drivers competed at the Goodyear International 500K at the new Calder Park Thunderdome in Melbourne, Australia. The February 28 exhibition race took place between events at Richmond and Rockingham during the 1988 regular season. Allison led a contingent of Winston Cup stars including Neil Bonnett, Dave Marcis, Kyle Petty, and Michael Waltrip, along with Winston West drivers. There was also an assemblage of Aussie starters led by Alan Grice, Robin Best, and Terry Byers. The race was spiced up by a nine-car wreck after Lap 60 of the 218-circuit contest. Bonnett held off a charging Allison with Marcis taking third. Americans swept the first nine places with Aussie Robin Best in 10th.

655 With attendance estimated at nearly 50,000 for the 1988 Goodyear International 500 at Thunderdome, the stock car crowd headed down under again to Calder Park on December 18 that year. The Christmas 500 saw Morgan Shepherd lead 203 of 280 laps to take home $87,500, the bulk of an $850,000 total purse. American racers again dominated, taking the top-7 spots with Aussie Allan Grice taking an eighth-place finish. IndyCar star Johnny Rutherford finished 17th, his Oldsmobile 28 laps down at the finish.

656 After winning his first Winston Cup race at Phoenix International Raceway November 6, 1988, Alan Kulwicki took the checkered flag and drove counterclockwise around the 1-mile oval saluting the fans. When asked about the unusual gesture, Kulwicki (a Wisconsin native of Polish descent) called it his "Polish Victory Lap." Kulwicki repeated the salute after each of his five Winston Cup career wins.

657 November 20, 1988, proved bittersweet day for NASCAR legends Cale Yarborough and Benny Parsons, both retiring after the *Atlanta Journal* 500 at Atlanta International Raceway. Yarborough finished 10th in his Oldsmobile while Parsons' bad luck saw him finish 34th after crashing out early on. Both drivers are in the NASCAR Hall of Fame; Yarborough was enshrined in 2012 and Parsons is scheduled for 2017.

658 The 1989 Winston All-Star Race at Charlotte Motor Speedway proved to be a perfect finish to a decade of amazing growth for the event and NASCAR. Contact between Darrell Waltrip and Rusty Wallace coming off Turn 4 to the checkered flag sent Waltrip spinning and Wallace to a $200,000 payday. The incident ignited a shoving match just outside Victory Lane between the pit crews and when Waltrip uttered, ". . . hope Wallace chokes on that 200 thousand," it became an instant classic. Waltrip (long loathed by many for outspoken public comments, leading to the nickname "Jaws") became a fan favorite, winning his only two Most Popular Driver Awards in 1989 and 1990.

659 Darrell Waltrip had to settle for second behind Terry Labonte in the Talladega DieHard 500, July 30, 1989. Waltrip's $47,965 runner-up prize money must have been a salve for the Franklin, Tennessee, driver. The second-place take makes him the first driver to eclipse the $10 million mark in Winston Cup competition.

660 Rusty Wallace filed a lawsuit against car owner, Raymond Beadle, on July 25, 1989. Wallace wanted out of the last year (1990) of his contract with Beadle. In October, after Wallace announced he had secured funding for the next four seasons from Miller Genuine Draft Beer, the two sides came to an agreement on a new contract and Wallace's suit dropped. In spite of the outside distractions, Wallace took 6 wins and posted 20 top-10 finishes in 29 events, winning the final Winston Cup championship of the decade by just 12 points over Dale Earnhardt.

Chapter 7

The 1990s: America's Motorsports Pastime

The dawn of the 1990s saw the population of the United States of America grow to almost 249 million, up from more than 226 million just a decade before.

The populace was in for a wild ride in the 1990s as emerging digital-age devices, personal computers (PCs), and cell phones were changing their lives on both personal and financial levels.

Consider that in 1980, computers and the Internet had yet to integrate into the daily life of most Americans. There were slightly more than one million computers in use worldwide in 1980. Contrast that to 1990 when PC laptops with high-speed browsers and infinite information search engines found their way into 54 million American homes with more than 94 million registered Internet users.

The results were life-changing as Americans were getting "connected" in record levels, exploring new forms of global communication and entertainment while sitting at their home or office desk.

The condominiums standing tall over Turn 2 were just some of the amenities that greeted fans when Texas Motor Speedway hosted its first NASCAR race in 1997. (John Close Photo)

The integration of computers was rivaled only by the assimilation of cell phone use into society. In 1990, less than six million Americans had cell phones. In 2000, more than 109 million people were using them.

Americans drew a third and unexpected benefit of financial gain from the new technology. Fueled by tech stocks, the economy boomed, adding 1.7 million jobs a year from 1992 to 1999. Personal wealth grew as the median American household income increased 10 percent throughout the decade. In short, there was plenty of cash for laptops, flip phones, and exciting diversions such as NASCAR races.

NASCAR entered the 1990s as a folksy, down-home, good-old-boy sport that gained national attention thanks to the technology of the 1980s, cable television. Now national in scope, NASCAR sped into the new decade at full throttle and experienced astounding growth not unlike the digital industry counterparts.

From 1993 through 1998, the Winston Cup Series experienced a 57 percent increase in track attendance at new, modern race palaces in major cities including Dallas/Fort Worth, Miami, and Las Vegas.

Longtime NASCAR racetracks such as Charlotte, Atlanta, and even Bristol couldn't build seats fast enough to accommodate demand as NASCAR's popularity exploded. Crowds in excess of 100,000 were commonplace and at one point, NASCAR owned nine of the top-10 biggest sports events by annual attendance in the United States with the only exception the Indy 500 and its 300,000-plus fans.

By the end of the 1990s, NASCAR eclipsed all forms of racing in America in terms of public recognition and popularity. It was a time when NASCAR connected with the country like never before and in the process became the national pastime of American motorsports.

CARS

661 Prior to the start of the 1990 season, Bobby Allison announced the formation of Bobby Allison Motorsports. This marked Allison's return to NASCAR after an accident in a 1988 Cup event ended his driving career. The new team featured driver Mike Alexander, and fielded Buick racers out of Concord, North Carolina.

Unlike the "one-size-fits-all" body styles of today, Winston Cup cars in the early 1990s retained individual brand identities requiring multiple templates, evidenced by the different rooflines of these Pontiac, Oldsmobile and Ford Cup cars on pit road at Bristol in 1991. (John Close Photo)

662 Mark Martin scored the second win of his career when he captured the Pontiac Excitement 400 at Richmond International Raceway February 25, 1990. After the event, runner-up Dale Earnhardt and his team owner, Richard Childress, protested Martin's victory claiming the Jack Roush Ford had an oversized carburetor spacer plate. NASCAR determined that the plate was not oversized, but was bolted on instead of welded, technically illegal by rule. Martin kept the win, but was assessed a 46-point penalty for the infraction. Earnhardt won the 1990 title by 26 points over Martin. Earnhardt's season winnings of $3.3 million, including more than $1 million in championship bonuses, made Martin's spacer plate one of most expensive parts in NASCAR history.

663 The 1990 movie *Days of Thunder*, "camera cars" were inserted into several NASCAR races including the Daytona 500. The camera cars of Bobby Hamilton and Tommy Ellis started at the back of the field, were not scored as participants, and were both

parked after 40 laps. At the April 1, 1990, TranSouth 500 at Darlington Raceway, two cars, the No. 51 Exxon Chevy driven by Hut
Stricklin and the No. 46 City Chevrolet piloted by Greg Sacks, officially competed in the race. Neither of the Rick Hendrick–owned
cars had cameras mounted in them, but were instead filmed by
cameras positioned around the track. Stricklin finished 36th, completing 61 laps, while Sacks was 37th after falling out of the race on
Lap 52 with a broken crankshaft.

664 After a rash of pit road incidents late in the 1990 Winston
Cup season that left one crewmember injured and another
dead, the organization enacted sweeping pit road changes for the
1992 season. The revisions mandated that signboard crewmembers
remain behind the pit wall instead of standing at the front of the pit
box. In addition, over-the-wall crewmembers were now relegated to
staying behind the pit wall until their vehicle was one pit stall away.

665 In an effort to reduce traffic congestion and crashes on pit
road, NASCAR implemented the use of two pace cars at the
start of the 1991 season. One pace car circled the track with the
field in tow while the other led groups of cars down pit road for
servicing. Those qualifying in an odd position (1, 3, 5, etc.) were
given a blue sticker and followed the second pace car down pit road
first. Even-numbered qualifiers (2, 4, 6, etc.) had an orange sticker
and were led to pit road in a second group a few laps later. The
system had several flaws and the concept was scrapped a few races
into the season.

666 One of the more controversial pit road rule changes implemented mandated that teams could not change tires under
caution. In an extension of the Odd-Even/Blue-Orange rule, a blue
flag was waved, allowing odd-numbered qualifiers to pit for fresh
rubber after two laps of green-flag racing were completed following
a caution. After three laps under green, an orange flag allowed the
even-qualified cars to pit for tires. The rules confused competitors
and fans alike, proving unworkable after Bill Elliott suffered a flat
tire in the season-opening Daytona 500. Instead of safely changing

the tire under a yellow flag, Elliott's blue-stickered Ford was forced to wait for two green-flag laps to be completed before pitting for new tires. By the sixth race of the season, the rule had been changed and teams were allowed to change tires under caution.

667 Another 1992 pit road rule gave a one-lap penalty to any competitor who pitted with the wrong group. In addition, any competitor overshooting or pitting out of their box was held on pit road for an additional 15 seconds.

668 Rusty Wallace drove a Pontiac in 293 consecutive starts from 1984 to 1993, winning 31 times. This included a single-season career-high 10 victories in 1993. In spite of this success, Penske Racing jumped to Ford for the 1994 season, where it won eight times. Wallace spent the final 12 years of his career in the Penske Blue Oval racer, winning 24 times.

669 Most NASCAR fans don't know who Andy Papathanassiou is and even fewer can spell his last name, but the former Stanford University football player and graduate had a profound impact on the sport in the 1990s. Papathanassiou was NASCAR's first pit crew coach, hired to supervise Jeff Gordon's Hendrick Motorsports over-the-wall team in 1993. Papathanassiou revolutionized common pit crew practices by replacing regular team mechanics with former college and professional athletes to execute pit stops for Gordon. He then instituted diet and nutrition programs as well as pit stop practices, something few teams were doing at the time. During the practices, Papathanassiou (along with crew chief Ray Evernham) selected crew members by size and athletic ability for each position, meticulously scripting the movements of each member to maximize their efforts while minimizing time-consuming actions and mistakes.

Nicknamed the "Rainbow Warriors" because their uniforms matched Gordon's No. 24 DuPont Chevrolet, the team became practically unbeatable on pit road. By the end of the decade, almost every team had emulated Papathanassiou sport-changing methods by instituting their own pit crew training programs.

670 In 1992, NASCAR introduced new rules that forever took the word "stock" out of a stock car. The fourth-revision racer, known as the Gen 4, was the sport's greatest departure from the original Strictly Stock mantra introduced by Bill France Sr. in 1949. The Gen 4 was, for all intents and purposes, a prototype racer with few parts remotely resembling its production-car counterparts. Only the hood, roof, and rear deck lid needed to match Detroit manufacturer specifications, leaving the rest of the body open to interpretation. Items such as hand-crafted molded plastic nose and tail items replaced the metal parts previously purchased from the manufacturer. Along with NASCAR's insistence on retaining V-8 power and rear-wheel-drive configuration in a time when no Detroit automaker offered an intermediate-sized model with that engine and drivetrain, the Gen 4 ushered in an era of wind-tunnel testing during which aerodynamics became paramount. The Gen 4 remained the NASCAR vehicle template until the Car of Tomorrow (COT) was introduced in 2007.

671 Developed by Jack Roush and introduced into competition in 1994, roof flaps were a welcome safety device designed to keep the Generation 4 Winston Cup cars on the ground. The vehicles had a tendency to get airborne when sliding backwards, the aerodynamic shape acting like a wing instead of hugging the track. After several violent flips in 1993, NASCAR approved the 12 x 8-inch roof panels that opened as the car rotated to kill lift and equalize air pressure over and inside the vehicle.

672 In the early 1990s, Baja 1000 Ford Truck racer Jim Smith approached off-road racing buddies Frank "Scoop" Vessels, Jim Veneble, and Dick Landfield with an idea for a truck series. The group initially wanted the vehicle configuration to resemble the mid-engine stadium racers of the day, but California short-track stock car racer Gary Collins convinced them that a Winston Cup version with a modern truck body would be a better platform and have the most marketing appeal. The group commissioned Collins to build a prototype and display it at the *Circle Track* Magazine Trade Show the week of the 1994 Daytona 500. Collins' creation was a huge hit and would be the genesis of the 1995 NASCAR Craftsman Truck Series.

673 On May 14, 1994, the first Truck Series vehicle was introduced in a press conference at Sears Point Raceway in Sonoma, California. Built by California racer Gary Collins and North Carolina chassis builder Ron Hutcherson, the 1994 Ford F-150 used a body skin straight off the assembly line. A Winston Cup chassis wheelbase was stretched from a 110 inches to 112 inches to accommodate the stock sheet metal. Under the hood, the 358-ci V-8 featured 9:1 compression, down from the 12:1 ratio used in Winston Cup at the time. The rest of the 3,400-pound vehicle was basically a Cup vehicle, using the same suspension, steering, braking, running gear parts, and electrical components, right down to the gauges.

674 "The Big One," a 10-car crash, broke out at the front of the field just laps from the finish in the July 21, 1996, DieHard 500

The cockpit of Winston Cup cars got much busier in the 1990s as evidenced by the wide array of dash toggle switches, gauges, and the steering wheel-mounted radio talk button on this car. (John Case Photo)

at Talladega Superspeedway. When the melee came to a grinding halt, the roof on former race leader Dale Earnhardt's No. 3 Chevrolet was crushed, having taken several direct blows in the dust up. Earnhardt had to be extricated from the car and suffered a broken sternum in the crash. Afterward, NASCAR mandated the installation of an extra roll bar to reinforce the center windshield area from the top of the cage to the chassis bars below the windshield. It was immediately named the "Earnhardt Bar."

675 In May 1996, NASCAR quickly reacted to the deaths of three fans after being struck by a flying wheel off a car competing in an Indy Car race at Charlotte Motor Speedway. All cars in the Busch Series event at Charlotte two weeks later were required to have wheel tethers, heavy-duty steel-braided cables with a loop on each end attaching the front spindle and wheel assembly to the frame. The devices were mandated in the Cup Series by late June; hood and trunk tethers were added to the mix prior to the Pepsi 400 at Daytona International Speedway the first week in July.

676 In a tribute to one of his racing heroes, Darrell Waltrip's Chevrolet wore the No. 300 when unloaded for the March 12, 1998, TranSouth Financial 500 at Darlington Raceway. Tim Flock, one of NASCAR's all-time great drivers, piloted the No. 300 Carl Kiekhaefer Chrysler to 15 wins and the Grand National Championship in 1955. Waltrip drove the No. 300 *Tim Flock Special* in practice for the Darlington event, then changing back to No. 17 for the race, as three-digit numbered cars are not allowed in NASCAR competition.

677 Despite competing in just one event, Hendrick Motorsports (HMS) chassis No. 2429 is considered one of the most creative race cars ever built. It was nicknamed *T-Rex* in part because its paint job touted Universal Studios new movie *The Lost World: Jurassic Park*. The car's name also honored its designer, Rex Stump. The car was built with larger frame rails, a lowered floor pan, different rear shock/spring, and front strut mounting points. Even the door bars were moved to improve the rigidity of the chassis. Stump and the HMS team scrutinized every part in an effort to exploit any holes in the NASCAR rulebook.

In testing, the front of the car, which sat higher than its counterparts, sucked down to the track while keeping the rear at a higher angle. The resulting negative air under the car provided superior handling, especially in the corners' landing zone. Gordon debuted *T-Rex* at the 1997 Winston All-Star race at Charlotte Motor Speedway, easily beating the rest of the field on the way to a $207,500 first-place payday. The car was technically legal under rules of the day, but sanctioning officials made it clear in post-race inspection that Hendrick Motorsports should never bring *T-Rex* to the track again.

Later on, NASCAR closed several gray areas in the rulebook to prevent anyone else from bringing their own *T-Rex* to the track. After several years as an HMS show car, *T-Rex* was restored to original condition and is now part of the rotating display of vehicles at the Hendrick Motorsports Museum.

678 Throughout the 1990s, Chevrolet and Ford battled for the Manufacturers' Championship. Chevrolet came out on top winning six times (1990, 1991, 1993, 1995, 1996 and 1998) while Ford captured four titles (1992, 1994, 1997, and 1999).

679 Other than Ford and Chevy, the only other Detroit brand in Winston Cup at the end of the 1990s was Pontiac. "The Chief" won a division-high 11 events in 1993 but was still nosed out for the Manufacturers' Championship. Pontiac visited Victory Lane nine times in 1999, the big finale for the brand before leaving the sport prior to the 2004 season.

680 The Ford Taurus was introduced in 1984 as a 1985 model and by the end of the 1990s it was already in its third generation and the best-selling car in the United States. In 1998, the Taurus was approved for NASCAR competition, replacing the Thunderbird, Ford's racer of choice since 1977. The introduction of the Taurus at Daytona International Speedway on February 8, 1998, marked the first time a four-door sedan competed in a Modern Era event.

Rusty Wallace made the car's debut a success, getting the jump on Jeff Gordon's Chevy on a late restart to win the Bud Shootout.

681 On August 4, 1999, Reynard Motorsport introduced its new "seven-post shaker" test rig to NASCAR. At a media demonstration at the company's Indianapolis, Indiana, Auto Research Center, Steve Park's No. 1 Winston Cup Chevrolet was tested on the vehicle dynamics device that simulates on-track race car chassis movements. The controlled variable test equipment quickly became a must-have piece of equipment and is used extensively in NASCAR today.

682 In 1999, NASCAR instituted a "one engine only" rule in the Busch Series. Teams now had to practice, qualify, and race with the same engine. Previously, teams used high-power, limited-durability engines in qualifying, while running a separate detuned and more reliable engine in the race. In addition, any powerplant changes had to be approved by NASCAR. Teams opting to change engines rolled off at the back of the starting field. The rule proved a cost effective benefit in an era in which a BGN race engine priced out between $20,000 and $40,000. In 2002, the Nextel Cup Series adopted the one-engine-rule, saving teams millions of dollars in related engine costs annually.

683 Any racer, mechanic, or fan that ever fantasized about working on a NASCAR team saw that dream come a bit closer when NASCAR announced in May 1999 that it was going to develop a $7 million NASCAR Training Institute. NASCAR planned to build as many as six campuses nationwide with the first one opening in Charlotte, North Carolina, in 2001. The school would have NASCAR specific training as well as basic automotive technician training provided by Universal Technical Institute, who partnered with NASCAR in the educational project. Tuition cost for the 57-week program when the school opened in 2002 was $24,350.

684 In 1998, Chevrolet announced plans to redesign the Monte Carlo and launch the new model in 2000. That meant

NASCAR teams needed to start working on switching over the new model. On August 29 and 30, 1999, Chevrolet conducted a two-day test of the first 2000 NASCAR Monte Carlo. The test was held at Gateway International Raceway with Winston Cup drivers Dale Earnhardt, Ken Schrader, Bobby Hamilton, Sterling Marlin, Jerry Nadeau, David Green, Mike Skinner, and Geoff Bodine taking turns driving the cars.

TRACKS

685 Despite qualifying 12th for the 1990 Daytona 500, Derrike Cope was hardly considered a favorite to win the February 18, 1990, event. Cope managed to overcome the odds by staying close to the front of the pack while Dale Earnhardt dominated, leading all but 44 of the first 199 laps. On the final circuit, Earnhardt cut a passenger-side rear tire while entering Turn 3, allowing Cope to slip by and win the 500, scoring his first Winston Cup Series triumph. Cope collected $188,000 for the victory, one of two Winston Cup wins he scored in a 29-year career featuring 409 starts. Cope's other Cup win came the same season when he captured the Budweiser 500 at Dover Downs International Speedway on June 3.

686 A 24-car wreck on Lap 2 took the fizz out of the 1990 Pepsi 400 at Daytona International Speedway. Dale Earnhardt took advantage of the thinned field and led five times for 127 of the 160 laps on the way to his first Winston Cup points race victory at The World Center of Speed.

687 Michael Ritch, a crewman for Bill Elliott, was struck and killed on pit road by the spinning car of Ricky Rudd during the 1990 Atlanta Journal 500. It was the third time tragedy had struck the Atlanta Motor Speedway pit lane; Randy Owens (1975) and Dennis Wade (1979) had also died while serving as pit crew members. After the 1990 season, NASCAR introduced the first of what became many rules and equipment regulations in an effort to improve pit road safety. Fortunately, there have been no additional fatalities on pit road at Atlanta since Ritch's death.

688 Dale Earnhardt scored the 46th victory of his Cup career in the 1990 Heinz Southern 500 at Darlington Raceway. Earnhardt's winning purse of $210,350 was boosted by an additional $30,400 in Unocal 76 Challenge bonus bucks for winning pole position. The giant payday makes Earnhardt the first driver to win more than $11 million in Winston Cup prize money.

689 Dale Earnhardt was in a championship battle with Mark Martin, trailing by just 16 points as the Series headed to Charlotte Motor Speedway and the Mello Yello 500 on October 7, 1990. Earnhardt proved to be an also-ran, bringing out the third caution of the day when he hit the Turn 4 wall on Lap 116. A quick trip to pit road had Earnhardt quickly heading back onto the track only to have all four tires come off his car at the end of pit road. Thanks to quick thinking by his pit crew who ran down pit road to put the tires back on, Earnhardt salvaged a 25th-place finish, losing just 33 points to Martin. Earnhardt rallied through the final three events to win the title, beating Martin by 26 points.

690 An unintended glitch in the 1991 "odd-even" rules helped Rusty Wallace score a late-race victory in the Valleydale Meats 500 at Bristol International Raceway. NASCAR had mandated that odd-qualified cars would restart in the inside lane after a caution period while those in even-qualified cars would restart on the outside. Wallace was running seventh when the 17th caution flag flew on Lap 472. Per the rules, Wallace (in an odd-qualified car) moved to the inside lane and advanced, passing five even cars in the outside lane when the odd cars in front of him pitted. Wallace, who didn't pit, then took the green flag restart at the front of the field and held it to the finish, jumping from the seventh spot to Victory Lane without ever passing a car under green-flag conditions.

691 Kenny Wallace's first Winston Cup start was a memorable one, but for the wrong reason. Wallace's crash with 19 laps remaining in the 1990 First Union 400 brought out a yellow flag and sent leader Brett Bodine to pit road for fresh tires. Meanwhile, second- and third-place drivers Dale Earnhardt and Darrell

Waltrip stayed on the track and the pace car picked up Earnhardt as the leader. A 17-lap delay followed while NASCAR officials tried to figure out the correct running order, finally putting Bodine back in front. Bodine, the only driver among the leaders with four fresh tires, made quick work of the final two circuits to win the event. Waltrip, who got by Earnhardt to finish second, immediately protested the results to see his appeal denied. Bodine's victory was his only win in 480 career starts.

692 The 1.349-mile Suzuka International Racing Course located in Ino, Japan, played host to NASCAR Winston Cup non-points paying exhibition races in 1996 and 1997. NASCAR visited Japan for the first time November 24, 1996, when Rusty Wallace won the pole and the 125-lap Thunder Suzuka Special. Dale Earnhardt, Jeff Gordon, Terry Labonte, and Wally Dallenbach Jr. rounded out the top-5. One year later, Mike Skinner lead the final 23 laps, beating Mark Martin to the checkered flag at Suzuka. In 1998, NASCAR held a third Thunder event, this one at Twin Ring Motegi. Skinner came home the winner again with Gordon, Jeremy Mayfield, Jeff Burton, and Rusty Wallace in tow.

693 Prior to the 1991 NASCAR season, ESPN decided to not renew its broadcast rights to five Winston Cup races. This allowed The Nashville Network (TNN) to expand its motorsports-programming platform by picking up the castoff events at Rockingham, Phoenix, Dover, New Hampshire, and Phoenix that season. Over the next decade, TNN televised Winston Cup, Busch Grand National, and Craftsman Truck Series events until NASCAR signed a new six-year deal with FOX, NBC, and TBS.

694 J. D. McDuffie made his NASCAR debut at Rambi Speedway in Myrtle Beach, South Carolina, in 1961, wheeling an ex-Curtis Turner Ford to a 12th-place finish. Winless in 652 starts throughout the next 27 seasons, McDuffie was killed August 11, 1991, at Watkins Glen International after his No. 70 Pontiac's driver-side front suspension failed and he crashed into a steel guardrail. McDuffie's best race finish was in third-place at Albany-Saratoga Speedway in

Switching the racing surface from asphalt to concrete didn't keep the crowds down at Bristol International Raceway, as evidenced by this photo from a 1993 Busch Series race. Actually, tickets to a race at Bristol were among the hardest to get even with the track doubling the seating capacity from more than 70,000 to 150,000 in the 1990s. (John Close Photo)

1971. The 52-year-old McDuffie also won a celebrity race at Shangri-La Speedway in Oswego, New York, the night before he died.

695 After a disappointing 27th-place finish in the 1992 Daytona 500, Bill Elliot won his next four Winston Cup events. Driving for Junior Johnson, Elliott scored consecutive victories at Rockingham, Richmond, Atlanta, and Darlington. Despite the solid showing, Elliott still wasn't the season point's leader; he trailed Davey Allison by 48.

696 Frustrated with constant repairs to its asphalt surface, Bristol Motor Speedway owner Larry Carrier repaved the half-mile Tennessee oval with concrete in the summer of 1992. On August 29, Darrell Waltrip won the Bud 500, the first race on the new surface. It was the first time a Winston Cup race was run on an all-concrete raceway.

697 On March 13, 1993, the day before the Motorcraft Quality Parts 500 at Atlanta Motor Speedway, northern Georgia was hit by a massive blizzard, dumping nearly 3 feet of snow. The rogue storm, which claimed 15 lives across the state, paralyzed the area, forcing cancellation of the race. One week later, Morgan Shepherd passed rookie Jeff Gordon with a dozen laps to go and sprinted away to a 17.38-second win over runner-up Ernie Irvan. Gordon, in his fifth Winston Cup start, finishes fourth, his best Winston Cup finish to date.

698 After a night of drinking in the Pocono Raceway infield, Chad Blaine Kohl escaped serious injury when he ran across the racetrack under green-flag conditions during the 1993 Champion Spark Plug 500 NASCAR Winston Cup race. Kohl, a 24-year-old computer programmer from Ephrata, Pennsylvania, hopped over the infield-retaining fence and ran across the track in front of race leader and eventual winner Kyle Petty. He then jumped the outside retaining wall and disappeared into a marsh. Lost in the thicket, Kohl lit a signal fire so that a search helicopter could find him. He was later charged with public drunkenness, trespassing, disorderly conduct, risking a catastrophe, and arson.

699 On July 30, 1994, the Mesa Marin 20 took the green flag at the Bakersfield, California, half-mile paved oval. The exhibition race debuted NASCAR's Truck Series with four Fords driven by Gary Collins, P. J. Jones, Dave Ashley, and Rob MacCachren with one Chevrolet piloted by Craig Huartson. Jones slipped by Collins for the lead on Lap 14 and went on to the $900 first-place victory.

700 The Mesa Marin 20 was the first of four exhibition events that NASCAR used to examine and approve the viability of the new vehicles as race-worthy. Rob MacCachren and Gary Collins won the second and third events at Portland Speedway (Oregon) and Saugus Speedway in Santa Clarita (California) without incident. In the final exhibition, California Late Model stock car ace Ron Hornaday Jr. piloted a Spears Manufacturing Chevrolet to a win at Tucson Raceway Park (Arizona).

701 The success and acceptance of the truck exhibition races allowed NASCAR to take the next step with the new form of racing. A series of three 200-lap Winter Heat events were scheduled; they were real races with larger fields to be run at Tucson Raceway Park. All three races, which featured a unique halftime break at the end of the first 100 laps, were televised live by The Nashville Network. The races were an immediate hit with fans seeing the (now titled) NASCAR SuperTrucks race for the first time.

702 Sterling Marlin made his Winston Cup career debut May 8, 1976, finishing 29th in the Music City 400 at Nashville Fairgrounds Speedway. Marlin made 277 starts over the next 17 seasons before winning the Daytona 500 February 20, 1994. Marlin held Ernie Irvan at bay in the final laps, taking his first career Cup victory in his 279th start, the longest time taken by a driver to post his first win.

703 Jeff Gordon became the second driver in NASCAR history to score his first Cup win in the Coca-Cola 600 at Charlotte Motor Speedway. His No. 24 Hendrick Motorsports Chevrolet visited Victory Lane on May 29, 1994. The other driver notching his first win in the 600-mile classic was David Pearson, in the former World 600 Grand National race in May 1961. Gordon's first win was in his 42nd Winston Cup start.

704 In 1990, after nine months of construction to add a 1-mile oval track to the former Bryar Motorsports Park road course facility, New Hampshire International Raceway opened. That added NASCAR's first appearance on the Magic Mile on July 15, 1990, with the Budweiser 300 Busch Series event. Tommy Ellis took home the checkered flag, .29 seconds in front of Harry Gant, Chuck Bown, Morgan Shepherd, and Rick Mast.

705 Sterling Marlin dominated the early portion of the Slick 50 300, but it was Rusty Wallace who came on strong to win the event at New Hampshire International Speedway July 11, 1993. The race is the first Cup competition at the flat 1.058-mile paved oval.

Since then, New Hampshire has hosted a top-division event every year, with two races every season since 1997.

706 NASCAR had flirted with the idea of an event at Indianapolis Motor Speedway for years but could never quite pull the trigger. On April 6, 1992, the International Race of Champions (IROC) stock cars conducted a test. NASCAR drivers Dave Marcis, Dick Trickle, and Jim Sauter drove identically prepared Dodge Daytonas around the 2.5-mile Indy oval. Based on the results, nine Winston Cup drivers (Rusty Wallace, Dale Earnhardt, Ernie Irvan, Ricky Rudd, Mark Martin, Bill Elliott, Darrell Waltrip, Davey Allison, and Kyle Petty) headed to Indianapolis for an unofficial Goodyear tire test June 23 and 24. On the second day, more than 40,000 fans watched a 15-lap "gang tire test." With test results in, NASCAR officially announced on April 14, 1993, that it would sanction its first Winston Cup event at The Brickyard in August 1994.

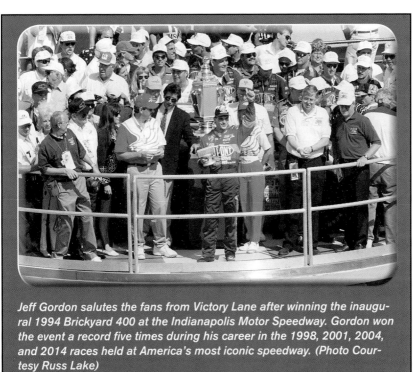

Jeff Gordon salutes the fans from Victory Lane after winning the inaugural 1994 Brickyard 400 at the Indianapolis Motor Speedway. Gordon won the event a record five times during his career in the 1998, 2001, 2004, and 2014 races held at America's most iconic speedway. (Photo Courtesy Russ Lake)

707 On August 6, 1994, the inaugural Brickyard 400 at Indianapolis Motor Speedway broke all Winston Cup single-event attendance records with a staggering 340,000 fans. The perfect Indiana day saw surprise pole winner Rick Mast lead the 43-car field to the green flag and the first lap. Indiana's favorite son, Jeff Gordon, took the lead five laps from the finish, beating Brett Bodine, Bill Elliott, Rusty Wallace, and Dale Earnhardt to the checkered flag by .53 seconds. Gordon's second career Cup win earned him a staggering $613,000, nearly 2½ times more than Sterling Marlin's take for winning that season's Daytona 500.

708 As the centerpiece of economic revitalization after Hurricane Andrew's devastation in 1992, the Miami Dade Homestead Motorsports Complex (Homestead, Florida), hosted its first NASCAR race November 5, 1995. The 1.5-mile flat, square-shaped oval saw 63 cars attempt to qualify for Busch Series Jiffy Lube 300's 43-car starting field. Dale Jarrett took the win under caution going from fourth to Victory Lane after leaders Kenny Wallace, Hermie Sadler, and Larry Pearson crashed in Turn 3, two laps from the finish.

709 Constructed in 1995 on the grounds of Walt Disney World Resort outside Orlando, Florida, primarily for the Indy Racing League (IRL), Walt Disney World Speedway hosted Craftsman Truck Series events in 1997 and 1998. The 1997 Chevy Trucks Challenge was a 200-lap battle on the 1-mile triangle-shaped "Mickyard" oval, and was won by Joe Ruttman. The race was marred by the death of John Nemechek when his No. 8 Chevrolet hit its driver's side flush with the Turn 1 outside retaining wall. One year later, Ron Hornaday Jr. beat Ruttman to the finish in the final truck event at the track.

710 After remaining winless in his first 73 Winston Cup starts, Bobby Labonte scored his first series victory May 28, 1995, in the Coca-Cola 600 at Charlotte Motor Speedway. Labonte also won family bragging rights by finishing 6.28-seconds in front of older brother and runner-up Terry. The sweep of the top 2 spots earned the brothers the distinction of being the first since Bobby and

Donnie Allison finished 1–2 24 years earlier in the May 30, 1971, World 600 at Charlotte.

711 Originally built at a cost of more than $72 million, Las Vegas Speedway opened in September 1996. NASCAR came calling soon afterward with Ken Schrader capturing the Winston West Las Vegas 300K on November 2, 1996, with the Truck Series a day later when Jack Sprague took first-place honors. On March 13, 1997, Jeff Green nabbed the first Busch Series event while Mark Martin ruled supreme in the first Cup race held March 1, 1998. That year, Speedway Motorsports, Inc. acquired the facility at a cost of $215 million. In 2006, the large oval track was reconfigured, adding 12 to 20 degrees of progressive banking in the corners in addition to a modern media center and multiple fan amenities to make LVMS one of the most unique and advanced racing facilities in the United States.

Since its NASCAR debut in 1996, Las Vegas Motor Speedway has undergone several makeovers, with the last one including one of the coolest-fan infield experiences anywhere, the "Neon Garage." (John Close Photo)

712 Matt Kenseth made his Lycos-sponsored Chevrolet supporters happy when he won the Lycos.com 250 at Pikes Peak International Raceway (PPIR) on June 14, 1998. The Busch Series event was the first NASCAR-sanctioned race at the 1-mile Fountain, Colorado, oval. The Busch Series raced eight times at PPIR through 2005 with eight different winners. The Truck Series competed at the track five times from 1998 through 2002. Greg Biffle is the only driver to win both series at the track (the Truck Series in 2000 and the NBS in 2004).

713 Originally opened in 1967 as a 1/8-mile drag strip, St. Louis Raceway Park, a road course (with a 1.25-mile egg-shaped oval added later) was added to the Gateway Motorsports Park mix by the 1997 season. NASCAR invaded the Madison, Illinois, track for the first time with the Busch Series Gateway 300 on July 26, 1997. Elliott Sadler won ahead of Jason Keller, Dale Shaw, Elton Sawyer, and Mike McLaughlin. The track hosted 15 NBS events throughout the 2010 season. Rick Carelli won the first Truck Series race at Gateway in 1998. Kyle Busch Motorsports driver Christopher Bell wheeled a Toyota to victory in the 2016 Truck Series Drivin' For Lineman 200 on June 25.

714 Built at a cost of more than $250 million, Texas Motor Speedway hosted its first NASCAR race on April 5, 1997; Mark Martin captured the Coca-Cola 300 Busch Series event. A day later, Jeff Burton earned his first career Winston Cup victory when he beat the 43-car starting field to the finish in the Interstate Batteries 500. Since then, the 1.5-mile oval has hosted nearly 100 Cup, Xfinity, and Truck Series events.

715 The NASCAR Craftsman Truck Series made its first appearance at Texas Motor Speedway on June 6, 1997. Mike Bliss won the pole for the Pronto Auto Parts 400K with a lap of 175.667 mph, nearly 18 mph more than the previous qualifying mark of 157.909 mph set by Michael Waltrip at Las Vegas Motor Speedway in 1996.

716 Heartland Park in Topeka, Kansas, opened in 1989 with multiple road course layouts, a drag strip, and a third-mile dirt oval. The 1.8-mile road course hosted five Truck Series events in the 1990s, the first in the division's inaugural 1995 season. The July 29 Heartland Tailgate 175 was the first Truck Series race run on a road course and was won by Ron Hornaday Jr. Mike Skinner (1996), Joe Ruttman (1997), Stacy Compton (1998), and Mike Bliss (1999) all captured Truck Series races there before the track fell off the schedule prior to the 2000 season.

717 NASCAR's dreams of returning to Southern California were realized when California Speedway in Fontana opened in 1997. Owned by Roger Penske, the 2-mile, D-shaped oval is built on a former Kaiser Steel mill site, which required a $6 million fee to remove hazardous waste before construction is permitted. On June 22, 1997, NASCAR made its first appearance at the track with Jeff Gordon winning the California 500 Presented By NAPA. Since then, more than 65 Winston Cup, Xfinity, and Truck Series races have been contested at the renamed Auto Club Speedway.

718 Greg Biffle scored his first and only NASCAR REBCO Northwest Tour Series win when he captured the NAPA 150 at Magic Valley Speedway on December 20, 1997. Biffle, who joined the Roush Racing NASCAR Craftsman Truck Series effort full-time in 1998, dominated at the first touring series race held at the Twin Falls, Idaho, paved oval. In all, 12 NASCAR Northwest Tour races were held at Magic Valley throughout 2006 with Garrett Evans winning four of them.

719 NASCAR's 50th Anniversary season (1998) got off to a flying start with the 40th Annual Daytona 500. The landmark events were overshadowed by the sport's biggest star when Dale Earnhardt finally captured NASCAR's most highly-prized race. Earnhardt, who had often come close to winning in his 19 previous 500 starts, took the checkered flag under caution in front of Bobby Labonte, Jeremy Mayfield, Ken Schrader, and Rusty Wallace. The win, Earnhardt's only Daytona 500 triumph, earned him $1,059,809 in prize money, nearly three times the $377,410 prize money Jeff Gordon banked after winning in 1997.

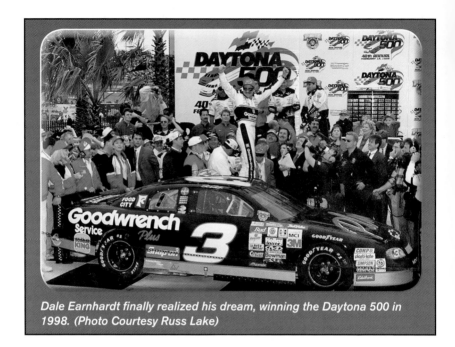

Dale Earnhardt finally realized his dream, winning the Daytona 500 in 1998. (Photo Courtesy Russ Lake)

720 The 1998 Pepsi 400 at Daytona International Speedway was scheduled for July 4 only to be canceled due to the wildfires sweeping northern Florida the week prior. Rescheduled for October 17, the event was slowed down three times due to wet weather, the last time just five laps from the finish. Jeff Gordon eventually took the victory in a green-white-checkered-flag finish.

721 The 5/8-mile "round rectangle" Flemington Speedway (New Jersey) was converted from dirt to asphalt costing $500,000 prior to the 1991 season. Speeds increased nearly 10 mph average and two seconds a lap. After several Modified drivers suffered injuries in high-speed crashes into the retaining walls, promoter Paul Kuhl contracted Buffalo, New York, company Thermol Foams, Inc. to manufacture and attach 8 x 3 x 3-foot blocks of Styrofoam insulation to the racetrack's outer walls. The blocks, costing $90 each, worked to perfection, disintegrating upon hard contact and absorbing much of the impact. The barriers are considered the forerunner to modern SAFER Barriers used at all major NASCAR tracks today.

PIT PASS

722 During the August 1989 Winston Cup race weekend at Watkins Glen International, team owner Junior Johnson approached Alan Kulwicki with a three-year offer to pilot the No. 11 Budweiser Ford, starting with the 1990 season. Kulwicki, winless in 1989 and driving his own equipment to a 14th-place finish in the points, turned Johnson down. Citing his personal investment and an inability to give up on his own dreams, Kulwicki won four times over the next three seasons, capturing the 1992 Winston Cup championship. After Kulwicki declined, Johnson hired Geoff Bodine and that association produced four wins over two seasons. Bill Elliott joined Johnson's team in 1992, winning five times, finishing second to Kulwicki in the title chase.

723 L. D. Ottinger won the 1990 Budweiser 200 NASCAR Busch Series race at Bristol International Speedway, but the April 7 event is remembered as the day Michael Waltrip cheated death. On Lap 170, Waltrip's No. 30 Kool-Aid Pontiac tore through the crossover gate on Turn 2's outside wall. The dead stop–impact all but disintegrated Waltrip's car, leaving his legs hanging out of the wreckage. Crews rushed to the scene assuming the worst, instead found him conscious and virtually unhurt. Amazingly, Waltrip started and finished 20th the next day in the Valleydale 500 event.

724 While Michael Waltrip escaped serious injury during the 1990 season the same cannot be said for his brother, Darrell. The elder Waltrip suffered multiple leg fractures, a broken arm, broken ribs and a concussion in final practice the day before the July 7 Pepsi 400 at Daytona International Speedway. Waltrip spun after Dale Earnhardt (driving A. J. Foyt's car) broke an oil line, and Waltrip's prone racer was hit in the driver's door at full speed by Dave Marcis. Marcis, who suffered a broken leg in the incident, started the 400 the next day for points, completing the pace lap before being relieved by J. D. McDuffie. Waltrip made his 500th career start two weeks later at Pocono, also completing one lap before turning the car over relief driver Jimmy Horton. Waltrip returned to the cockpit full-time in September, starting 27th and finishing 3rd in the Pontiac Excitement 400 at Richmond International Raceway.

725 Morgan-McClure Motorsports was one of the more successful Winston Cup teams during the 1990s, with 14 victories, two in the Daytona 500. The Abingdon, Virginia-based team notched its first Cup win at its hometown track August 25, 1990, as Ernie Irvan wheeled the No. 4 Kodak Film Chevrolet to victory in the Busch 500 at Bristol International Speedway.

726 Rob Moroso, the 1989 Busch Series champion, was having a successful Winston Cup rookie year, finishing 21st in the Holly Farms 400 at North Wilkesboro Speedway September 30, 1990. Later that evening, Moroso lost his life when his car skidded into the path of another vehicle on Highway 150, north of Charlotte. The driver of the other car, Tammy Williams of China Grove, North Carolina, was also killed in the crash. At season's end, Moroso was posthumously named the Winston Cup Rookie of the Year.

727 Dale Earnhardt was six laps from winning his first Daytona 500 when Ernie Irvan motored past The Intimidator and won the February 19, 1991, classic. The race ended under caution after Earnhardt crashed with two laps left, allowing Irvan to idle to the checkered flag. The victory was the second of Irvan's Winston Cup career and earned him $233,000 in prize money.

728 Ricky Rudd and Davey Allison waged an epic battle late in the 1991 Banquet Frozen Foods 300 at Sears Point International Raceway's 2.520-mile road course. Contact between the two drivers with slightly more than a lap remaining sent Allison spinning off the track. Rudd raced on to an apparent victory as Allison righted his machine, finishing in the runner-up position, 4 seconds behind Rudd. After the race, NASCAR assessed a 5-second penalty to Rudd for the on-track incident, giving Allison the second of five Winston Cup victories that season.

729 Brothers Rusty, Kenny, and Mike Wallace raced a total of 1,247 Cup Series events. The first time the brothers competed in the same event was November 3, 1990, in the Pyroil 500 at Phoenix International Raceway. Rusty won bragging rights with a 5th-place finish while Mike (in his first Winston Cup start) wheeled Jimmy Means' Pontiac to 31st. Kenny Wallace had nothing to brag about, finishing 43rd (last) with steering problems after one lap.

730 The newest member of the "Alabama Gang," Clifford Allison was 22 races into his Busch Series career when he headed to Michigan International Speedway for the 1992 Detroit Gasket 200. The son of Bobby and Judy Allison, Clifford Allison was practicing August 13 when his Chevrolet Lumina crashed head-on into the Turn 3 outside retaining wall. The impact was so great that it tore Allison's seat from its mounting. Suffering severe head injuries in the crash, he was pronounced dead en route to the hospital. Allison's death was the first driver fatality in the history of MIS, open since 1969. He was 27.

731 After 1,185 top-tier races in 35 seasons, Richard Petty retired at the end of the 1992 season. The undisputed King of NASCAR, Petty was the leader in nearly every statistical category at that time. These included nearly 1,200 starts, wins (200), pole positions (127),

Richard Petty looks like he'd rather be fishing than riding out a rain shower at Bristol's 1992 spring event. Petty made 60 Cup series career starts at Bristol, winning three times while posting a whopping 37 top-10 finishes. (John Close Photo)

victories in a single season (27 in 1967), victories in a row (10), Daytona 500 victories (7), and championships (7), to name a few. Petty made his final start in the November 15, 1992, Hooters 500 at Atlanta Motor Speedway, starting 35th in his iconic No. 43 STP Pontiac. On Lap 95, Petty was caught in a multi-car crash on the main straight, his car briefly catching fire as it rolled to a stop at the end of pit road. Petty returned to the race with two laps remaining to avoid a DNF and took a final Victory Lap to the delight of the 160,000 fans in attendance.

732 The 1992 Hooters 500 at Atlanta Motor Speedway will be remembered as Richard Petty's final event and the race at which the next great NASCAR star, Jeff Gordon, made his Winston Cup debut. Gordon, who posted three wins and 11 pole positions to finish fourth in the 1992 Busch Series championship standings, was the fastest in second-round qualifying, and took the green flag at Atlanta from the 21st position. It was his first start in a Chevrolet after running a Ford in NBS competition and his first for Hendrick Motorsports. Gordon and his No. 24 DuPont stocker finished 34th, crashing out on Lap 161.

733 Less than six months after capturing the Winston Cup championship, Alan Kulwicki died in an airplane crash on April 1,

Alan Kulwicki left his native Wisconsin with little more than a truck full of personal items in 1985, ultimately to become a driver/owner prototype in the Winston Cup Series by the end of the decade. Kulwicki's career culminated with the 1992 Winston Cup championship. (John Close Photo)

1993. Kulwicki was en route to Bristol, Tennessee, when the private aircraft plunged into a hillside just short of Tri-Cities Regional Airport in Blountville, Tennessee. Also killed in the crash were Hooters' marketing manager Mark Brooks, Hooters' director of sports management Dan Duncan, and pilot Charlie Campbell. Kulwicki, the 1986 Winston Cup Rookie of the Year, competed in 207 Cup races from 1985 to 1993, winning five times. The Greenfield, Wisconsin, native was 38 at the time of his death.

734 Davey Allison was a solid fifth in the 1993 point standings after finishing third in the Slick 50 300 at New Hampshire International Speedway July 11, 1993. The following day, Allison, an accomplished pilot who had recently earned his helicopter certification, crashed the chopper he was piloting while attempting land in a confined area of the Talladega Superspeedway infield. Allison suffered traumatic head and lung injuries as well as a broken pelvis in the crash. Veteran racer Red Farmer, a passenger in the helicopter, received non-life-threatening injuries. Both were transported to Caraway Methodist Medical Center in Birmingham, Alabama. Allison immediately underwent surgery to relieve the pressure on his brain. He never regained consciousness and died the morning of July 13. Allison had 191 Winston Cup starts, winning 19 races and 14 pole positions. He competed in 86 Busch Series races. In 1998, Allison was named one of NASCAR's 50 greatest drivers in the first 50 years of the sport.

735 Dennis Huth was NASCAR's point man in developing what became the Craftsman Truck Series in 1994. Huth, NASCAR vice-president of administration at the time, was dispatched to California in April where he committed the organization's marketing might in exchange for rights to the idea. Within a month, Huth had introduced the new series to the press and scheduled the first Exhibition Races for later that fall. As his personal project, Huth presided over the Truck Series as director from the first point's event at Phoenix International Raceway in 1995 through December 1999, when he resigned due to objections regarding NASCAR's plan to change the division from a short-track to a superspeedway entity.

736 After rain delayed the start of the 1996 DieHard 500 at Talladega Superspeedway (Alabama), CBS abandoned its live coverage, instead cutting to a professional golf tournament. That meant nobody saw the grinding 10-car wreck near the finish in which Dale Earnhardt cheated death. In the era before Internet integration and smart phone technology, most found out about the results and the crash on the late-evening news. CBS aired the race two weeks later. It is the last NASCAR Cup race to have been televised on a tape-delayed basis.

737 Veteran Norwalk, Connecticut, driver Randy Lajoie competed in 80 Busch Series races in eight seasons before scoring his first win in the Meridian Advantage 200 at Nazareth Speedway on May 19, 1996. The win kicked off a wave of success as Lajoie went on to win four more times and capture the 1996 Busch Series Championship. Lajoie, with a previous best finish in points of 16th, turns in an almost mirror image of his 1996 season, winning five times on his way to a second-straight BGN championship in 1997.

738 Randy Lajoie's 1997 Busch Series championship proved profitable when he became the first driver in division history to win more than $1 million in a single season. Lajoie banked a record $1,105,201 in prize money for the 1997 BGN crown; it was nearly doubling his previous best of $532,823 payday after winning the 1996 division title.

739 Susanville, California, native Mike Skinner moved to North Carolina to work as a Winston Cup crewman before making his first Cup start as a driver in 1986. Unfortunately, his career never took off. Skinner made less than 20 Cup and Busch Series total starts over the next eight seasons. He got his big break in 1995 after signing to drive the No. 3 Richard Childress Chevrolet in the all-new SuperTruck Series. Skinner won 8 of 20 events that season, capturing the first Truck championship. A year later, Skinner had another eight Truck Series wins, finishing third in the standings. The efforts solidified his position as one of the early greats of the Craftsman Truck Series.

740 A native of Tomi, Japan, Keiichi Tsuchiya was an accomplished road racer and veteran of the 24 Hours of Le Mans when he took the green flag in the NASCAR Thunder Suzuka Special at Suzuka, Japan, November 23, 1996. Tsuchiya and his No. 1 Harry Ranier–owned Thunderbird battled their way to 15th, the highest finish of four Japanese-born drivers in the non-points race. Tsuchiya was the highest-finishing native again in the 1997 NASCAR Suzuka Special with an 11th-place finish. His good luck ran out in the 1998 Thunder exhibition at Twin Ring Motegi when he crashed on Lap 49 and finished 35th.

741 From 1995 through the 12th race of 1998, Craftsman Truck Series races featured a "half-time break" for a 10-minute mandated stop in the action. During the break (the brainchild of Brian France) teams could service their trucks, giving the media the opportunity to interview drivers mid-race, a rarity in an era before the development of sophisticated driver cockpit communications. The breaks, which saved teams money for special over-the-wall pit crews, ended when the division staged live pit stops in the July 25, 1998, Tempus Resorts 300 at Pikes Peak International Raceway (Colorado). The Truck Series has had live pit stops in its events ever since.

742 Math whiz Jack Roush carried the Ford banner into NASCAR competition, fielding his first Winston Cup entry in 1988. By the end of the 1990s, Jack Roush Performance Enterprises was one of the top teams in all of NASCAR with 44 series wins to its credit and multiple teams in each event. In addition, Roush's Busch Series cars dominated the 1990s by winning 40 times. Today, Roush has fielded more than 5,500 combined Cup, Xfinity, and Truck Series entries.

743 Charlotte, North Carolina–based auto dealership mogul Rick Hendrick saw his dreams of multi-team Winston Cup success come to pass from 1994 through 1999. Led by driving sensation Jeff Gordon, Hendrick's Chevrolets scored 60 victories in six seasons. The most memorable win came when Gordon, Terry Labonte, and Ricky Craven swept the first three spots in the 1997 Daytona 500.

The efforts resulted in four-straight Winston Cup titles as Gordon won the 1995, 1997, and 1998 laurels with Labonte grabbing the HMS championship crown in 1996.

744 Jeff Gordon and Ray Evernham first teamed up as part of the Bill Davis Racing Team's Busch Series in the early 1990s. In 1992, Gordon began fielding offers to jump to the Winston Cup division in 1993. Ford, who paid Evernham's salary while he worked for Davis, seemed to have the inside track with Gordon going to Jack Roush's stable. Roush, however, would not agree to Gordon's demand to include Evernham in the deal. That opened the door for Rick Hendrick to lure Gordon away by offering Gordon more money and the opportunity to bring Evernham along as his crew chief. Gordon and Evernham went on to win 49 Winston Cup races and three championships for Hendrick through the 1999 season.

745 After 38 years working for NASCAR, Doyle Ford retired after the 1997 Coca Cola 600 at Charlotte Motor Speedway. Ford flagged races all over the South including his home track, Nashville Fairgrounds Speedway. Ford had been the chief starter for all Winston Cup events since 1990.

746 After a driving career spanning 27 years and 535 Winston Cup starts, Elmo Langley took over pace car-driving duties at all Winston Cup events during the 1989 season. On November 21, 1996, Langley suffered a massive heart attack while pacing the NASCAR exhibition race at Suzuka, Japan. He was pronounced dead at Suzuka General Hospital. Langley was 68 years old.

747 For its 50th Anniversary season in 1998, NASCAR commissioned a special logo honoring the event. It also launched a massive merchandising campaign signing licensing agreements with more than 40 companies to produce commemorative souvenirs for the season-long celebration. The market was flooded with hundreds of anniversary die-cast cars, clothing, and card sets. Some of the more unique items were anniversary Christmas ornaments and a special edition Barbie doll.

748 As part of NASCAR's 50th Anniversary season, R.J. Reynolds Tobacco created "The Winston No Bull 5." Qualified drivers who won the Daytona 500, Brickyard 400, Coca-Cola 600 at Charlotte, Pepsi Southern 500 at Darlington, and the Winston 500 at Talladega received an extra $1 million. Jeff Gordon collected the bonus twice for victories at Indy and Darlington while Dale Jarrett got $1 million bag-o-cash for his victory at Talladega. In addition, R.J. Reynolds held a contest pairing fans with the five drivers eligible for the No Bull bonus, enabling fans earn a $1 million prize if their driver won. The program continued through the 2002 season, awarding the $1 million bonus, 13 times. Gordon won four times, with Jeff Burton taking three. Dale Jarrett and Dale Earnhardt Jr. earned the bonus twice, with Mark Martin and Dale Earnhardt each winning once.

749 Kenny Irwin Jr. took over the wheel of the No. 28 Ford fielded by Robert Yates Racing in 1998, rolling all the way to the Winston Cup Rookie of the Year Award. Irwin beat out Steve Park, Dennis Setzer, Kevin Lepage, and Jerry Nadeau for the honor.

750 Darrell Waltrip was selected as the most popular Winston Cup driver in 1990. The fans then voted the honor to Bill Elliott, "Awesome Bill From Dawsonville," throughout the remainder of the decade (1991 through 1999). Elliott was also the fan's choice as Mr. Popularity for five straight years from 1984 to 1988 and again in 2002.

751 During the 1999 season, Lowes Motor Speedway president Humpy Wheeler suggested that all over-the-wall pit crew members wear a number on their uniforms, similar to football, baseball, and basketball. His plan would identify crewpersons by position (crew chief, front tire changer, etc.), with numbers 1 through 8. Alternate members would be assigned numbers 9 through 12. The suggestion never gained traction and was never implemented.

752 Indicating how far NASCAR had come since its motor oil and cigarette sponsorship days, food giant General Mills launched the Betty Crocker Racing Family in 1999. Comprised of NASCAR wives Nancy Andretti, Debbie Benson, Kim Burton, Flossie Johnson, Andrea Nemechek, Pattie and Lynda Petty, and Stevie Waltrip, the women and their favorite dishes created with Betty Crocker products were featured on various General Foods product packages. The special products were highlighted in a national television and magazine advertising campaign.

MILESTONES

753 Released June 27, 1990, *Days Of Thunder* was a NASCAR-themed major motion picture starring Tom Cruise and Nicole Kidman. Loosely based on the Hendrick Motorsports team and the career of driver Tim Richmond, the movie was plagued by production delays and cost overruns that nearly doubled the film's original $35 million budget. Dismissed as Hollywood tripe by most NASCAR insiders, the film won public acclaim, grossing more than $157 million in its original release. More important, the movie spurred a mainstream interest in NASCAR, fueling an entire decade of public acceptance of the sport.

754 Darrell Waltrip won at least one race each season from 1975 to 1989, a total of 79 victories. The 15-season streak ended in 1990 when the Franklin, Tennessee, driver was forced to sit out six events after a huge practice crash for the Pepsi 400 left him with significant injuries.

755 Prior to the 1989 season, Unocal 76 (the official fuel provider of NASCAR) created the Unocal 76 Challenge, a Winston Cup contingency program that awarded an additional $7,600 to the purse of any driver who won an from pole position. If unclaimed, the prize rolled over to the next event. After pole sitter Kenny Schrader failed to win the bonus in the season-opening Daytona 500, Rusty Wallace grabbed double bonus of $15,200 one week later when he notched the pole and the win in the Goodwrench 500 at North Carolina Motor Speedway in Rockingham.

Kyle Petty proved to be a competent wheelman in the 1990s, winning six times. Three of Petty's eight Winston Cup career victories were at North Carolina Motor Speedway in Rockingham from 1990 to 1992. (John Close Photo)

756 After Rusty Wallace's victory at North Carolina Motor Speedway, the Unocal 76 Challenge bonus went unclaimed for the remainder of the 1989 season. By the time the Winston Cup Series pulled into Rockingham for the third race of 1990, the $7,600 bonus had "rolled over" 29 times. That meant a $228,400 bonus to the winner of the pole and the March 4 GM Goodwrench 500, in addition to the regular racing purse. Kyle Petty not only scored his first pole in 277 career starts, but led a staggering 433 of 492 laps to collect the giant Unocal bonus and a total winner's purse of $284,450. At the time, it was the biggest single-race payday in Winston Cup history.

757 In 1990, consumer goods giant Proctor and Gamble (the sponsor for Darrell Waltrip's Winston Cup efforts) announced plans to produce 1.5 million boxes of Tide laundry detergent featuring Waltrip and his Hendrick Motorsports Monte Carlo. The promotion was so popular with fans and consumers that the company ultimately printed and sold 7.5 million limited-edition boxes of laundry soap.

758 "Handsome" Harry Gant earned another title in the fall of 1991, speeding his way to four-consecutive Winston Cup victories. "Mr. September" wheeled his No. 33 Skoal Bandit Oldsmobile to victory in the Heinz Southern 500 at Darlington Raceway before rolling home first at Richmond (Virginia), Dover (Delaware), and Martinsville (Virginia) over the next three weeks. On September 29, Gant led 350 of the 400 laps in the Tyson Holly Farms 400 at North Wilkesboro Speedway, only to have Dale Earnhardt slip past with nine laps remaining, taking the win, and preventing Gant from scoring a fifth-straight victory.

759 After leading nearly 100 consecutive laps in the 1992 Hooters 500 at Atlanta Motor Speedway, Alan Kulwicki's crew chief Paul Andrews determined that if the team paced the field and held off pitting until Lap 310, Kulwicki would earn five bonus points for leading the most laps in the race. He also determined that if Kulwicki returned for the final 18 laps of the race and finished no worse than second, he would win the 1992 championship regardless of where title rival Bill Elliott finished. Kulwicki pitted on Lap 311 and returned to finish second (8.06 seconds behind Elliott). The finish earned Kulwicki the title by 10 points, the smallest championship margin of victory in the pre-Chase era.

760 On February 14, 1993, Dale Jarrett gave Winston Cup team owner Joe Gibbs his first win in the "Super Bowl of Stock Car Racing," the Daytona 500. Gibbs, the former Washington Redskins coach, guided the National Football League team to wins in the Super Bowl in 1982, 1987, and 1991. Gibbs was elected to the NFL Hall of Fame in 1996.

761 Jeff Gordon (1993) and Tony Stewart (1999) proved they were the real deal, capturing Winston Cup Rookie of the Year Awards before going on to win Cup Series championships. Meanwhile, top rookies Bobby Hamilton (1991), Jeff Burton (1994), Ricky Craven (1995), and Johnny Benson Jr. (1996) went on to post Cup wins during their careers.

The cream of the 1993 Winston Cup rookie crop, Jeff Gordon, Kenny Wallace, and Bobby Labonte share the spotlight in an ESPN interview. (Photo Courtesy Russ Lake)

762 Rusty Wallace had the kind of year any Winston Cup driver would dream about in 1993, posting division-high marks of 10 wins, 19 top-5, and 21 top-10 finishes. Despite a stellar season, Wallace came up second in the championship standings when Dale Earnhardt captured the crown by 80 points. Earnhardt's sixth championship was won on the strength of six wins, two fewer DNFs producing 147 more laps, and an 8.2 average finish to Wallace's 9.4.

763 In 1994, Ricky Rudd won the Slick 50 300 at New Hampshire International Speedway. The win was his first as a car owner and the 15th of his career. The triumph extended his Winston Cup winning streak to 12 straight seasons. The streak ended in 1998, after he had captured a Cup race in 16 consecutive seasons.

764 Dale Earnhardt achieved what most thought impossible after tying Richard Petty's mark for most championships in a career when he won the 1994 Winston Cup championship. Earnhardt's victory in the October 23 AC Delco 500 at Rockingham gave him the record-tying title and an insurmountable 448-point lead in the standings despite the fact there were two races remaining on the schedule.

765 Neil Bonnett built a successful television career in the early 1990s after racing injuries prevented him from competing in Winston Cup. In 1994, healthy and ready to resume a career that began in 1974 at Talladega, Bonnett took to the track in his No. 51 Country Time Lemonade Chevrolet for Daytona 500 practice on February 11. Moments later, Bonnett crashed hard in Turn 3 and was later pronounced dead at nearby Halifax Memorial Hospital. Bonnett, 47, ended his career with 18 victories in 362 Winston Cup career starts.

766 An outgrowth of O. Bruton Smith's business empire, Speedway Motorsports didn't incorporate until December 1994. Two months later, on February 24, 1995, Speedway Motorsports, Inc. (SMI) authorized the sale of company shares at $18 each in a $68-million initial public offering on the New York Stock Exchange.

767 The enormous amount of cash generated by SMI's public stock offering allowed the company to go on a spending spree over the final five years of the 1990s. The company purchased Bristol International Speedway and Sears Point Raceway in 1996, following up with the construction of NASCAR's most modern track (Texas Motor Speedway) in 1997. In 1999, SMI outbid both International Speedway Corporation (ISC) and NASCAR's parent company by $15 million, to acquire Las Vegas Speedway.

768 The Copper World Classic, a multi-division event held each February at Phoenix International Raceway (PIR), had an extra division in 1995 when the SuperTruck Series by Craftsman held its first points-paying race. The February 5 Skoal Bandit Copper Classic featured 33 starters (17 Chevrolets, 13 Fords, and 3 Dodges) in an 80-lap event on the 1-mile PIR oval. Pole sitter Ron Hornaday Jr. paced the first 32 laps in his Dale Earnhardt-owned Chevy before Mike Skinner took over on Lap 62 and never looked back, racing the Richard Childress-owned No. 3 Chevy to the win. Skinner earned $15,750 for the landmark win.

769 While Mike Skinner will be remembered as the winner of the first Truck Series regular season race, John Borneman has the distinction of finishing last in the same event. Borneman, an El Cajon, California, veteran driver who competed in eight Winston Cup events in the late 1970s and early 1980s, crashed out of the Skoal Bandit Copper Classic on Lap 22, finishing 33rd (last) in the inaugural race. He earned $1,200 in prize money.

770 In the six seasons from 1990 through 1995, Dale Earnhardt won 29 races. He also took two wins in the first four events of the 1996 season before a winless streak of 59 straight races. He broke out of the slump, winning the 1998 Daytona 500 on February 15, 1998. After the Daytona triumph, Earnhardt was again winless in his next 40 races; not seeing Victory Lane again until Talladega on October 17,1999.

771 When Ken Schrader wheeled to victory in the April 15, 1995, Craftsman Truck Series Scott Irwin Chevrolet 200 at Saugus Speedway, he became the first driver to win in all three NASCAR top series. Schrader's first Winston Cup victory was at Talladega in 1988; his first Busch Series triumph a year later at Dover.

772 The digital age exploded from 1994 through 1997 when the number of registered websites grew from slightly more than 2,700 to nearly 1.2 million. Among them were Yahoo.com, CNN.com, and NASCAR.com, all launched in late 1995.

773 Tony Stewart, the 1997 Verizon Indy Racing League champion, captured the 1999 Winston Cup Rookie of the Year title on the strength of three wins and 21 top-10 finishes in 34 races. "Smoke's" first Cup win happened September 11 in the Exide Batteries 400 at Richmond International Raceway. The win propelled Stewart through the final third of the season, winning two more times (Phoenix and Homestead back-to-back) and posting two runner-up finishes (New Hampshire and Dover) to finish fourth in the 1999 championship standings.

774 From 1968 through 1999, Dave Marcis made 32 consecutive starts in the Daytona 500. The record-holding consecutive starts began when Marcis wheeled a Larry Wehrs–owned Chevrolet to a 20th-place finish in the 1968 500 and ended with a 16th-place finish in the 1999 event. Marcis' best finish in the 500 was in 1975, a third-place effort behind the wheel of the No. 71 K&K Insurance Dodge.

775 In 1999, International Speedway Corporation (ISC) was the second-largest track owner behind Speedway Motorsports, Inc. when it swung a deal to acquire Penske Motorsports. ISC already owned 12 percent of Penske's holdings, which included Michigan Speedway, California Speedway, Nazareth Speedway, and North Carolina Speedway (Rockingham), with a 45 percent share in Homestead Speedway (Florida). ISC purchased the remaining 88 percent of Penske common stock, approximately 12.2 million shares, at $50 per share in a deal worth $623 million. The acquisitions vaulted ISC over SMI as the largest NASCAR facility ownership entity.

776 Throughout the 1980s and 1990s, tracks negotiated individually with the television networks to swing the best deal for their facility. By the end of the 1990s, NASCAR as a "product" had grown to the point at which the races could be collectively bargained in a single package, much like the NFL had done. On December 15, 1999, NASCAR agreed to a six-year package with television giant NBC and newcomer FOX. Both entities featured the Cup and Busch Series on their cable television platforms (FOX Sports, FX, and TBS). The estimated value of NASCAR's new television deal that started in 2001 was $2.4 billon.

777 NASCAR wasn't the only one headed to the bank with a truckload of money at the end of the 1990s. Dale Jarrett banked $6,649,596 by winning the 1999 Winston Cup championship, more

than double the $3,308,056 Dale Earnhardt collected for the 1990 title. Race purses skyrocketed throughout the decade. In 1990, just one event, the Daytona 500, featured a total purse of more than $1 million ($1,746,392), while 20 of the 29 races on the 1990 schedule featured purses of less than $500,000. In 1999, every race on the 34-event tour featured a purse of more than $1 million, with the biggest at Daytona ($7,287,146) and the smallest at Michigan ($1,588,750).

778 Jeff Gordon dominated many NASCAR statistical categories in the late 1990s. Over three seasons (1996–1998), Gordon led a staggering division-high 5,678 laps. For these efforts, Gordon collected $781,150 in bonuses; 81.4 percent of $900,000 available in lap leader cash during the span.

779 In the summer of 1999, the New York Division of Motor Vehicles announced that it would offer a line of custom license plates featuring eight Winston Cup drivers including Jeff Burton, Mark Martin, Tony Stewart, and Bobby Hamilton. In addition to drivers, the NASCAR logo was also incorporated into the plate design, making New York the first state to feature the sport's marketing brand on a vehicle identification tag.

Chapter 8

The 2000s: Changing Times, the New Millennium

January 1, 2000: the dawn of the new millennium.

While the world fretted over predictions of a massive computer malfunction and the subsequent "Y2K" lost-data apocalypse, NASCAR had nothing but a clear-windshield outlook speeding into the new decade.

And why not? The sport was flush with success enjoying aesthetic and financial success well beyond the imagination of its founder, Bill France Sr. Meanwhile, the future seemed just as bright as a new television contract all but guaranteed billions of dollars in future revenue and untold fan converts, too.

In retrospect, the Y2K global computer scare proved little more than that, a mirage that never really happened. The continued and unrestricted growth of NASCAR didn't happen either.

In what can only be described as a harmonic convergence of expansion-killing events, NASCAR suffered a series of blows during the 2000s that not even previous decades of vertical, record growth could overcome. Untimely events such as the death of Dale Earnhardt, the sport's most recognizable star, and the passing of Bill France Jr. proved to be watershed moments. Other turning points, were seen in the retirements of longtime stars Rusty Wallace, Mark Martin, Bill Elliott, Sterling Marlin, Kyle Petty, Ricky Rudd, Dale Jarrett, and Ken Schrader.

One of the biggest hits came from within industry as automakers moved further away from NASCAR's once V-8–powered rulers of the road

Due to rule changes that made cars nearly identical in performance, Sprint Cup events often featured three-wide "Pack Racing" on the superspeedways. (Photo Courtesy Russ Lake)

with a new form of car, the hybrid. Later, the 2007 global monetary crisis financially crippled much of the sport's blue-collar fan base.

The decade also produced a wave of personal entertainment choices with the introduction of the iPod (2001), YouTube (2005), iPhone (2006), and Kindle reader (2007) forever changing the way Americans spent their free time.

These unforeseeable events were just some reasons for the NASCAR slow-down in the 2000s. New leadership took the sport in different directions during the decade, boldly tweaking its core elements: the cars, race rules, and championship formats. Meanwhile, the persona of the sport changed losing much of its folksy, down home charm to a more buffed corporate veneer demanded by sponsorship benefactors and new television partners.

To say that NASCAR lost its way in the 2000s is probably an unfair assessment. In retrospect, the world changed exponentially at that time. To think the sport would continue the unfettered expansion of the three previous decades in the new millennium was fool's gold at its best and unrealistic at its worst.

To be sure, the events of the 2000s were unlike anything NASCAR or its fans could have envisioned. It was the dawn of the new millennium, a decade in which everyone was no longer trying to stay ahead of the curve, but, rather, just trying to keep up.

CARS

780 In 2000, the Toyota Prius became the first mass-produced hybrid four-door sedan sold in the United States. The energy-saving vehicle combined a gas engine with an electric motor to power the car, alternating use depending on driving needs. The car became the ultimate expression of a new "green" gas-saving culture, selling more than 2 million units worldwide throughout the decade. More important, it reshaped the public's core belief of what a car should and could be, further distancing NASCAR and its V-8–powered, fuel-gulping, full-size vehicles from mainstream passenger car buyers.

781 The next generation Monte Carlo was introduced in 2000, bringing with it a new race car. The NASCAR version got off to a slow start with just three finishing in the top-10 at the 2000 season-opening Daytona 500. After missing two more shots at victory, Dale Earnhardt gave the car its first Cup win in the Cracker Barrel Old Country Store 500 at Atlanta Motor Speedway on March 12. By season's end, the new Monte Carlo won 9 Cup races in 2000, second in the GM camp to Pontiac's 11.

782 Midway through the 2000 season, NASCAR informed teams in the Busch Grand National and Craftsman Truck Series that in 2001, both divisions would switch from a 9.5:1-compression engine to the 12.0:1 model currently used in the Cup division. While the bigger engine increased horsepower, it also exploded the engine bill for teams by as much as $300,000 per season.

783 One of the first safety improvements implemented after Dale Earnhardt's death was the six-point safety harness system. The newest generation featured a wraparound leg design wherein an

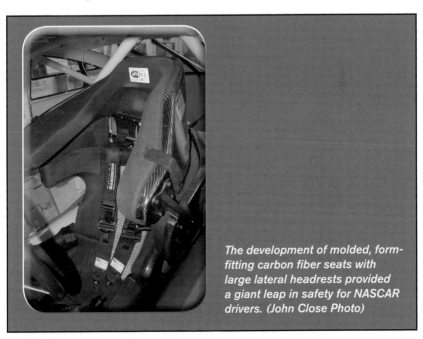

The development of molded, form-fitting carbon fiber seats with large lateral headrests provided a giant leap in safety for NASCAR drivers. (John Close Photo)

additional belt prevented the driver's lower torso from sliding down (or submarining) in a hard impact. The new system tied all the belts together with a single, quick-release latch design that assisted drivers in making a hasty retreat from their wrecked vehicles after a crash.

784 The evolution of the driver's seat design and construction proved to be one of the biggest safety developments of the 2000s. Single-piece carbon-fiber seats that formed to the shape of each driver emerged, replacing aluminum models. The new seats held the torso in place much better and provided much superior head and neck protection with the addition of giant side headrests covered with impact-resistant foam.

785 Based in large part on its success in the Craftsman Truck Series, Dodge returned to Winston Cup competition in 2001. The effort is spearheaded by Ray Evernham (with drivers Bill Elliott and Casey Atwood), and featured teams fielded by Bill Davis Racing (Ward Burton and Dave Blaney), Melling Racing (Stacy Compton), Petty Enterprises (John Andretti, Kyle Petty, and Buckshot Jones), and Chip Ganassi Racing with Felix Sabates (Sterling Marlin and Jason Leffler).

786 Like Ford, Dodge broke with the traditional two-door hard-top body style, campaigning the Dodge Intrepid (a four-door family sedan) in its return to Winston Cup racing. While NASCAR approves the Intrepid R/T quickly, the same can't be said for the new V-8 engine submitted for approval. After several rejections, the Dodge R5-P7 engine is approved in November 2000, just three months before Mopar returned to the track in the 2001 Daytona 500.

787 NASCAR took a giant step toward preventing fatalities due to basilar skull fracture by mandating the use of head and neck restraints in 2002. The device, which initially came in various configurations, keeps the head stable, not allowing it to whiplash forward in a sudden-stop impact. In the decade prior to the NASCAR mandate, drivers Neil Bonnett, Kenny Irwin Jr., Adam Petty, John Nemechek, Tony Roper, and Dale Earnhardt all died because of basilar skull fracture injuries. Not a single driver has died of basilar skull fracture injuries since the restraints became a fixture in 2002.

788 As part of sweeping safety changes in 2003, NASCAR mandated that all vehicles competing in Winston Cup, Busch and Craftsman Truck series be outfitted with a second cockpit fire extinguisher. The device is heat-activated and created specifically to prevent fires in the fuel cell area.

789 The HANS (Head and Neck System) Device is the approved restraint system used in NASCAR today. Developed by Michigan State University professor Dr. Robert Hubbard in the early 1980s, the carbon-fiber U-shaped device fits behind the driver's neck in an upside down position with the ends of the "U" pointing down the driver's chest. The driver's helmet is then anchored to the HANS and the entire unit secured by placing the upper belts in the six-point harness system above it. Today, the HANS device is used in nearly every form of amateur and professional motorsports around the world.

A Penske Racing crewmember helps Ryan Newman put on his Hutchens Device prior to a 2003 NASCAR Winston Cup race. (Photo Courtesy Russ Lake)

790 Many drivers preferred the Hutchens head and neck restraint system to the HANS device. Bobby Hutchens at Richard Childress Racing developed the device after the death of team driver Dale Earnhardt. Unlike the HANS that featured a bulky neck collar, the Hutchens Device used a series of straps fastened around the driver's upper torso that looped up and attached to the driver's helmet. NASCAR allowed both the HANS and the Hutchens system through the 2004 season before making the HANS the single mandatory unit for drivers in 2005.

791 NASCAR introduced modern crash data analysis to the sport in 2002, requiring vehicles in all touring series to have an on-board black box system. Nicknamed "The Witness," the battery-powered unit consists of multiple sensors that measure and record crash data such as angle of impact, G-forces expended, roll, pitch, and yaw of the car. The $499 waterproof, heat-resistant unit is slightly smaller than a videotape and is mounted on the lower left frame rail adjacent to the driver's seat.

792 Launched in 1975 as the Baby Grand National Division, the 4- and later, 6-cylinder engine series went through several name changes, the most recognizable being Goody's Dash Series from 1992 to 2003. NASCAR shut down the division after the 2003 season. During the 29-year series run, Dean Combs and Robert Huffman proved to be the most successful drivers, winning five championships each.

793 Before Toyota's success in NASCAR's top three divisions, the Japanese carmaker won races and a championship in Goody's Dash Series. Robert Huffman gave Toyota Racing Development (TRD) its first win in a Dash race at Kentucky Speedway, capturing the Kentucky 100 on June 16, 2001. Huffman followed up with Toyota's first title, wheeling the No. 37 *White House Apple Juice* Toyota Celica to the 2003 Dash Series championship.

794 After 155 top division wins, Pontiac left the Nextel Cup prior to the 2004 season. The best season for "The Chief" was in 1961, winning 30 of 52 NASCAR Grand National events.

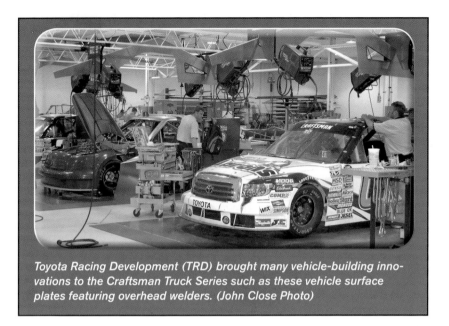

Toyota Racing Development (TRD) brought many vehicle-building innovations to the Craftsman Truck Series such as these vehicle surface plates featuring overhead welders. (John Close Photo)

795 The 2004 season saw Toyota enter the Craftsman Truck Series. The Japanese automaker, constructing all its Tundra trucks in the United States, earned its first win in the Line-X Spray-On Truck Bedliners 200 at Michigan International Speedway, the 13th race of the 2004 season. Travis Kvapil had his name added to the record books as he rolled his Alexander Meshkin–owned Tundra to Victory Lane on July 31.

796 Roush Racing made a statement when its five Fords took half the spots in the 2005 Chase 10-car lineup. Greg Biffle, Mark Martin, Matt Kenseth, and Carl Edwards swept the top four spots in the final Chase race at Homestead-Miami Speedway, but Tony Stewart grabbed the championship with a 20th-place finish.

797 In August 2005, the all-new Ford Fusion four-door, five-passenger mid-size sedan starts production as a 2006 model. The car also becomes Ford's Nextel Cup model of choice, replacing the Taurus. The double debut is the first time since the introduction of the 1968 Torino that Ford launches a new passenger car and designates it as its NASCAR racer of choice in the same year.

798 New to NASCAR in 1971, the Monte Carlo has been a mainstay of the Chevrolet effort ever since. On September 17, 2006, the marque picked up its 400th victory when Kevin Harvick captured the Sylvania 500 at New Hampshire International Speedway.

799 Introduced at Bristol in March 2007, NASCAR's fifth-generation Cup racer, the Car of Tomorrow (COT), was a significant advance in safety. The 2-inch taller and 5-inch wider car moved the driver closer to the center of the car and incorporated energy-absorbing crumple zones. The COT's body took several styling cues from the Truck Series with the nose having an adjustable splitter (a heavy plastic shelf the width of the nose), replacing the valance, and creating more downforce. It wore a rear wing instead of a spoiler, the first time that NASCAR Cup cars used such a device since the winged Dodge Charger Daytonas and Plymouth Superbirds of the late 1960s and early 1970s. Drivers complained about the car's handling characteristics while the fans never accepted the boxy shape over the previous slick aerodynamic models. After trying for five years, NASCAR scrapped the COT at the end of 2012 in favor of the current Gen 6 model, which incorporates nearly all of the COT's safety features.

Jimmie Johnson was a quick study in adapting to the new Car of Tomorrow (COT) by winning the 2007 Nextel Cup championship in the car's first season. (John Close Photo)

800 The COT's 2007 introduction brought some new names to the sport. Chevrolet, which had campaigned the Monte Carlo for most of the last 35 years, debuted its COT as an Impala SS, while Dodge ditched the Charger for the Avenger model. Ford continued to run the COT as a Fusion while Toyota continued using the Camry.

801 Beginning in 2007, each new chassis was subject to NASCAR approval before hitting the track. NASCAR laser measured each chassis to certify it ready for competition. As many as 220 measurements, accurate up to 1/10,000th of an inch, are taken and recorded in a permanent file for each chassis. Once approved, each chassis is assigned a serial number that is affixed to the roll bar for identification. Any chassis damaged in a crash and rebuilt must go through another recertification measurement process by NASCAR before being allowed to compete again.

802 Toyota's entrance into NASCAR forced the sanctioning body to approve parts with no links to Toyota's passenger car line. That opened the door for Chevrolet to introduce the first engine designed specifically for NASCAR, the R07 (short for Racing 2007). The fourth-generation small-block Chevy powerplant used what GM engineers called "computational fluid dynamics," a design to optimize high-speed airflow. The R07 featured several enhancements over the previous model (SB2), with larger cylinder bore centers to improve coolant flow, a new head bolt pattern to reduce cylinder bore distortion, and a raised camshaft to improve valve train performance and reliability. The new Chevy engine took off with a bang as Jeff Burton wheeled a Richard Childress Racing R07-powered car to a win in the 2007 Samsung 500 at Texas Motor Speedway.

803 Prior to the COT's introduction in 2007, every vehicle brand had a set of body templates specific to that car. With the development of the COT, NASCAR also introduced the Claw (a cage-like single grid of templates) to its technical inspection process. Now, instead of positioning multiple single templates over the car to see if it conformed to rules and passed, the Claw was lowered over the whole car and a Laser Inspection System (LIS) measured the car's

"The Claw," a one-piece cage-like template, modernized NASCAR's inspection process by replacing individual templates for each brand of racecar. (John Close Photo)

fit. The Claw and its LIS technology are still used today to measure the body specs of the Gen 6 racer.

804 The COT made its competitive debut in the fifth race of the 2007 season at Bristol Motor Speedway. Kyle Busch scored the fourth win of his Cup career in a Rick Hendrick–owned Chevrolet Impala SS over Jeff Burton, Jeff Gordon, Kevin Harvick, and Greg Biffle. Busch's win in the March 27 event was the first time a Chevrolet Impala had been to Victory Lane since December 1, 1963, when Wendell Scott won the Jacksonville 200 at Jacksonville Speedway Park (Florida).

805 Launched in 2004, iRacing.com announced in April 2009 that it would partner with NASCAR to create an online racing series. It rolled out in 2010 with a mix of seven amateur and pro divisions including the NASCAR i-Racing Pro Series (NiPS) and the NASCAR i-Racing World Championships (NiWS). Today, thousands of fans compete in NASCAR Cup, Xfinity, Truck, and Modified division iRacing contests. The iRacing World Championships bring together the top 50 pro division drivers.

806 After years of trial and error, NASCAR decided to ditch the wing on the COT's rear deck lid early in the 2010 Sprint Cup season. Beginning with the March 29 Goody's Fast Pain Relief 500 at Martinsville Speedway, the aerodynamic wing device was replaced with a tried-and-true metal air deflection spoiler attached to the trunk of each racer. Denny Hamlin was the first to win with the new spoiler, coming in .670 seconds ahead of runner-up Joey Logano.

807 In total, NASCAR's winged COT competed in 93 Sprint Cup events. Jimmie Johnson proved to be the most successful driver, winning 22 times, 9 more wins than COT runner-up Kyle Busch.

808 The 2007 Sylvania 300 at New Hampshire International Speedway was won by Clint Bowyer, earning the Emporia, Kansas, driver his first Cup career victory. The win was the first in Cup competition for his car number (07).

TRACKS

809 Located 30 miles west of Nashville in Gladeville, the Nashville Superspeedway never lived up to its potential, opening in 2001 and closing in 2012. The 1.333-mile all-concrete oval owned by Dover Motorsports, Inc. started out a NASCAR staple with 21 Busch/Nationwide Series and 13 Craftsman/Camping World Truck events raced there from 2001 to 2011. Eight Indy Car races were also held there from 2001 to 2008. Unfortunately, the track's inability to attract a Cup Series race and its lack of proximity to Nashville's fan base doomed the track financially, forcing it to give up the 2012 Busch and Truck division dates. Carl Edwards won the last NASCAR race at the track, Nationwide, on July 23, 2011. The track has been sitting idle since and is currently for sale.

810 Constructed at a cost of $153 million, Kentucky Speedway opened in 2000. Located near Sparta, the 1.5-mile track flew the green flag June 16 with Billy Bigley Jr. winning the Kentucky 150 NASCAR Slim Jim All Pro Series event. The next day, Greg Biffle added his name to the Kentucky Speedway record book, winning the Kroger 225 Craftsman Truck Series race. The trucks have competed at Kentucky every year since its opening, while the Xfinity division started at the track in 2001, with the Cup Series a regular attraction since 2011.

811 Dale Earnhardt Jr. led 106 laps, including the last 39, to score his first Winston Cup victory on April 2, 2000. The DirecTV 500 at Texas Motor Speedway pays Earnhardt $374,675, considerably more than the $19,800 his father Dale earned for his first Cup win at Bristol in 1979.

812 The worst fan injury disaster in the history of NASCAR happened on May 20, 2000, after the conclusion of The Winston All-Star race at Lowes Motor Speedway. More than 100 fans were injured when an 80-foot section of a pedestrian bridge connecting the track to a parking lot on the other side of North Carolina Highway 29 collapsed and plunged 17 feet to the roadway. More than 50 lawsuits were filed by injured fans after investigators determined that Anti-Hydro, a drying agent, had been used at a rate of 40 times more than the acceptable amount. Curing the concrete in the bridge had corroded the steel reinforcement cables of the bridge. Most of the lawsuits were settled out of court.

813 Bobby Labonte got the biggest gift of his career when he won the 2000 Pepsi Southern 500 at Darlington Raceway. Labonte never led a green-flag lap, taking the lead under yellow. Eight laps later, the race is red-flagged and called complete as rain washes out the final 39 circuits. The win is Labonte's only triumph at Darlington in 33 career starts.

814 Jeff Burton scored 21 victories in 695 Cup Series starts. His most impressive win came September 17, 2000, when he led all 300 laps, capturing the DuraLube 300 at New Hampshire International Speedway. Burton's wire-to-wire victory is the first in a NASCAR top series event since Fireball Roberts led all 178 laps on the 1.4-mile Marchbanks Speedway in Hanford, California, March 12, 1961.

815 October 15, 2000, became a watershed moment in NASCAR history as Dale Earnhardt rallied from deep in the field to win the Winston 500 at Talladega Superspeedway. The victory, number 76 of Earnhardt's storied career, is his last as he perishes in the 2001 season-opening race at Daytona International Speedway.

816 Constructed on a 1,200-acre site near Kansas City, Missouri, Kansas Speedway hosted its first NASCAR race July 7, 2001. The Craftsman Truck Series, the O'Reilly Auto Parts 250, was won by Ricky Hendrick. The 1.5-mile International Speedway Corporation (ISC) oval hosted its first big NASCAR weekend later that year with Jeff Green and Jeff Gordon winning their Busch and Cup events on September 29–30, respectively. Today, Kansas Speedway is the hub of a giant entertainment and shopping complex including a casino built in 2012. The speedway's economic impact on the Kansas City area is estimated at $250 million annually.

817 On May 27, 2001, Tony Stewart became the third NASCAR driver in history to race in the Indianapolis 500 and the Coca-Cola 600 on the same day. Following in the footsteps of John Andretti (1994) and Robby Gordon (1997), Stewart finished sixth in the Indy classic and then flew to Charlotte from which he brought home a third in the marathon NASCAR event.

818 NASCAR expanded its footprint into the Chicago, Illinois, market in 2001 with the opening of Chicagoland Speedway. Constructed by Raceway Associates, LLC, a partnership between International Speedway Corporation, the Indianapolis Motor Speedway Corporation, and Dale Coyne's Route 66 Raceway. The 1.5-mile track was built adjacent to Route 66 Raceway drag strip and dirt oval facility near Joliet. Rookie Kevin Harvick won the first NASCAR Winston Cup race at the track on July 15, 2001.

819 Located in Cicero, Illinois, on the grounds of the old Sportsman's Park, Chicago Motor Speedway was originally a dog-racing track funded and partially owned by Al Capone. Horse racing became the bill of fare at the CMS until 1998 when it was purchased by a group of investors led by Chip Ganassi. The 7/8-mile oval was paved for auto racing, hosting Truck Series events in 2000 (won by Joe Ruttman) and 2001 (won by Scott Riggs). The opening of Chicagoland Speedway in 2001 ended NASCAR's involvement with Chicago Motor Speedway, which continued to hold CART Indy Car events through 2002. The city of Cicero purchased the facility in 2003 for $18 million, but demolished it in 2009. Today, a Wal-Mart Superstore is located on the site of the former racetrack.

820 Developed by a team of researchers at the University of Nebraska between 1998 and 2001, Steel and Foam Energy Reduction (SAFER) barriers were first installed at the Indianapolis Motor Speedway in 2002. The system, installed in front of a track's retaining walls, extends 30 inches away from the hard barrier, gives when impacted at high speed, and effectively absorbs the kinetic energy of the crash. Originally installed in the turns at most raceways hosting NASCAR Cup races by the middle of the decade, the soft wall system now encircles both the inside and outside retaining barriers at nearly all Cup Series tracks.

821 Kyle Busch began his NASCAR career in 2001 at 16 years old competing for Roush Racing in the Craftsman Truck Series. After posting the fastest time in practice for the final season race (the Auto Club 200 at California Speedway) Busch was told he would not be able to participate. As a companion event to a CART event sponsored by Marlboro, he was ineligible to race as mandated by the 1998 Master Settlement Agreement prohibiting anyone under the age of 18 to compete in events sponsored by a tobacco firm. In 2002, NASCAR mandated a minimum participation age of 18, which forced Busch to compete in the American Speed Association that year. Busch returned to NASCAR in 2003 (now 18) wheeling a Rick Hendrick–owned Chevy to a fifth-place finish in the Carquest Auto Parts 300 Busch Series race at Charlotte Motor Speedway.

Having to sit out the 2002 NASCAR season due to new minimum age restrictions, Kyle Busch headed to the American Speed Association in which he finished eighth in the championship standings that year. (Photo Courtesy Russ Lake)

822 Veteran racer Shawna Robinson and her No. 49 BAM Racing Dodge qualified 39th and finished 24th in the 2002 Daytona 500. This made Robinson the second woman to compete in NASCAR's signature event. Janet Guthrie broke the gender barrier when she finished 12th in the 1977 Daytona 500 classic.

823 In 2002, Speedway Motorsports, Inc. shareholder, Francis Ferko filed a lawsuit against NASCAR stating the sanctioning body failed to live up to a promise of a second race date at Texas Motor Speedway, an SMI property. Although NASCAR denied the allegation, it was announced that a settlement was reached in May 2004. The agreement provided for the sale of North Carolina Speedway (Rockingham; owned at the time by NASCAR parent International Speedway Corporation) to SMI. In turn, Speedway Motorsports moved Rockingham's remaining Cup date to Texas, giving it two NASCAR weekends each season. The settlement all but finished the Rockingham track, which has only held two Camping World Truck Series events (2012 and 2013) and little else since.

The Daytona International Speedway media center was graced with NAS-CAR royalty when 13 past Cup Series champions visited prior to the 2005 event. Included in the group were (first row, left to right) Bobby Allison, Rex White, Benny Parsons, Richard Petty, Ned Jarrett, and Darrell Waltrip. (Back row), Dale Jarrett, Tony Stewart, Bill Elliott, Terry Labonte, Rusty Wallace, Jeff Gordon, and Bobby Labonte. (Photo Courtesy Russ Lake)

824 Tony Stewart purchased Eldora Speedway (Ohio) in 2004. The half-mile dirt oval had been owned and operated by Earl Baltes since its opening in 1954.

825 Joe Ruttman started 40th in the 2004 Subway 500 at North Carolina Speedway, the last Cup race at the Rockingham track. Ruttman completed one lap before his No. 09 Phoenix Racing Dodge was black-flagged for not having a pit crew. Ruttman earned $54,196 for his efforts, slightly less than the $56,410 paid to Kenny Schrader who finished 27th after completing 389 of the 393 laps.

826 The 2006 Busch Series season schedule got tweaked when International Speedway Corporation (ISC) purchased Pikes Peak International Raceway in Fountain, Colorado, and immediately awarded its date to Martinsville Speedway. The Martinsville BGN race was short-lived, when, one year later, the date was shipped north to Canada and the Circuit Gilles Villeneuve.

827 In 2006, *Talladega Nights: The Ballad of Ricky Bobby* became the number-one movie in the country, grossing $47 million in sales in its first weekend. The NASCAR-themed comedy beat out *Barnyard: The Original Party Animals* ($16 million) and *Pirates of the Caribbean: Dead Man's Chest* ($11 million) for most box office money earned that weekend.

828 Designed by former driver Rusty Wallace, Iowa Speedway was one of the first tracks in the country to implement SAFER Barriers around the entire outside of the track during construction. The 7/8-mile paved tri-oval raceway opened in 2006 with a USAR Hooters Pro Cup won by Woody Howard. The K&N Pro Series East and West Series were the first divisions to compete at the Newton, Iowa, track May 20, 2007 at which 17-year-old Joey Logano took the victory. Both the Xfinity and Camping World Truck Series have competed at Iowa every year since 2009 with the IndyCar Series a regular since 2007.

829 In an unusual turn of events, none of the top-10 starters in the UAW-Daimler Chrysler 400 held March 11, 2007, at Las Vegas Motor Speedway finished in the top-10. The last time the top-10 starters were shut out of was in the Firecracker 400 at Daytona International Speedway on July 4, 1965.

830 Fan darling Kasey Kahne drove his Gillette Evernham Dodge to a win in the May 17, 2008, Sprint All-Star Race at Lowes Motor Speedway, becoming the first driver to capture the non-points event after being voted in by the fans. One week later, Kahne does the heavy lifting by himself, spanking the field by more than 10 seconds to win the Coca-Cola 600.

831 The 2008 Brickyard 400 at Indianapolis Motor Speedway featured 11 caution flags in 52 of the 160 laps. NASCAR purposely threw the "competition caution" flag 6 of the 11 times when the tires brought by Goodyear proved to be unsafe, coming apart in just a few laps. The longest green-flag run of the race was 13 laps with an average green flag period lasting just nine laps (22.5 miles). Jimmie Johnson won the race with an average speed of 115.117 mph.

832 Early events required little more than an ambulance and fire truck, but as the sport grew more sophisticated, the way NASCAR handled driver injuries became an issue. By 2001, when Dale Earnhardt died at Daytona, all NASCAR tracks had Infield Care Centers. Stocked with the latest in emergency equipment and staffed by qualified doctors and support staff, the care centers of today can manage almost any critical injury. Whether injured or not, all drivers whose vehicles can't continue after a crash are required to visit the infield care center. They are cleared, treated, or determined to need transportation to a local hospital.

833 In 1999, Lowes Home Improvement Company acquired title rights to Charlotte Motor Speedway, making it the first track with a corporate sponsor in its name. The $35 million, 10-year agreement was extended one year in 2009 while the track and the big box home improvement corporation worked out a new deal. The speedway wanted $9 million a year and the company wanted to reduce its $3.5 million annual commitment, the deal didn't happen and the association came to an end before the 2010 season. The track reverted back to the name it had for 39 years prior, Charlotte Motor Speedway.

834 In an effort to spice things up, NASCAR introduced double-file shootout-style restarts at the 2009 Pocono 500. Previously, all lead-lap cars started in the outside lane while cars one-lap down were rode the inside lane.

835 Kyle Busch captured his first Nationwide Series win in the 2008 O'Reilly Challenge at Texas Motor Speedway. Busch went on to win four Nationwide races in a row, giving him five-straight victories, the longest string of consecutive wins in any division in the history of the Fort Worth track.

PIT PASS

836 While Mike Wallace will go down in history for winning of the first Craftsman Truck Series race at Daytona International Speedway, the February 18, 2000 event is remembered for the 13-truck crash on Lap 57. The 190-mph wreck was punctuated by Geoff Bodine's airborne Ford F-150 ripping through the front-stretch catch fence. Bodine, his truck a pile of rubble, suffered a concussion, a fractured back, ankle, wrist, and cheekbone in the horrific crash. In addition, nine fans were also injured.

837 Prior to the 2001 season, NASCAR sold the rights of NAS-CAR.com to Turner Interactive Group, a division of Time Warner Company. The six-year deal is estimated to be worth $100 million to NASCAR. As part of the agreement, America Online, owned by Time Warner, will feature NASCAR Online content to more than 20 million of its subscribers. The deal ended NASCAR's digital association with ESPN, which had controlled NASCAR.com since its launch in 1995.

838 With a Winston Cup debut and 43 Busch Series starts to his credit, Adam Petty was destined to be a bright star for years to come. Unfortunately, as he rolled out for an NBS practice run at New Hampshire International Speedway on May 12, 2000, he experienced mechanical problems and hit the Turn 3 wall at full speed. The son of Kyle Petty and grandson of Richard Petty was killed instantly. He was just 19 years old.

839 The 9/11 terrorist attacks in 2001 touched every part of American society including NASCAR. NASCAR postponed its September 16 event at New Hampshire International Speedway. The New Hampshire 300, the final of race of the 2001 season, was held November 23 with Robby Gordon taking his first Winston Cup victory.

840 Joe Gibbs Racing had enormous success in both the Cup and Xfinity divisions, winning more than 125 races in each series. However, the team competed in 65 Truck Series events from 2000 to 2002, never once visiting Victory Lane.

841 Martin Truex Jr. punched his ticket to a full-time seat in the Cup Series in 2006 by winning back-to-back Busch

Series championships in 2004 and 2005. Truex wheeled the Dale Earnhardt, Inc. Chevrolet to six wins each season, and posted a top-10 finish in 48 of 69 NBS events contested over the two seasons. His 2005 championship earnings of $3,143,692 marks the first time a driver eclipsed $3 million in a single Busch Grand National season.

842 Jack Sprague, nicknamed "One-Track Jack" for his Late Model Stock Car success at Concord Motor Speedway (North Carolina), won 28 races and three championships in the Craftsman Truck Series. Sprague never replicated his success in Winston Cup, scoring no wins and no top-5 or top-10 finishes in 24 starts. In 10 Busch Series seasons, Sprague notched just one victory in 108 starts.

843 Truck Series driver Brendan Gaughan earned a closet full of 10-gallon hats after winning four-straight division races at Texas Motor Speedway in 2002 and 2003. He improved his bank account as well, taking $245,490 for the quartet of victories.

844 All 1,221 residents of tiny Cambridge, Wisconsin, could be heard cheering when hometown hero Matt Kenseth won the

Wisconsin short-track rivals Robbie Reiser (left) and Matt Kenseth teamed up to win the 2003 NASCAR Winston Cup Championship. (Photo Courtesy Russ Lake)

2003 Winston Cup championship. Kenseth only won one race that season (UAW-Daimler Chrysler 400 at Las Vegas Motor Speedway) but still earned the title by completing 97 percent of all laps raced in Sprint Cup competition that season. Incidentally, Kenseth was on the sidelines when he won the title after falling out on Lap 28 of 267 in the final race of the season at Homestead-Miami Speedway. It was just his second DNF of the year.

845 The August 17, 2003, Michigan 400 at Michigan International Speedway resembled a pro wrestling match when Jimmy Spencer punched Kurt Busch while sitting in his car on pit road after the race. The fight was a culmination of a three-season feud between the two drivers. Spencer's actions earned him a one-race suspension for the next event, the 2003 Winston Cup tour at Bristol.

846 Dale Earnhardt Jr. was plenty excited after winning the October 3, 2004, EA Sports 500 at Talladega Superspeedway and taking the Cup points lead in the process. Earnhardt was so enthusiastic that he uttered a swear word during a post-race television interview. NASCAR promptly fined him $25,000 and 25 points, dropping him to second in the standings after the race.

847 Tony Hirschman Jr. scored 9 of his 35 career Whelan Modified victories in 2004 and 2005, in the process winning the open-wheel division championship each season. The Northampton, Pennsylvania, driver also won Whelan Modified titles in 1995, 1996, and 1999. The 1995 championship-winning margin over Steve Park by just three points remains the closest finish in Whelan Modified history.

848 Todd Bodine, nicknamed "The Onion," made his fellow NASCAR Craftsman Truck Series competitors cry by winning championships in 2005 and 2007. Bodine, one of the most consistent drivers in the division, notched 19 of 22 NCTS wins from 2005 through 2010 by posting six-straight top-5 championship points finishes.

849 Former Formula 1 racing star Juan Pablo Montoya proved that racing a full-bodied stock car was no problem when he won the 2007 Nextel Cup Rookie of the Year Award. The Columbia-born driver finished 20th in the final standings after winning one event, the SaveMart 300 at Infineon Raceway in Sonoma, California. The victory was the first for a foreign-born driver in NASCAR's top series since Canadian Earl Ross captured the 1974 Old Dominion 500 at Martinsville Speedway.

850 Red Bull energy drink was introduced in 1984 by Austrian businessman Dietrich Mateschitz. He built the brand into a global leader in part through a Formula 1 racing ownership/sponsorship program. In 2006, Mateschitz, along with Danny Bahar, brought the business model to America and joined the Cup Series as Team Red Bull. From 2007 through 2011, the team participated in 224 Cup events scoring two wins. Team Red Bull ceased operation in December 2011, selling all its assets to Ron Devine who formed BK Racing.

851 After winning the Indianapolis 500 and the IndyCar championship in 2007, Dario Franchitti joined NASCAR in 2008, competing in 10 Sprint Cup events. Franchitti found NASCAR tougher to tame, finishing 32nd or worse in nine of 10 events. By mid-season, his Chip Ganassi team had run out of funding so Franchitti finished out the year running a handful of NASCAR Nationwide events. Franchitti returned to the IndyCar ranks in 2009 with renewed success, winning both the 2009 and 2010 IndyCar titles.

852 Nashville, Tennessee, native Bobby Hamilton, one of NASCAR's most popular drivers, took four Cup Series wins in his 15-year career. His greatest success occurred in the Craftsman Truck Series in which he won 10 times in 101 starts, grabbing the 2004 NCTS championship along the way. Just over a year later, Hamilton was diagnosed with cancer and succumbed to the disease January 7, 2007. He was 49.

853 Oakland, California, native Bill Lester was a veteran driver in five Craftsman Truck Series seasons when he made his first Nextel Cup start in the Golden Corral 500 at Atlanta Motor Speedway March 20, 2006. Lester started 19th and finished 38th in the race, and became the first African-American to compete in a NASCAR top-division race since Willy T. Ribbs ran in the Miller American 400 at Michigan International Speedway in 1986.

854 Driving a Dodge owned by Rusty Wallace, Chase Austin was the first African-American to race in the Busch Series when he took the green flag in the Sam's Town 250 at Memphis Motorsports Park (Tennessee) October 27, 2007. Austin, just 18 at the time, started 43rd and finished 41st, after crashing out on Lap 86.

855 After four seasons as title sponsor of NASCAR's top division, Nextel Communications bowed out prior to the 2008 season. Sprint Corporation, acquiring Nextel in 2004 for a cool $35 billion, took over in 2008 and renamed the division the NASCAR Sprint Cup Series.

856 In a move that shocked the NASCAR community, Dale Earnhardt Jr. announced early in 2007 his plans to leave Dale Earnhardt, Inc., and race for Hendrick Motorsports in 2008. Earnhardt's deal with HMS was for five years and in late 2011, the agreement was extended for five more years, through 2017.

857 Galesburg, Illinois, driver Aaron Fike made 12 starts during the 2007 Camping World Truck Series season, posting a career-best fifth-place spot at Memphis Motorsports Park. One week later, Fike was arrested after he and his girlfriend were observed using heroin in the parking lot of an Ohio amusement park. Fike, immediately banned from NASCAR competition, later admitted that he had used heroin before several races, including the Memphis event. His arrest and admission invalidated NASCAR's "reasonable suspicion" drug policy and played a big part in the implementation of a strict drug-testing program two years later.

858 Prior to the 2008 season, all fines imposed by NASCAR were added to each division's championship point fund. That changed in 2008 when the sanctioning body chose to instead redirect the cash to the NASCAR Foundation, a 501c non-profit charitable organization.

859 Before the start of the 2009 season, NASCAR announced that all race officials, drivers, at-track mechanics, over-the-wall pit crew, and spotters would be subject to mandatory drug testing. All tests will be conducted prior to the start of the season while at-track testing throughout the year will be conducted randomly with a computer selecting those to be tested.

860 By the time Ricky Carmichael made his debut in 2009, he was already a legend in American Motorcycle Association (AMA) competition, having won more than 270 AMA Supercross and Motocross events. Nicknamed "The Goat" (greatest of all time) for his

American Motocross legend Ricky Carmichael joined the NASCAR ranks piloting a Camping World Truck for three seasons beginning in 2009. (Photo Courtesy Russ Lake)

two-wheel racing exploits, Carmichael made NASCAR his home from 2009 to 2011, primarily in the Camping World Truck Series. Unfortunately, Carmichael never replicated his AMA success, remaining winless in 68 division starts. His best Truck finish was fourth, something he did twice, (Dover in 2009 and Talladega in 2010).

861 Joey Logano appeared on the Sprint Cup scene in 2009 as a 19-year-old driver with a ton of potential. The Middletown, Connecticut, teenager didn't disappoint, posting seven top-10 finishes and his first Cup victory June 29 Lennox Industrial Tools 301 at New Hampshire Motor Speedway. Logano was chosen as the 2009 Sprint Cup Rookie of the Year, becoming the youngest driver to win the award.

MILESTONES

862 After televising 262 Winston Cup races from 1981 to 2000, NASCAR's new 2001 television deal. The 19-year association proved mutually beneficial as NASCAR gained national prominence, while ESPN, a fledgling enterprise in the early 1980s, became the "Worldwide Leader In Sports." In a separate agreement, ESPN still featured Craftsman Truck Series events in 2001 and 2002 before disappearing from NASCAR's television landscape in 2003.

863 NASCAR's oldest television partner, CBS, was also left out of the new television deal. CBS was the first to televise parts of the Daytona 500 in 1960 and showed the first live flag-to-flag coverage in 1979. Fittingly, CBS ended its association with NASCAR by televising the 2000 Daytona 500.

864 Bristol, Virginia, native Mike Helton began his career in 1980 as public relations director at Atlanta International Raceway. Helton joined the NASCAR corporate ranks in 1994 and in 1999 was named NASCAR's senior vice-president and chief operation officer, the first time someone from outside the France family was in charge of the sport. One year later, on November 28, 2000, Bill France Jr. named Helton as his successor as president.

865 In a financial deal of epic proportions, NASCAR contracted a new television deal with FOX and NBC in 2001. The six-year agreement allowed the networks, along with their partners FX and TBS/TNT, to televise the Sprint Cup and Busch Grand National divisions on a rotating basis in the first collectively bargained NASCAR television contract. The deal was valued at about $2.4 billion, approximately four times more than the previous television package.

866 Dale Earnhardt, one of NASCAR's greatest drivers and public figures, was killed on the final lap of the 2001 Daytona 500 at Daytona International Speedway. Earnhardt was third in the race when he impacted the Turn 3 wall. He was immediately transported to Halifax Memorial Hospital, where he was pronounced dead. Earnhardt owned the cars of his son, Dale Earnhardt Jr., and Michael Waltrip who placed second and first in the race, respectively. The final stat sheet for the seven-time Cup Series champion showed 76 victories, 281 top-5s, and 428 top-10 finishes in 676 starts over 27 seasons.

Dale Earnhardt and his son, Dale Earnhardt Jr. share a laugh during Speedweeks at Daytona International Speedway in 2001. The senior Earnhardt perished in a last-lap wreck in the Daytona 500 later that week. (Photo Courtesy Russ Lake)

867 It took 23 races for Dodge to reach Victory Lane after Chrysler's brand returned to Winston Cup racing in 2001. Sterling Marlin did the job for the Dodge Boys when he won the rain-shortened Pepsi 400 at Michigan Speedway August 19, 2001. The breakthrough win was the first for Dodge since the *Los Angeles Times* 500, the last race of the 1977 season.

868 Prior to the 2002 season, NASCAR required spotters be present and accounted for during a race but had no such edict for practices. That changed when ARCA driver Eric Martin died in a practice crash on October 9 at the Lowes Motor Speedway in Charlotte. A week later, NASCAR changed the rules for spotters, requiring one be in place for all practices. In addition, all spotters must collect a pass to a designated spotter's stand at each track and be in place for roll call prior to the start of practice. Teams without a spotter in place would not be allowed to practice.

869 NASCAR had to take a hard look at safety procedures in the wake of top star Dale Earnhardt's death in 2001. One long overdue change was a revision of pit crew safety, with a new rule being instituted that required all over-the-wall pit members to wear helmets.

870 R.J. Reynolds not only supported NASCAR's highest division throughout its long-time sponsorship, but also poured millions of dollars into NASCAR's local short-track program. Prior to the 2000 season, the tobacco company announced it could no longer support the short-track program due to 16- and 17-year-olds being allowed to compete in Winston events. The company cited the 1998 Master Settlement agreement that forbade participants under 18 years of age to compete in a tobacco company–sponsored event.

871 Despite a new contract in July 2002 extending its sponsorship of the Winston Cup division through 2007, R.J. Reynolds announced in February 2003 that its support of NASCAR's top division would be discontinued as soon as a new title partner was found. That opened the door for communications giant Nextel to become the Cup Series sponsor in 2004. In a three-decade association beginning in 1971, R.J. Reynolds contributed more than $125 million in purse, point fund, and bonuses to NASCAR, most in the Winston Cup division.

872 After 30 years presiding over the enterprise started by his father, Bill France Jr. relinquished his roles as NASCAR chairman and chief executive officer of on September 13, 2003. In keeping with family tradition, France Jr. named his son Brian his successor.

873 In the interest of safety and fair play, NASCAR announced in late 2003 that racing back to the caution flag would no longer be allowed. Previously, lead-lap drivers or lapped competitors did this to try to improve their position. The edict came after multiple near misses when speeding cars race past through crash sites. The new rule freezes the field in current running order when the caution flag is waived.

874 As part of the 2003 rule regarding racing back to the caution flag, NASCAR introduces the Beneficiary Free Pass Rule. This provision allows the first car to become a lap down to regain that lap by passing the leader and the pace car once the field is safely under caution. It's almost immediately nicknamed the "Lucky Dog Rule" in the garage area.

875 In 1952 the Pure Oil Company became one of the first product sponsors in Grand National competition by providing racing fuel for the competitors. Union 76 and Unocal, later incarnations of Pure Oil, remained the official racing fuel provider until 2003 when NASCAR announced that Sunoco would replace Unocal in 2004. The 51-year association was one of the longest sponsorship agreements in the history of NASCAR.

876 In 2004, NASCAR does a complete overhaul of the way a Cup Series champion is determined. Attempting to emulate the playoff-type system used in professional and college sports, the Chase for the Cup features a 10-race showdown between the top-10 drivers in the points standings after the 26th race of the season at Richmond International Raceway (Virginia). Jeff Gordon, Jimmie Johnson, Dale Earnhardt Jr., Tony Stewart, Matt Kenseth, Elliott Sadler, Kurt Busch, Mark Martin, Jeremy

Mayfield, and Ryan Newman make up the inaugural 2004 Chase field. In the end, five drivers have a mathematical chance of winning the championship heading into the final Chase race at Homestead-Miami Speedway, but Kurt Busch comes away with the title after a fifth-place finish.

877 In 2004, Kyle Petty opened Victory Junction Gang Camp to celebrate the life of his son, Adam Petty, killed in a NASCAR practice crash in 2000. The charitable non-profit 84-acre camp in Randallman, North Carolina, assists children ages 6 to 16 with chronic medical issues. To date, the camp has hosted more than 23,000 children from all 50 states.

878 Aviation disaster struck NASCAR again when a plane crash killed 10 Hendrick Motorsports associates on October 24, 2004. The HMS Beachcraft Super King aircraft crashed into a mountainside near Stuart, Virginia, en route to Blue Ridge Airport and the Subway 500 NASCAR Nextel Cup race at Martinsville Speedway. Due to heavy fog, the plane missed the landing strip on its first attempt and crashed after redirecting for a second landing attempt. Among those lost in the crash were Ricky Hendrick, Rick Hendrick's son, John Hendrick, HMS team president and Rick Hendrick's brother, and HMS chief engine builder Randy Dorton.

879 NASCAR president Mike Helton opened the door for "hard liquor" companies to serve as sponsors of the sport when he lifted the ban on participation prior to the 2005 season. Jack Daniels and Jim Beam immediately signed up as team sponsors for the 2006 Nextel Cup season for drivers Clint Bowyer and Robby Gordon, respectively.

880 After 55 victories, 202 top-5, and 349 top-10 finishes in 706 career top-division starts, Rusty Wallace called it a career after the 2005 season. Wallace, who earned $14,250 for finishing second in his first start at Atlanta International Raceway in 1980, ended his career with more than $49 million in total earnings. Wallace was inducted into the NASCAR Hall of Fame in 2013.

881 Andy Santere made 166 NASCAR K&N Pro Series East starts from 1992 through 2005. The Cherryfield, Maine, driver notched 23 victories throughout the period, 13 in 2002–2005 when he won four-straight NKNPSE championships. Santere's "four-peat" breaks the record of three-straight East titles set by Jamie Aube from 1988 to 1990.

882 Jimmie Johnson scored his first Daytona 500 victory motoring the No. 48 Hendrick Motorsports Chevrolet on February 19, 2006. Johnson captured the Great American Race with interim crew chief Darian Grubb on top of his pit box. Regular crew chief Chad Knaus sat out the race after a suspension for cheating when a post-qualifying inspection determined Knaus had altered the rear window of Johnson's racer. Johnson was forced to start the event in a back-up car at the end of the 43-car field.

883 Charlotte, North Carolina, hosted NASCAR's first Strictly Stock race in 1949, so it was no surprise when the Queen City was chosen to be home to the new NASCAR Hall of Fame on March 6, 2006. Charlotte won the right to host the Hall, beating out Atlanta, Georgia; Kansas City, Missouri; Richmond, Virginia; and Daytona Beach, Florida; for the honor. The $160 million facility was to be built and owned by the city of Charlotte and was projected to open in 2010.

884 NASCAR continued rolling in the dough making an announcement that it had inked a new $4.48 billion television contract on December 7, 2005. The eight-year agreement expanded NASCAR's deal with FOX and TNT, while adding the ABC to the mix. The deal paved the way for ESPN (a subsidiary of ABC) to telecast NASCAR events again as part of the 2007 Nextel Cup season.

885 In 2006, Jimmie Johnson became the only driver in Sprint Cup history to win the Daytona 500, Brickyard 400, and the Sprint Cup Series championship in the same season.

886 NASCAR made its first major tweaks to its Chase championship format in 2006, starting by expanding the field of competitors to 12. The finalists will start the final 10-race showdown with 5,000 points while drivers scoring regular-season victories receive an extra 10 points for each win. At the end, Jimmie Johnson won the 2006 Nextel Cup championship by 56 points over runner-up Matt Kenseth. The title was Johnson's fourth and the first for Jeff Gordon as a Nextel Cup team owner.

887 Longtime official scorer Morris Metcalfe died August 30, 2007. Metcalf began scoring NASCAR races in the early 1950s and retired as the Chief of Timing and Scoring after the 2002 Daytona 500. In addition to his longtime NASCAR service, Metcalf is credited with creating the sports first fan club when he launched Lee Petty's Fan Club in 1955. Metcalf, a Morristown, Tennessee, native, passed away at the age of 81.

888 In 2008, Coors replaced Budweiser as the "Official Beer of NASCAR." As such, Coors becomes the sponsor of NASCAR's pole award. Coors' cost of the five-year deal is reported to be a thirst-quenching $20 million.

889 One of NASCAR's most unusual statistical anomalies occurred from 2006 through 2010. In 2006, Kasey Kahne captured the most Cup wins with six, going winless in 2007. Jeff Gordon, the leading Cup winner with six in 2007, scored no wins in 2008, while Carl Edwards, the kingpin in 2008 victories with nine, didn't win any in 2009. Mark Martin closed out a "hero-to-zero" streak winning five Cup races in 2009 only to get shut out of Victory Lane in 2010.

890 Ron Hornaday Jr. earned his record fourth Truck Series championship in 2009. Hornaday also captured Truck titles in 1996, 1998, and 2007. His 2009 title broke the record a mark previously shared with Jack Sprague.

891 Jimmie Johnson added his name to the list of Cup Series champions when he won the 2006 title. Johnson then pulled off three more in 2007, 2008, and 2009 giving him four-straight titles breaking Cale Yarborough's record of three-consecutive championships from 1967–1978. Johnson broke his own record with a fifth-straight in 2010 earning him the nickname "Five-Time" in the garage area.

892 Starting with the 2003 Bass Pro Shops 500, Ryan Newman won six consecutive Cup poles at Atlanta Motor Speedway. The pole streak ended for the "Rocket Man" on October 30, 2005, at the Bass Pro 500. Newman's best finish in six races was fifth, with a dismal 19.6 finishing average.

893 Mike Stefanik won his first Whelan Modified Tour championship in 1989. In 2006, Stefanik picked up a seventh Whelan

Seven-time Whelan Modified champion Mike Stefanik is all business while his crew thrashes on his car during a practice run at New Hampshire Speedway. (John Close Photo)

Mod title adding to his 1991,1997, 1998, 2001, and 2002 championships. Stefanik's seven Modified crowns are the most of any driver in the Modern Era (that began in 1985) and second only to the all-time Modified Division championship record of nine set by Richie Evans.

894 After years of medical problems, Bill France Jr. passed away Monday June 4, 2007, in Daytona Beach. His death came during the running of the rain-delayed Autism Speaks 400 Nextel Cup race at Dover International Speedway. On Lap 261 of the event, France's death was announced to the crowd and a national television audience. France was 74.

895 NASCAR expanded its footprint internationally in 2006 with the purchase of the Canadian Association for Stock Car Auto Racing (CASCAR). The group, founded in 1981, had started a multi-year marketing relationship with NASCAR in 2004, which opened the door for the Nationwide Series to compete north of the border beginning in 2007 while the Camping World Truck Series followed suit in 2013. NASCAR's 12-race Pinty's Series, an offshoot of the first CASCAR division, held 12 events in 2016.

896 Kyle Busch reached two milestones in the 2008 Kobalt Tools 500 at Atlanta Motor Speedway. Busch piloted a Toyota Camry to the brand's first Sprint Cup win. It was also the first victory for a foreign car in NASCAR's top division since June 13, 1954, when Al Keller drove a Jaguar to a win in a Grand National race on a makeshift track at the Linden Airport in New Jersey.

897 Tony Stewart notched his first win as a Cup owner on June 7, 2009, when he drove his No. 20 Office Depot Chevrolet to victory in the Pocono 500 at Pocono International Raceway. The win is the first time in more than a decade that a driver won a top division race in his own vehicle. Ricky Rudd was the last to pull it off at Martinsville Speedway September 27, 1998.

Chapter 9

The 2010s: Racing for Relevancy

Since its inception, NASCAR has faced, and weathered, just about every imaginable crisis and somehow managed to land on its feet. That said, the challenges of a new decade beginning in 2010 may have been some of the most difficult the sport has ever faced.

Let's face it; NASCAR has struggled in recent years. The economic crash of 2007–2008 still impacts the sport. Fan that used to travel to multiple NASCAR events each year now attend one or two races annually (or none) because of income that has become even more discretionary. NASCAR tracks that once sold out months in advance now have thousands of empty seats. This has prompted some facilities to remove entire grandstands that have sat vacant in recent years.

In addition to the fans' financial crisis, the sport has suffered aesthetically. Many lament that, "it's not the way it used to be." They've moved on because NASCAR vehicles no longer resemble, even remotely, what's in their driveway. Others cite their disappointment with once relatable "regular-guy" drivers who have morphed into polished corporate millionaire spokespersons.

Even television, the engine that drove NASCAR to the top of the sports food chain in the 1980s, has become unable to connect with fans. It has lost its ratings share despite bringing viewers closer to the action than ever.

NASCAR is shooting for the moon in the new millennium, just like these military jets during a pre-race show for the 2014 Daytona 500. (Photo Courtesy Russ Lake)

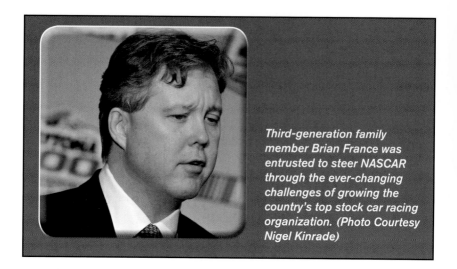

Third-generation family member Brian France was entrusted to steer NASCAR through the ever-changing challenges of growing the country's top stock car racing organization. (Photo Courtesy Nigel Kinrade)

If the thought of reversing these trends isn't daunting enough, NASCAR has the unenviable task of moving forward in an era in which personal entertainment choices are as close as the palm of someone's hand. That's especially true of the New Millennials (those born in the early 1980s through 2000); many aren't even interested in owning a car much less watching them race.

To its credit, NASCAR hasn't stood around hoping for the best. New-age facility improvements, such as the "Daytona Rising" project completed in 2015 at DIS, rival those of any other sports entertainment facility in the country. Meanwhile, the sanctioning body, its drivers, and teams have embraced social media and other digital communication platforms as a direct link to the fans.

Finally, a new crop of young, talented, culturally and ethnically diverse drivers has emerged in recent seasons. These stars of the future are ready to carry the sport into the 2020s and beyond.

NASCAR has proven that it's big enough to absorb change and succeed. However, it will face challenges trying to keep up and stay relevant, just as everyone else does. Public tastes are more fickle, short-lived, and harder to predict than ever before.

Meanwhile, the fate of NASCAR may have already been cast. Partially autonomous cars can park and stop themselves. It's not difficult to imagine vehicles 20 years from now that can operate with no driver input other than programming and entering travel coordinates. If that occurs, will anyone want to watch them race? You may laugh, but it could happen. So might a new form of vehicle not centric to the internal combustion engine. What happens then? Either outcome could make NASCAR obsolete in a heartbeat.

Regardless of the next season or the next decade, NASCAR has survived more than 80 years since stock cars first raced on the sandy shores of Daytona Beach. Based on that, there's reason to believe that quite a few laps are yet to be run before NASCAR's final facts are written.

CARS

898 In 2007, Ford Motor Company and Roush-Yates Racing began developing the FR9 engine, the first FoMoCo powerplant in NASCAR not specifically designed for a passenger car. Fully integrated into NASCAR by the 2009 season, the new engine replaced the (Cleveland/Windsor) R452 block–based powerplant and featured a 357-ci graphite-iron block with 4.175-inch bore and 3.260-inch stroke. Rated at 850–900 hp, the FR9 improved block and cylinder head coolant flow significantly thanks to cast-in water passages that delivered coolant directly from the water pump to each individual cylinder bore. Meanwhile, the aluminum heads are compartmentalized so that each combustion chamber has its own water jacket. The improved engine cooling properties provide Ford NASCAR teams with an aerodynamic benefit. They can use more tape on the front of their cars.

899 After six seasons of competition, NASCAR retired its first version of the Car of Tomorrow (COT), replacing it with a new model for 2013. The sixth-generation racer ("Gen 6") incorporated all of the COT's safety innovations. It also provided a necessary return to brand identity; the cars resembled their street-legal counterparts much more closely. The slimmed down Gen 6 Cup car (160 pounds lighter than the COT), featured a reduction in downforce and handling qualities that were less dependent on aerodynamics. Outfitted with a taller spoiler and new tires designed specifically for the car by Goodyear, the car is more reliant on mechanical grip, which puts more of the vehicle's performance back in the hands of the driver. Drivers and fans welcomed the car as a replacement for the COT, which was never fully accepted by either group.

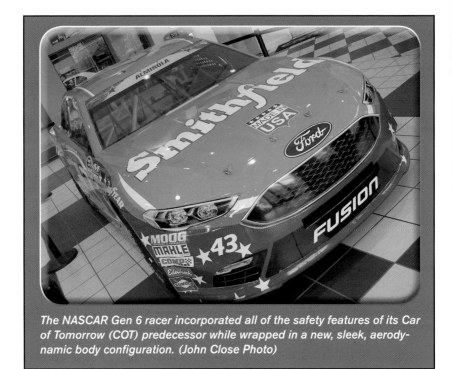

The NASCAR Gen 6 racer incorporated all of the safety features of its Car of Tomorrow (COT) predecessor while wrapped in a new, sleek, aerodynamic body configuration. (John Close Photo)

900 In 2011, NASCAR made the switch from unleaded fuel in all three top divisions (Cup, Nationwide, and Truck) to a new green fuel featuring a 15-percent ethanol blend. The new fuel, Sunoco Green E15, replaces the Sunoco 260 GTX 98-octane gas used since NASCAR introduced unleaded fuel in 2008.

901 Unofficial records indicate that Carl Wilkerson was the first driver to wheel a Dodge in NASCAR's top division; he finished 25th in the Poor Man's 500 at Canfield Speedway (Ohio) on May 30, 1950. At the end of the 2012 Sprint Cup season, Dodge announced that it would no longer participate in NASCAR. Brad Keselowski retired the brand with a bang by capturing five races and the 2012 Sprint Cup championship.

902 The last American-built car with a carburetor instead of electronic fuel injection (EFI), the Ford Crown Victoria Police Cruiser, rolled off the assembly line in 1991. Meanwhile, NASCAR stubbornly held on to the old carburetor-based technology until 2012 when it finally made the switch to EFI. The new fuel delivery system, based on a model produced by McLaren Electronic Systems and Freescale Semiconductor specifically for NASCAR, allows fuel to be injected directly into the engine's intake runners where it mixes with air from a Holley throttle body.

The EFI system, metered by an electronic control unit (ECU, or "black box") controls the amount of fuel injected into the engine and when to fire the spark plugs. The ECU receives information from a group of oxygen sensors at a rate of up to 100 times per second and automatically adjusts the air/fuel mixture, which makes it significantly more efficient than its NASCAR carburetor predecessor. In an effort to ensure that the system is tamperproof from "creative" engineers and crew chiefs, NASCAR incorporates a special authorization code for the computer-driven system. Matt Kenseth won the first race using the new fuel delivery system: the 2012 Daytona 500.

Here's a look at today's modern NASCAR engine, topped with a McLaren electronic fuel injection (EFI) system. In addition to replacing the carburetor, the EFI system eliminated the need for a distributor, thanks to eight individual coils that send electricity to each spark plug. (John Close Photo)

903 In an effort to keep speeds in check at its superspeedways, Talladega Superspeedway and Daytona International Speedway, NASCAR still requires the use of a restrictor plate in combination with the new electronic fuel injection system. Required in normally aspirated carburetor-fed superspeedway engines since the late 1980s the plate is placed below the EFI throttle body to limit the amount of air available to the engine. In its first application in the 2012 Daytona 500, Carl Edwards won the pole with a lap of 194.738 mph, 3 mph slower than the top qualifying speed set in Daytona during the restrictor plate era.

904 Chevrolet continued to own the Sprint Cup Manufacturers' Championship, winning for the 10th consecutive season in 2012. The streak, which started in 2003, broke the old record of nine-straight manufacturers' titles also set by Chevrolet from 1983 through 1991.

905 In an effort to curtail unwanted team "tandem drafting" on superspeedways, NASCAR changed the rules for Sprint Cup car cooling systems for the 2012 season. The edict reduces the radiator's capacity from 5 gallons to just 2, with the overflow tank also reduced in size. Moreover, the front bumper air dam locations are changed in conjunction with the cooling system adjustments in an effort to force cars to do less drafting and run more in "clean air" to keep engine temperatures down.

906 David Ragan's victory in the 2013 Aaron's 499 Sprint Cup Series race at Talladega Superspeedway conjured up memories of an important milestone. When Ragan wheeled car No. 34 to the May 5 triumph, it was the first time that car number captured a top-division NASCAR race since December 1, 1963, when Wendell Scott won at Jacksonville.

907 To make NASCAR Camping World Trucks race ready for the first Mudsummer Classic dirt-track race at Eldora Speedway, NASCAR enacted several rule changes. Teams were allowed to remove front splitters, close off the grilles, and add mesh shields to protect the radiator from debris. An 8 x 12-inch deflector was added to the hood to keep debris from impacting the windshields, which were retained for the event. Meanwhile, the rear spoiler was raised and enlarged to provide better rear downforce and under-chassis skid plates were installed to keep dirt from building up under the truck. Most important, Goodyear developed a new Wrangler racing tire for the event. It was bigger and used a softer-compound 11-inch-wide bias-ply block-tread pattern model that featured a 3-inch stagger between the right and left side (88.5 to 85.5 inches).

908 In a string of successes reminiscent of the dominance by cars using a Banjo Matthews chassis in the 1970s and 1980s, Troyer Race Cars captured 11-straight Whelan Modified Series championships from 2004 to 2014. Established as Troyer Engineering in 1977 by Modified driver Maynard Troyer, the company produces both asphalt and dirt chassis and bodies today in its Rochester, New York, facility.

909 NASCAR banned private testing in 2015. The move is an effort to reduce spiraling research and development costs

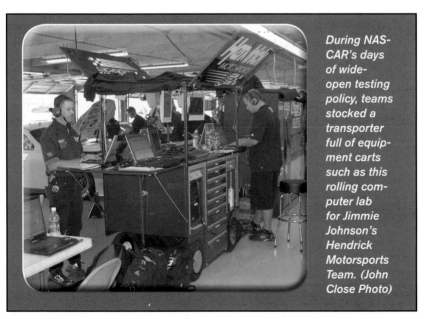

During NASCAR's days of wide-open testing policy, teams stocked a transporter full of equipment carts such as this rolling computer lab for Jimmie Johnson's Hendrick Motorsports Team. (John Close Photo)

incurred though testing. Teams that violate the new rules will be subject to a P6 penalty, the most severe of all NASCAR punishments with a loss of 150 championship points, no less than a $150,000 fine, and six-week suspensions for offending crew chiefs and team members.

910 NASCAR first flirted with using rain tires in road course events after using them in practice and qualifying for the 1997 Winston Cup exhibition race in Suzuka, Japan. In 2014, NASCAR approved wet-weather tires and associated equipment such as windshield wipers in both the Nationwide and Camping World Truck Series divisions. One year later, the Goodyear D-4215 rain tire is selected for use in the Sprint Cup Series road course events at Watkins Glen International and Sonoma Speedway (California). However, the wet-weather rubber stays behind pit wall because neither event is impacted by rain.

911 In 2015, NASCAR enacted new engine rules reducing the horsepower of a Sprint Cup engine from approximately 850 to 725. A tapered spacer is mounted on the intake manifold to accomplish the throttling back. The 2015 rules reduction in ponies is the first for NASCAR's top division since it made the move from big-block to small-block engines in the early 1970s.

912 The 2015 Southern 500 at Darlington (South Carolina) Raceway marked the debut of the first digital dashboard in Sprint Cup competition. Kurt Busch's Stewart-Haas Chevrolet was the only car in the race using the new hardware. This new dashboard gives the same RPM, voltage, oil, water, and fuel pressure as the old analog model and also provides up to 25 data options to the driver including analysis of lap and pit times. The system allows the driver to customize up to 16 different screens, including one resembling the conventional analog dial and gauge view. Weighing slightly more than of the old analog instrument cluster, the electronic readout will be required in all NASCAR Sprint Cup cars beginning in 2016.

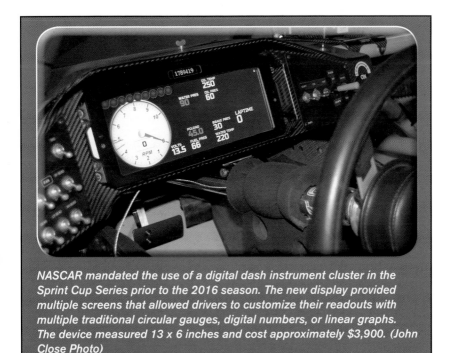

NASCAR mandated the use of a digital dash instrument cluster in the Sprint Cup Series prior to the 2016 season. The new display provided multiple screens that allowed drivers to customize their readouts with multiple traditional circular gauges, digital numbers, or linear graphs. The device measured 13 x 6 inches and cost approximately $3,900. (John Close Photo)

TRACKS

913 Hoping to give fans a more uniform schedule and attract more television viewers in the process, NASCAR standardized the starting time for its Sprint Cup races in 2010. All races held on the East Coast were slotted in for a 1 p.m. green flag while events on the West Coast were scheduled for noon local time, and 3 p.m. on the East Coast. Meanwhile, all night races (except the Memorial Day weekend Coca-Cola 600 at Charlotte) rolled off at 7:30 p.m.

914 One of America's most storied road racing facilities (Road America, located near Elkhart Lake, Wisconsin) returned to the NASCAR schedule in 2010 with the Bucyrus 200 Nationwide Series event. Carl Edwards took home the victory. It was the first time a major NASCAR event was held at the 4.048-mile road course since August 12, 1956, when Tim Flock piloted a Bill Stroppe Mercury to the win in a NASCAR Grand National clash.

915 Historically, the majority of winning drivers in Sprint Cup races at Daytona International Speedway start from a top-10 spot. That wasn't the case in the 2014 Coke Zero 400 when not a single top-10 qualifier finished in the top 10. Aric Almirola won the race from the 15th slot while Jeff Gordon came in 12th, proving to be the best finish of the top-10 qualifiers.

916 Kyle Busch was the first driver in NASCAR history to sweep all three top divisions in a single weekend in 2010. Busch scored a triple at Bristol Motor Speedway August 18–21 where he won the O'Reilly 200 Truck race, the Food City 250 Nationwide event, and the Irwin Tools Race Night 500 Cup clash. Busch and his three Toyotas led 515 of the total 956 laps contested in the three events.

917 The Camping World Truck Series made its first appearance at Pocono International Speedway July 31, 2010. Elliott Sadler won the race, which used a multi-truck qualifying procedure in which several trucks were allowed to be on track taking time trial runs at the same time.

918 Trevor Bayne competed in just one Sprint Cup Series event before taking the green flag in the 2011 Daytona 500. Wheeling a Wood Brothers Ford, he became one of the most unlikely winners in the 53-year history of the event. Bayne, who never led until the final six laps, became the second driver to win in his first start in the classic event; the other was Lee Petty in the first Daytona 500, in 1959. Bayne celebrated his 20th birthday the day before the February 20 race, becoming the youngest driver to win the 500.

919 The 2011 Daytona 500 became a caution-fest as 16 yellow flags totaling 60 laps punctuated the event. Both numbers were all-time records as was the 150 miles run under caution. The average race speed of 130.326 mph was the slowest Daytona 500 run since Junior Johnson won in 1960 at a turtle-like pace of 124.740 mph.

920 With 107,000 tickets sold in advance for the Quaker State 400, Kentucky Speedway officials were giddy with excitement prior to the track's first Sprint Cup race on July 11, 2011. Their smiles turned to frowns, however, when the throng of spectators became entangled in a massive traffic jam on race day. An estimated 10,000 never made it to the track. The track owners immediately lobbied the state for a road-widening project, and purchased land adjacent to the speedway to construct additional parking prior to the 2012 Kentucky event.

921 The 2012 Daytona 500 was the first race in the 53-year history of the event postponed because of rain. The race, scheduled for Sunday, February 26, was washed out and run the next day with Matt Kenseth taking the 500 victory beating Dale Earnhardt Jr., Greg Biffle, Denny Hamlin, and Jeff Burton to the checkered flag.

922 One of the most bizarre incidents in the history of the Daytona 500 came in 2012 on Lap 160 when Juan Pablo Montoya collided with one of the track's jet dryers. Montoya was speeding into Turn 3 under caution, trying to catch up to the field when he plowed into a safety truck towing a jet dryer. The impact ruptured the dryer's 200-gallon fuel tank causing fuel to cascade down the track and catching fire in the process. The event was red-flagged for nearly 2 hours while NASCAR removed the debris and repaired the track surface, which was damaged by the fire's intense heat. Fortunately, Montoya was uninjured in the incident while Duane Barnes, driver of the truck pulling the jet dryer, was shaken but not seriously injured in the frightening crash.

923 The August 5, 2012, Pennsylvania 400 Sprint Cup event was red-flagged on Lap 98 of 160 and declared an official race after severe thunderstorms hit Pocono International Raceway. Later, one fan was killed and nine others injured when they were struck by lightning in the parking lot behind the main grandstand while heading to their vehicles.

Kyle Larson (42) and fans on both sides of the catch fence survived this crash during the 2013 Nationwide Series race at Daytona International Speedway. (Photo Courtesy Russ Lake)

924 In an effort to curtail negative public attention to falling attendance numbers, NASCAR announced it would no longer provide on-site crowd estimates in 2013. Another reason for the policy change has to do with tracks not wanting to provide attendance figures that could give the government a clearer view of earnings at tax time.

925 After decades of adding seats to tracks, International Speedway Corporation (ISC) removed more than 100,000 seats from its tracks in 2013. Talladega Superspeedway seating was reduced from 108,000 to 78,000 while Richmond International Raceway removed 20,000 seats (91,000 to 71,000). At Chicagoland Speedway, the number of seats was cut from 69,000 to 55,500; Michigan Speedway seating was reduced from 84,000 to 71,000. California Speedway dropped from 81,000 to 68,000, Darlington Raceway went from 60,000 to 58,000, and Homestead-Miami Speedway's decrease from 56,000 to 46,000 round out the list.

926 On July 24, 2013, NASCAR staged the Mudsummer Classic at Eldora Speedway, a 150-lap Camping World Truck Series race. This marks the first time a major touring series event is held on a dirt track since September 30, 1971, at the clay-surfaced half-mile State Fairgrounds Speedway in Raleigh, North Carolina.

927 In what can only be described as strange circumstances, NASCAR fan Kirk Franklin dies of a self-inflicted gunshot wound during the NRA (National Rifle Association) 500 at Texas Motor Speedway April 14, 2013. Franklin, who had been involved in an altercation with other fans earlier in the evening, was found dead in his pick-up truck, in the TMS infield that night. He was 42 years old.

928 After winning his first Daytona 500 in 2004, it took Dale Earnhardt Jr. 10 years to get back to Victory Lane in the Great American Race. Earnhardt won the 2014 500 in dominating fashion, leading six different times including the final 18 laps. Earnhardt, who finished second in both the 2012 and 2013 Daytona 500 classics, earned a whopping $1,506,363 for the 2014 victory.

Dale Earnhardt Jr. won the 2014 Daytona 500, his 15th start in the racing classic at Daytona International Speedway. (Photo Courtesy Russ Lake)

929 In an effort to expand its menu, Darlington Raceway added a southern "delicacy" to the 2015 concession mix: a $3 pimento cheese sandwich. The item's success prompted the speedway to step out of the standard burger and hot dog box; it added the Southern 500 Egg Roll in 2016. The $4 item is a combination of smoked pulled pork, cheddar and Monterey jack cheeses, black-eyed peas, and collard greens served in a deep-fried tortilla.

930 With a cost of more than $400 million, the "Daytona Rising" renovation of DIS began in July 2013. Complete and open prior to the 2016 season, the updated speedway features fan amenities including facility-wide Internet connectivity, an application portal ('app'), and interactive stations allowing fans to easily navigate the massive facility. Old-school improvements such as wider seats, twice as many concessions, and three times the number of rest rooms are also part of the now 101,500-seat superspeedway.

931 While there have been many unusual event sponsors through the years, few compare to the one for the May 9, 2015, Sprint Cup race at Kansas Speedway. The SpongeBob SquarePants 400 featured the award-winning cartoon character headlining the race. After a rain delay lasting more than two hours, it was after midnight, local time, when Jimmie Johnson won the event; SpongeBob and the Fox Sports television audience were long gone to bed.

932 During his acclaimed Sprint Cup career, Jeff Gordon visited Victory Lane at every track where he competed, with the exception of one, Kentucky Speedway.

933 In an effort to bolster the Xfinity Series Dash 4 Cash program, NASCAR introduced heat races to the division in 2016. Qualifying set the field for two preliminary events at Bristol Motor Speedway, Richmond International Raceway, Dover International Speedway, and Indianapolis Motor Speedway. The finishing order in each would determine the starting grid for the main event. In addition, the two highest finishing Xfinity Series regulars in each heat race would automatically be eligible for the $100,000 Dash 4

Cash bonus, which was awarded to the top finisher among the four eligible drivers in the main event.

934 Denny Hamlin rolled to his first career Daytona 500 win in 2016 beating Martin Truex Jr. in a photo finish. Hamlin's margin of victory was .01 second, the closest finish in the 58-race history of the Daytona event.

935 As is generally the case when superstars retire, Tony Stewart received several interesting going-away presents during his final 2016 Sprint Cup season. Perhaps the most unique gift came from the Indianapolis Motor Speedway with the construction of a 3/16-mile dirt track inside Turn 3 of the 2.5-mile paved oval. The track was immediately nicknamed "Tony's Dirtyard."

936 Kyle Busch gave one of the most dominant performances in NASCAR history by becoming the first driver to earn the pole and win both the Xfinity and Sprint Cup races. He accomplished this in one weekend at Indianapolis Motor Speedway: July 23–24, 2016. Busch led 211 of the 233 contested laps to complete the milestone sweep.

PIT PASS

937 During the 2010 pre-season media tour, NASCAR Senior Vice-President of Competition Robin Pemberton stated, "Boys, have at it and have a good time." This referenced the sanctioning body no longer regulating bump drafting in superspeedway races at Talladega and Daytona. The comment went viral and was generally interpreted to mean that drivers should settle their differences between themselves. The statement was tested multiple times when several drivers were involved in physical confrontations. In 2011, the policy weakened when NASCAR fined team owner Richard Childress $150,000 and put him on probation for attacking Kyle Busch after a Truck Series race at Kansas Speedway. NASCAR all but ended the policy of self-policing in 2015. Once again, it took responsibility for its competitors when it issued Matt Kenseth an unprecedented two-race suspension after he intentionally wrecked Joey Logano in a Sprint Cup race at Martinsville Speedway.

938 After a non-specific list of banned substances contributed to the suspension of Truck Series driver Sammy Potaschnick in 2002, NASCAR published a list of non-compliant drugs in its 2010 rulebook. Included on the revised list are cocaine, marijuana, amphetamines (including methamphetamine), ephedrine, benzodiazepine, barbiturates, and 13 different narcotics including codeine and morphine.

939 In September 2009, nine months after Richard Petty Motorsports' merger with Gillett Evernham Motorsports, the team announced another merger with Yates Racing for the 2010 Sprint Cup season. The team switched to Ford and drivers Kasey Kahne, A. J. Almendinger, Elliott Sadler, Aric Almirola, and Paul Menard notched 11 top-5 finishes but no wins that season.

940 In 2010, NASCAR lowered the minimum age requirement for its weekly racing series from 16 to 14. South Dakota is the only state to issue a regular driver's license to 14-year-old drivers.

941 Despite a downturn in U.S. television ratings in the in 2010, NASCAR continued to expand its telecasts internationally to include numerous countries across the globe. In addition to Sprint Cup coverage in North America, the 2010 races are televised live in Latin America, Australia, France, Portugal, Sweden, and Finland.

942 With qualifying for the 2010 Daytona 500 originally scheduled for Sunday, February 7, NASCAR decided to move the event to Saturday, February 6, after discovering that the time trials would be in head-to-head competition with another major sporting event, Super Bowl XLIV.

943 The Coke Zero 400 at Daytona International Speedway was the first Sprint Cup Series race broadcast in 3-D on July 3, 2010. The three-dimensional programming was shown on DirecTV, TNT's "RaceBuddy," and NASCAR.com.

944 Blackmore, Virginia, driver John King started seven Camping World Truck Series races but never finished better than 15th. In 2012, King scored one of the most improbable wins in division history by capturing the NextEra Energy 250 NCWTS at Daytona International Speedway. Over the next three seasons, King never led another lap; he faded from the Truck Series in 2014 after 16 career races.

945 Matt Kenseth celebrated his 41st birthday in grand style by winning the Kobalt Tools 400 at Las Vegas Motor Speedway on March 10, 2013. Kenseth joined Cale Yarborough (1977) and Kyle Busch (2009) as the only drivers to win a NASCAR Cup race on his birthday.

946 In 2013, NASCAR took control of all its digital media, social media, and technical operations (including NASCAR.com), despite a contract with Turner Sports to manage them through 2016. Turner continued to oversee all NASCAR advertising and sponsorship related to digital property.

947 From 1992 through 2013, Whelan Modified Tour driver Ed Flemke never missed a race, competing in 382 consecutive events. Starting August 22, 1992, at Riverhead Raceway, the streak came to an end October 20, 2013 at Thompson Speedway (Connecticut), after which Flemke retired. Throughout an illustrious, and durable, racing career, Flemke captured 17 NASCAR Whelan Modified wins.

948 The 2013 Sprint Cup Rookie of the Year battle took on a new dimension when first-year drivers Ricky Stenhouse Jr. and Danica Patrick began dating. The initial revelation of their relationship set off a media frenzy in the garage area, but has since subsided despite erroneous reports that they married in 2014. As of the current 2017 season, Stenhouse and Patrick are still Cup's power couple.

949 Kurt Busch captured his first Sprint Cup victory for Stewart-Haas Racing on March 20, 2014, wheeling the No. 41 Haas Automation Chevy to victory in the STP 500 at Martinsville

Tony Stewart (14), Jeff Gordon (24), Kurt Busch (41), and Matt Kenseth (20) are part of "The Big One," a multi-car wreck at Daytona International Speedway. (Photo Courtesy Russ Lake)

Speedway. It was Busch's first Cup win since the 2011 fall race at Dover, and the first time a No. 41 car won a top division race since Curtis Turner sped to victory in the American 500 at North Carolina Motor Speedway in Rockingham October 31, 1965.

950 For 40 years, some of the best and most historic race cars came out of Smokey Yunick's garage on Beach Street in Daytona Beach, Florida. Sadly, the landmark building where Yunick built race cars from 1947 to 1987 burned to the ground on April 25, 2011.

951 More than 100 different "number" cars have visited Victory Lane since 1949. No. 11 has scored the most wins and is the only one with more than 200 Cup division triumphs. Denny Hamlin was behind the wheel for No. 11's historic 200th win in the Irwin Tools Night 500 at Bristol Motor Speedway on August 25, 2012.

952 Chase Elliott, son of NASCAR driving legend Bill Elliott, competed in nine 2013 Camping World Truck Series events, winning once on the road course at Canadian Tire Motorsports Park

Racing legacy Chase Elliott, son of Winston Cup champion Bill Elliott, won the 2014 Nationwide Series championship. (Photo Courtesy Russ Lake)

in Bowmanville, Ontario. The 19-year-old driver from Dawsonville, Georgia, moved to the Nationwide division in 2014 in which he promptly won the series title after earning three victories and 26 top-10 finishes in 33 events. After a second-place finish in the 2015 Xfinity Series championship, Elliott replaced Jeff Gordon in the No. 24 Hendrick Motorsports Chevrolet for the 2016 Sprint Cup season.

953 Louisville, Kentucky, driver Ben Rhodes scored one of the most unique triples in NASCAR history when he won the 2014 NASCAR K&N Pro East championship. The 17-year-old driver also won the Rookie of the Year and Most Popular Driver Awards, which made him the first to sweep all three titles in a single season.

954 In 2014, NASCAR made multiple changes to the post-season chase for the championship. The field was expanded to 16 participants, while a win in any of the 26 regular-season races became the top criteria to qualify for the 10-race championship round. Once underway, the finals featured a Challenger Round (races 27–29), Contender Round (races 30–32), Eliminator Round (races 33–35), and the Championship (race 36). Any driver who won a race automatically advanced to the next round; the bottom three drivers in each round were eliminated. This left four drivers to race for the title in the final race of the season at Homestead-Miami Speedway.

955 On June 14, 2015, Kurt Busch wheeled his way to victory in the Quicken Loans 400 at Michigan International Speedway. One week later his brother Kyle sped to a win in the SaveMart 350 at Sonoma Raceway. The double dip marked the seventh time the Busch siblings won back-to-back Cup events, the most by any brothers in NASCAR history.

956 A grinding crash in the season-opening Xfinity race at Daytona International Speedway on February 21, 2015 left Kyle Busch with multiple injuries to both legs. Sitting out the first 11 Sprint Cup events as he healed, Busch returned to Charlotte in May and proceeded to make one of the most courageous championship runs in NASCAR history, winning five races (with three in a row at Kentucky, New Hampshire, and Indianapolis). Busch then captured the final championship event at Homestead-Miami Speedway, winning his first Sprint Cup title by one point (5,043 to 5,042) over Kevin Harvick, who finished second in the Homestead race.

957 Prior to the 2016 season, NASCAR announced that races in the three top divisions (Cup, Xfinity, and Truck) would now feature "overtime" rules. The new, somewhat convoluted version of the green-white-checkered (GWC) flag rule introduced an "Overtime Line" positioned on a track-by-track basis. If the race leader passes the Overtime Line on the first lap of a restart before another caution flag is displayed, it will be considered a clean green-white-checkered attempt. If the yellow flag falls before the leader passes the Overtime Line after the green flag, another GWC attempt will be made. The rules require multiple Overtime GWC attempts until a clean restart occurs. If the yellow flag is displayed after a clean start, the field will be frozen and the race will conclude with the either a checkered/yellow or checkered/red flag at the finish line.

958 In 2016, NASCAR instituted a "20-minute clock" rule in the Camping World Truck Series. The edict produces an automatic caution period after 20 minutes of uninterrupted green-flag racing. The "Caution Clock" was used in all 2016 NCWTS events except the dirt race at Eldora Speedway. In addition, the clock is turned off at events with 20 laps remaining except at Pocono Raceway and Canadian Tire Motorsport Park, where it is shut down with 10 circuits remaining.

959 In March 2016, Dale Earnhardt Jr. announced that upon his death, his brain would be donated to scientists to assess the effects of concussions and the development of Chronic Traumatic Encephalopathy (CTE) in race car drivers. Earnhardt sat out the 2012 Kansas Speedway race after suffering the effects of serious concussions following two separate crashes in a six-week period; he was sidelined again midway through the 2016 season with concussion-like symptoms after wrecks at Michigan and Daytona.

960 On February 28, 2016, Jimmie Johnson rolled his No. 48 Hendrick Motorsports Chevy into Victory Lane in the Folds of

Jimmie Johnson proved to be the best at the new Chase championship formula, winning a record five-straight Cup Series championships from 2006 through 2010, sixth title in 2013, and seventh in 2016. (Photo Courtesy Russ Lake)

Honor 500 at Atlanta Motor Speedway. The win marked the 31st consecutive season of the Hendrick organization winning at the Cup level, the longest such streak in the history of the sport.

961 NASCAR fans got their own version of the *Love Boat* in 2017 when Kyle Petty hosted "NASCAR: The Cruise." The first officially licensed NASCAR cruise, the *Norwegian Pearl* cruise ship set sail from January 29 to February 3. It allowed fans to enjoy the Caribbean with top NASCAR stars of the past and present including Richard Petty, Bobby Allison, and Rusty Wallace; the entertainers included The Beach Boys and 38 Special. The cost of the cruise ranged from $975 to $7,500.

MILESTONES

962 The NASCAR Hall of Fame opened May 11, 2010. Built by the city of Charlotte, North Carolina, at an estimated cost of $195 million, the 150,000 square-foot facility showcases thousands of historic and current NASCAR artifacts in a multi-area facility including a Great Hall and the Hall of Honor. It also includes Glory Road, a 33-degree banked racetrack replica that holds up to 18 classic NASCAR race vehicles.

963 In 2009, NASCAR established a Hall of Fame voting process beginning with a 20-member committee that selects 25 nominees. Following that is a vote consisting of 48 ballots from the nominating committee plus 27 more from a group of select drivers, former owners, crew chiefs, manufacturers' representatives, and media members. The final vote is determined from the results of a nationwide fan vote. The top five vote getters will be inducted into the HOF.

964 NASCAR established eligibility requirements in 2009 for the Hall of Fame enshrinement. According to the rules, drivers must have competed in NASCAR for at least 10 years, and be retired for at least three years. All non-driver personnel must have worked in the sport for at least 10 years.

965 On May 23, 2010, Richard Petty, Dale Earnhardt, Junior Johnson, Bill France Sr., and Bill France Jr. were the first class of inductees in the NASCAR Hall of Fame. Nominated for this class but not selected were Bobby Allison, Richard Childress, Red Byron, Buck Baker, Richie Evans, Tim Flock, Rick Hendrick, Bud Moore, Ned Jarrett, Benny Parsons, Lee Petty, David Pearson, Fireball Roberts, Curtis Turner, Glen Wood, Herb Thomas, Joe Weatherly, Darrell Waltrip, and Cale Yarborough.

966 As part of the 2010 events at Charlotte Motor Speedway and the opening of the NASCAR Hall of Fame, the Actor's Theater of Charlotte brought *Heaven On Wheels* to the stage. The musical comedy about the history of NASCAR ran through May of that year.

967 Kevin Harvick probably wasn't too pleased with his 2008 and 2009 Sprint Cup results, going winless both seasons. Harvick finally broke his 115-race drought by winning the Aaron's 499 at Talladega Superspeedway on April 25, 2010. Harvick's last Cup victory prior to that win was the 2007 season-opening Daytona 500.

968 Cornelius, North Carolina, driver Kevin Conway finished 30th or worse in 24 of his 28 Sprint Cup starts in 2010. Despite the less-than-glowing record, Conway was named the Sprint Cup Rookie of the Year because, at season's end, he was the only driver who ran enough races to qualify for the award.

969 Introduced at the 2013 Daytona 500, NASCAR's Air Titan was hailed as a quantum leap forward in track-drying technology. Created by the NASCAR Research and Development Center, the system uses compressed air to push water off the track and onto the apron where vacuum trucks remove the remaining water. NASCAR estimates the system reduces track-drying time by as much as 80 percent.

970 A member of the 2012 Hall of Fame induction class, Dale Inman, first cousin to Richard Petty, grew up in Level Cross, North Carolina. With Inman serving as Petty's crew chief, the cousins went on to win seven Winston Cup championships (1964, 1967, 1971, 1972, 1974, 1975, and 1979). Inman later earned an all-time NASCAR Cup record eighth championship, as crew chief for Terry Labonte in 1984.

971 With a lap of 196.434 mph, Danica Patrick etched her name in the NASCAR record book by winning the pole position for the 2013 Daytona 500. Patrick's top qualifying run is the first for a woman in NASCAR Sprint Cup competition; she is the second woman to win a pole in a top NASCAR division. Shawana Robinson was the first when she captured the pole for the Busch Light 300 NASCAR Busch Series race at Atlanta Motor Speedway in 1994.

972 Originally called the Busch Clash for its 1979 debut, the exhibition race at Daytona International Speedway was retitled the Sprint Unlimited in 2013. Along with a new name, the race is reformatted using on-line fan voting to determine the length of the event's three segments (30, 25, 20 laps), pit stops (mandatory four-tire), and number of drivers eliminated after the first two segments (none).

973 Martin Truex Jr. won the 2013 Toyota/Save Mart 350 at Sonoma Raceway (California) and in the process gave the number 56 its second-ever top division victory. The only other time the number 56 visited a NASCAR Cup Victory Lane was March 27, 1966, when Indy Car veteran Jim "Herk" Hurtubise drove a Norm Nelson–owned Plymouth to a win in the Atlanta 500 at Atlanta International Raceway.

974 Jeff Gordon scored the 78th pole position of his career in qualifying for the 2015 Daytona 500. The effort marks the 23rd-straight season that Gordon captured a top-division pole (an all-time NASCAR record). Gordon notched a career-high of eight poles in 1995. The only year that Gordon didn't win a pole throughout his Cup career was in 1992, when he competed in just one race, his Cup debut at Atlanta Motor Speedway.

Jeff Gordon became a landmark figure in NASCAR history of both on and off the track. Gordon retired from full-time NASCAR competition at the end of the 2015 season but returned as a part-time fill in for the injured Dale Earnhardt Jr. in 2016. (Photo Courtesy Russ Lake)

975 Jeff Gordon started 10th in the 2015 Sylvania 300 at New Hampshire International Speedway, and in the process broke Ricky Rudd's record of 788 consecutive Cup Series starts. Gordon, who finished 7th at NHIS, went on to make 797 consecutive starts before retiring at the end of the 2015 season.

976 After trying for eight years, Toyota finally won NASCAR's pinnacle event when Denny Hamlin rolled to victory in the 2016 Daytona 500. Hamlin led the final 11 laps in his No. 11 Joe Gibbs Racing Camry, pacing a Toyota whitewash as Martin Truex Jr. and Kyle Busch came home 2nd and 3rd, respectively. Hamlin's victory was the Toyota's 80th in NASCAR Cup competition.

977 Driving for Roush-Fenway Racing, Ricky Stenhouse Jr. won the NASCAR Nationwide Series (NNS) championship in 2011 and 2012. Stenhouse became the sixth driver to win consecutive NNS championships joining Sam Ard (1983–1984), Larry Pearson (1986–1987), Randy Lajoie (1996–1997), Dale Earnhardt Jr. (1998–1999), and Martin Truex Jr. (2004–2005) as the only drivers to win back-to-back titles in NASCAR's junior circuit.

978 Matt Crafton spent most of his first 13 years in the Truck Series as an also-ran, winning just twice. In 2013 and 2014, Crafton became the first driver in the history of the division to win back-to-back championships with three wins and 20 top-5 finishes in 44 events in the two seasons.

979 Despite a wreck on Lap 134 of the FedEx 400, Greg Biffle came in 38th, still running at the finish of the June 1, 2014 Sprint Cup race at Dover International Speedway. The never-say-die effort allowed Biffle to break the record of 83-consecutive "running at the finish" Cup races set by Clint Bowyer. Biffle's streak began at Phoenix International Raceway on February 27, 2011.

980 Almost one month to the day after setting a new running at the finish in consecutive Sprint Cup races record, Greg Biffle sees his streak end after crashing on Lap 98 of the July 4, 2014, Coke Zero 400 at Daytona International Speedway. After repairs in the garage area, Biffle was about to return to the race when it was red-flagged for rain after 112 laps. The washout ends Biffle's DNF streak at 89 races. He was credited with 29th-place in the abbreviated event.

981 A post-race brawl wound up costing Hendrick Motorsports one of the biggest fines in NASCAR history. The incident was triggered when Brad Keselowski ran into Jeff Gordon's car late in the 2014 AAA 500 at Texas Motor Speedway. The contact cut down Gordon's left-rear tire relegating him to a 29th-place finish, and worse, all but eliminated Gordon from the championship battle. Gordon's HMS teammates were quick to react, confronting Keselowski's Penske Racing crew after the checkered flag, setting off a wild brawl in the process. Hendrick Motorsports was hit with a fine of $185,000, suspension of four HMS team members, and probation for two others. Keselowski and Penske Racing were not penalized for any actions in the incident.

982 In early 2015, Press Pass announced it would no longer produce NASCAR collectible trading cards. Launched in 1992, Press Pass was the last major card producer to offer NASCAR cards.

Among their most collectible sets was the 1996 edition, which featured a piece of a NASCAR racing tire.

983 Doug Coby etched his name into the Whelan Modified Tour record book after winning three out of four division championships from 2012 to 2015. Coby won his first Modified crown in 2012, finishing second in the 2013 title chase. The Milford, Connecticut, driver then won the 2014 and 2015 titles. He became the fourth racer since 1985 to win back-to-back Modified titles, joining Jimmy Spencer (1986–1987), Tony Hirschman Jr. (1995–1996 and 2004–2005), and Mike Stefanik (1997–1998 and 2001–2002).

984 In 2016, NASCAR reduced the starting field in Sprint Cup races from 43 to 40 cars. No rule actually mandated that 43 cars start a race, but the practice had been in place since the late 1980s.

985 In early 2016, sports trading card giant Panini America announced it would begin producing NASCAR trading cards later that year. The Italian-based company would add four sets of cards (Prizm NASCAR, Torque NASCAR, Certified NASCAR, and National Treasures NASCAR) to its worldwide distribution of books, magazines, comic books, and trading cards.

986 NASCAR extended the Chase format to the Xfinity Series in 2016. The seven-race championship playoff would feature 12 drivers and two elimination rounds, whittling the field down to 4 title-eligible drivers by the final race of the season at Homestead-Miami Speedway. All Xfinity Chase drivers started the championship round with 2,000 points, earning three bonus points for each win scored during the regular 26-race season. Point totals would be adjusted to 3000 for drivers advancing to the second elimination round; the 4 drivers advancing to the championship would start even with 4000 points. The highest-finishing driver, Daniel Suárez won the Xfinity title.

987 NASCAR put all its eggs in the Chase basket in 2016 when it brought the championship playoff format to the Camping

The NASCAR Truck Series made its first appearance at Daytona International Speedway in 2000. Since then, the "Tailgaters" have opened each season at the 2.5-mile high-speed oval. (Photo Courtesy Russ Lake

World Truck Series ranks. The system allows for a seven-race, two-elimination round title battle featuring eight drivers. As with the Xfinity Series Chase format, the four drivers who advance through the elimination rounds (each having 4,000 points) move on to the championship race at Homestead with. The highest finisher in the Truck final at Homestead, Johnny Sauter, was awarded the division crown.

988 NASCAR ditched its single-car Sprint Cup Series qualifying format in 2014, instituting new group qualifying procedures. Dubbed "Knockout Qualifying," a 25-minute first-round time-trial session is implemented with all entries allowed to take laps at their discretion. Cars qualifying outside the top 24 were eliminated, while the top 24 moved on to a second round, a 10-minute on-track time trial. Those inside the top-12 after round two move on to a final 5-minute round; the fastest car is determined the pole winner.

989 Kevin Harvick ended his 2014 Sprint Cup season with a second-place finish at Texas Motor Speedway and wins at Phoenix International Raceway and Homestead-Miami Speedway. The strong run earned Harvick the 2014 NSCS title and momentum into the 2015 campaign, with Harvick finishing either first or second in the first five races of the season. Harvick's run of eight-straight first- or second-place efforts ended with an eighth-place finish in the STP 500 at Martinsville Speedway, March 29, 2015.

990 From 2003 through 2016, Dale Earnhardt Jr. was selected as the Most Popular Driver in NASCAR's top division with an unparalleled run of 14 straight seasons. Bill Elliott holds a record Most Popular Driver Awards for Cup with 16 over 19 seasons, from 1984 to 2002.

991 At age 19 years 5 months 21 days, Erik Jones becomes the youngest driver to win the Camping World Truck Series championship. The 2016 titlist won three races and posted 20 top-10 finishes in 23 events capturing the crown by 15 points more than runner-up Tyler Reddick.

992 Prior to the start of the 2016 season, NASCAR established the Charter System for the Sprint Cup division. The new structure guarantees charter teams a starting spot in all division points-paying races. NASCAR awarded the charters to teams that attempted to qualify for every Sprint Cup race over the past three seasons.

993 NASCAR awarded 36 charters to 19 organizations for the 2016 Sprint Cup season. Thanks to a provision allowing teams to sell their charters, Michael Waltrip Racing sold two of its charter spots: one to Joe Gibbs Racing and another to Stewart-Haas Racing.

994 As part of NASCAR's new Charter System, the sanctioning body reduced the starting field in each Sprint Cup race from 43 to 40 cars. That left unchartered (or open) teams battling for just 4 available spots in each race.

995 Another provision of the NASCAR team charter rule called for a minimum performance standard. NASCAR reserved the right to revoke a team's charter if it finished in one of the last three spots in the owner's point standings for three consecutive seasons.

996 Norm Benning made 156 Camping World Truck Series career starts from 2002 to 2015. Throughout that period, the Level Green, Pennsylvania, driver never won a race, and never scored a top-5 or top-10 finish.

997 On June 24, 2016, Tony Stewart gave an interview in which he stated, "driving a Sprint Cup car does not make me happy right now" and "there are things in life I want to do other than be at a NASCAR track three days a week for 38 weekends out of 52 weeks a year." Two days later, the 18-year Sprint Cup veteran broke an 84-race winless streak and captured the Toyota/Save Mart 350 at Sonoma Raceway. The victory was the last of 49 Sprint Cup wins for Stewart, who retired from full-time NASCAR competition at the end of the season.

998 Kyle Bush led 190 of 200 laps to win the NASCAR Xfinity Series Lakes Region 200 at New Hampshire Motor Speedway on July 16, 2016. In the process, Busch eclipsed 17,000 laps led in Xfinity competition (17,064 out of 57,975 circuits completed in 321 division races). The win extended Busch's all-time record of Xfinity victories to 82, which is 33 more than runner-up Mark Martin's 49.

999 Monster Energy Drink is announced as the new title sponsor of NASCAR's top division on December 19, 2016. The company replaces Sprint and will debut as the Monster Energy NASCAR Cup Series at the 2017 Daytona 500. Also set to debut in 2017 is a new mark supporting the association replacing the familiar NASCAR "bar code" logo that has been in place since 1976.

1000 In 2017, the eighth assemblage of inductees was selected for the NASCAR Hall of Fame. Included in the group are drivers Benny Parsons and Mark Martin, along with team owners Raymond Parks, Richard Childress, and Rick Hendrick.

1001 NASCAR announced sweeping changes to the way championships are decided in the Monster Energy NASCAR Cup, Xfinity, and Camping World Truck Series beginning in 2017. Events in the divisions will now be completed in three Stages with the top 10 drivers in each of the first two Stages awarded championship "playoff" points on a 10-to-1 scale.

The leader at the end of the final Stage will be considered the winner of the event and receive 40 championship points. The 2nd-through 35th-place drivers will be awarded points on a 35-to-2 scale. Those finishing 36th through 40th place will be awarded 1 point.

Bonus points for leading a lap or leading the most laps will no longer be awarded. The 150-mile Cup division-qualifying races at Daytona will now award championship points.

The Monster Cup 10-race season-ending championship system will feature the top 16 drivers in points after 26 races. The "Playoffs" (replacing the "Chase" moniker) will still be divided into three three-race rounds with four drivers eliminated after each round. As in the past, a driver in a playoff round will automatically advance to the next round with the final four drivers determining the season champion in the final race for the year at Homestead–Miami Speedway. The highest-finishing driver among the four at Homestead will win the championship.

POSTSCRIPT

I hope you enjoyed reading *1001 NASCAR Facts* as much as I enjoyed crafting it.

As a lifelong follower of NASCAR, and as someone who was fortunate enough to be a part of it professionally for 30 years, I thought I knew a lot about the history of the sport. Boy, was I surprised. Time and again throughout the research and writing of this project, I discovered facts about NASCAR that I didn't know.

The biggest rush, however, came in having the opportunity of viewing countless classic stock car racing artifacts, files, and photographs. Just to see and touch some of the items was incredible and gave me a further appreciation of just how amazing NASCAR was, and is, as a sport.

To that end, here's a tip of the helmet to Steve Zautke, Randy Cadenhead, Ed Samples Jr., Jack Walker, Vaudell Sosebee and family, and the R. W. Hopkins family for graciously opening up their personal family racing archives.

In addition, many thanks to Gordon Pirkle and the Georgia Racing Hall of Fame, as well as the Public Relations Department at General Motors for access to their historic photo collections.

A special heartfelt thanks also goes out to the J. Murrey Atkins Library Special Collections and University Archives, the University of North Carolina at Charlotte, for providing the images shot by iconic NASCAR photographer and departed friend, T. Taylor Warren.

Speaking of friends, this book would not exist without the efforts of Greg Fielden, Brandon Reed, Russ Lake, and Wes Eisenschenk.

Greg is somewhat of a forgotten man in today's NASCAR, but his epic books, including *Forty Years Of Stock Car Racing*, were the bibles of statistical data for the sport before the Internet became the center of the information universe. As such, much of the information in this book was referenced from Greg's books in tribute to him.

Brandon's an amazing racing historian and his access to the rich past as well as the present Georgia racing community was invaluable in researching and obtaining some incredible historic content for this book.

Russ is, well, Russ. The legendary Wisconsin race photographer, who is still shooting in his 80s, has supported virtually every major work I've produced since he took me under his wing more than 30 years ago. Simple thanks seem hardly enough for one of the people I admire most, in life, not just racing.

Finally, I have to give a big shout-out to my "sponsor," Wes, and everyone at CarTech, for giving me the opportunity to run up front again after all these years.

Again, thanks to all for reading the book and in the process, supporting my lifelong racin' and writin' habits.

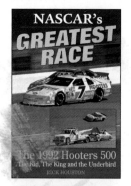

NASCAR's Greatest Race

The 1992 Hooters 500: The Kid, The King and the Underbird

Rick Houston On November 15, 1992, the entire NASCAR racing community tuned in to watch as six drivers strapped in for a chance to win the NASCAR Winston Cup. Davey Allison, Bill Elliott, and Alan Kulwicki each had a real shot at winning the Championship. On the track, Allison was in and out of contention until trouble found him, which left Elliott and Kulwicki to race for the title in a nail-biting finale. Author Rick Houston has gathered new interviews from Bill Elliott, Paul Andrews, Larry McReynolds, Ray Evernham, Rick Mast, Brett Bodine, Kyle Petty, and Tim Brewer. They all give fresh recollections and new information on the events leading up to and including the 1992 Hooters 500. Hardbound, 6 x 9 inches, 224 pages, 93 color and 26 b/w photos. *Item # CT568*

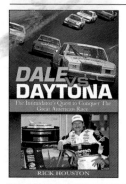

Dale vs. Daytona

The Intimidator's Quest to Win the Great American Race

Rick Houston Dale Earnhardt and Daytona International Speedway remain two of the most iconic names in the history of NASCAR, and are inevitably connected when either name is mentioned. Earnhardt's failed attempts to win the race have become folklore; each year brought its own unique set of circumstances for why he hadn't yet raised the Harley J. Earl Trophy. Author Rick Houston examines every Daytona 500 in which Dale competed from 1979 to 2001 with interviews from crew chiefs, competitors, rivals, crewmembers, and friends also offer their thoughts and recollections in this thrilling recap of the Intimidator's efforts to win the Great American Race. Hardbound, 6 x 9 inches, 224 pages, 111 photos. *Item # CT594*

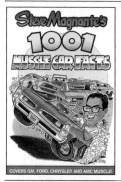

Steve Magnante's
1001 Muscle Car Facts

Steve Magnante Author Steve Magnante is well known for his encyclopedia-like knowledge of automotive facts. The details he regularly puts forth, both on the pages of national magazines and as a contributing host and tech expert at the popular Barrett-Jackson Auctions on television, are the kind of things muscle car fanatics love to hear. Covered are all the popular GM makes such as Chevy, Buick, Oldsmobile, Pontiac; Ford and Mercury cars; Chrysler, Plymouth, and Dodge cars; even facts about AMC and Studebaker. Softbound, 6 x 9 inches, 416 pages, 299 color photos. *Item # CT517*

1001 Drag Racing Facts

The Golden Age of Top Fuel, Funny Cars, Door Slammers & More

by Doug Boyce Spanning the 1950s through the 1970s, this book is packed with well-researched drag racing facts that even some of the most hard-core drag racing fans might be surprised to learn. Covered are all the popular classes of drag racing of the era, including Top Fuelers, Funny Cars, Pro Stocks, and Eliminators including Gassers and Altereds, Stocks, Super Stocks, and more. Softbound, 6 x 9 inches, 416 pages, 125 photos. *Item # CT539*